Reforming Sodom

Reforming Sodom

Protestants and the Rise of Gay Rights

HEATHER R. WHITE

The University of North Carolina Press *Chapel Hill*

Designed by Alyssa D'Avanzo
Set in Quadraat by codeMantra, Inc.

The University of North Carolina Press has been a member of the
Green Press Initiative since 2003.

Library of Congress Cataloging-in-Publication Data
White, Heather Rachelle, 1974–
Reforming Sodom : Protestants and the rise of gay rights/
Heather R. White. — 1 [edition].
pages cm
Includes bibliographical references and index.
ISBN 978-1-4696-2411-2 (pbk   ) —
ISBN 978-1-4696-2412-9 (ebook)
1. Homosexuality—Religious aspects—Christianity. 2. Protestant churches—
Doctrines. 3. Homosexuality—Religious aspects—Protestant churches.
4. Protestant gays—Religious life. I. Title.
BR115.H6W446 2015
261.8'357660973—dc23
2015006186

To KCB

Contents

Acknowledgments xi

Abbreviations xiii

Introduction
How the Bible Came to Speak about Homosexuality 1

Chapter 1
The Therapeutic Orthodoxy 15

Chapter 2
Writing the Homophile Self 43

Chapter 3
Churchmen and Homophiles 71

Chapter 4
Sanctified Heterosexuality 108

Chapter 5
Born Again at Stonewall 138

Epilogue
Afterlives of an Invented Past 171

Notes 187

Selected Bibliography 215

Index 229

Illustrations

Harry Emerson Fosdick, 1926 16

ONE, Inc., editorial staff, circa 1957–58 58

Rev. Robert Wood, 1958 64

Clergy participants in the Council on Religion
and the Homosexual, 1965 74

Annual Reminder demonstration, 1969 92

Gay Liberation Front meeting at
Washington Square United Methodist Church, 1970 95

John Charles Wynn, date unknown (likely late 1960s) 116

Sexuality education tract (1960s) 128

Craig Rodwell, 1970 143

Troy Perry, Steve Jordan, Edith Allen Perry,
and MCC members, 1970 151

Acknowledgments

A decade ago, when I was a graduate student researching the history of chapel cars, I contacted the director of a newly formed online archive project in LGBT religious history. Mark Bowmen persuaded me to abandon the trains, and the LGBT Religious Archive Network helped connect me to archivists, interviewees, scholars, and comrades who have shaped and supported this project along the way. Thanks go to John D'Emilio and Melissa Wilcox, in particular, for guidance in the earliest stages of the project. So many of the people I interviewed were generous with memories, contacts, and enthusiasm. I am grateful to Roy Birchard for ongoing e-mail updates and prayers and to Victor Jordan (in memory) for his guidance as an archivist and LGBT Religious Archive Network advisory board member. A dream team of religion scholars at Princeton University has been an encouragement to me, including Professors Marie Griffith, Leigh Schmidt, Albert Raboteau, Jeff Stout, Eddie Glaude, and Judith Weisenfeld and graduate school colleagues Josh Dubler, Micah Auerback, Katie Holscher, Anthony Petro, Melissa Proctor, Jenny Legath, and Tisa Wenger. Funding from various sources enabled research travel and writing time: the Princeton Center for the Study of Religion, the Princeton LGBT Alumni Society, the Historical Society of the Episcopal Church, and New College of Florida faculty development grants. Two research initiatives also emerged as I began working on the book revisions. Those attending the 2009 Religion and Sexuality Initiative at Emory University gave amazing feedback; successive gatherings of the Human Rights Campaign Summer Institute in Religion and Sexuality heard and read various drafts and chapters of this book. The scholars I came to know through these two initiatives have made this book better in many ways. Particular thanks go to Mark Jordan, patron saint of chapter drafts, and to Summer Institute team members Rebecca Alpert, Ken Stone, Ellen Armour, Kent Brintnall, Patrick Cheng, and Sharon Groves. Colleagues and students at Vassar College and the New College of Florida enlivened this project. Thank you to all the Novo Collegians who gave feedback over works-in-progress presentations. I give particular acknowledgment to Susan Marks, Miriam Wallace, and Emily Fairchild for illuminating conversations and draft feedback and to Fred Carriles for the astonishing feats of organization as my research assistant. I presented draft versions of chapters at annual meetings of the American Academy of Religion, the American Society of Church History, the American Historical Association, the American Studies Association, the Committee on LGBT History, and the Society for Biblical Literature; I thank respondents and audience members for helpful feedback and questions. Participants at several works-in-progress workshops also guided me through draft writing: the Religion in America seminar at Columbia University; the American Religious History symposium at Princeton University; the Seminar on Gender, Sex, Religion, and Politics at the University of Southern California Center for Religion and Civic Culture; and the Religion and Love conference at Georgia State University. Speaking invitations from the religion departments at Millsap College and North Carolina State University; the Center for the Study of Religion and Sexuality at Columbia University; and the Lang College of the New School of Social Research gave me great conversation partners. I am also grateful to the scholars and mentors involved with the Congregational Studies Project of the Hartford Institute for Religion Research for engaging with this project as they supported and advised my next project and to the staff at Burke Theological Library for hospitality during the spring of 2014 when I was a scholar in residence. Reviewers from the University of California Press and the University of North Carolina Press valuably shaped the project, and I am grateful to my editor Elaine Maisner for her support through the publication process. In addition to those already named above, several draft readers, conference paper respondents, and advice givers deserve mention: Gill Frank, Lynne Gerber, David Watt, Laura Levitt, Rebecca Davis, Bethany Moreton, Wallace Best, Michael Pettinger, Joe Marchal, Marc Stein, Jack Halberstam, Martin Kavka, and Kathryn Lofton. I thank Kathy Kravitz and Detta Penna for editing and egging on, Mark Larrimore for a sunlit corner of Brooklyn during the final writing stages, and the extended White/Gustafson families for being exemplars of unconditional love. And, finally, thanks go to my wife, KC Bitterman, for being pretty much perfect.

Abbreviations

CCSA	Council for Christian Social Action
CRH	Council on Religion and the Homosexual
ECHO	East Coast Homophile Organizations
GAA	Gay Activist Alliance
GLF	Gay Liberation Front
HYMN	Homophile Youth Movement in Neighborhoods
KJV	King James Version (of the Bible)
LGBT	Lesbian, Gay, Bisexual, Transgender
MCC	Metropolitan Community Church
NACHO	North American Conference of Homophile Organizations
NCC	National Council of Churches
NIV	New International Version (of the Bible)
PRIDE	Personal Rights in Defense and Education
PSR	Pacific School of Religion
RSV	Revised Standard Version (of the Bible)
SCCRH	Southern California Council on Religion and the Homophile
UCC	United Church of Christ
UFMCC	United Fellowship of Metropolitan Community Churches

Reforming Sodom

INTRODUCTION
How the Bible Came to Speak about Homosexuality

A certain mechanism, which was so elfin-like that it could
make itself invisible, . . . in a game that combined pleasure with
compulsion and consent with inquisition, made it tell the
truth about itself and others as well.

—Michel Foucault, *The History of Sexuality*

In 1946, the term "homosexuals" appeared for the first time in an English Bible. This new figure appeared in a list of sinners barred—according to a verse in the Apostles Paul's first epistle to the Corinthians—from inheriting the kingdom of God.[1] The word change was made by leading Bible scholars, members of the translation committee that labored for over a decade to produce the Revised Standard Version (RSV) of the Bible. With an approach inspired by text-critical scholarship, many of their choices upset readers of the older King James Version, the favored Bible of Protestant America since the colonial era. Amid the outrage over other changes—to the red-letter words of Jesus and the old Shakespearean idiom—another modernizing innovation went virtually unremarked. Two enigmatic Greek nouns, referenced in the King James as "effeminate" and "abusers of themselves with mankind," now appeared as a single, streamlined "homosexual."[2] Subsequent Bible commentaries approached the new term as age-old tradition. *The Interpreter's Bible*, in a side-by-side comparison of the RSV and KJV, insistently smoothed over the difference between translations. "Obviously," wrote the commentator on the Corinthians passage, "the apostle is perturbed by the influence of the immoral pagan community upon the lives of the church. . . . There is special reference to unnatural vice, homosexuality . . . against which Christianity set itself uncompromisingly from the first."[3] The cross-references regarding this passage linked it to a set of texts that similarly expounded upon this "obvious" biblical prohibition. The Genesis Sodom account, two verses in Leviticus, and the first chapter of Romans, along with the 1 Corinthians passage, together underscored that both Jewish and Christian teachings had, evidently, opposed homosexuality from their earliest origins.

Some Bible readers, however, responded with surprise to this textual change. In everyday use, the verse in 1 Corinthians had other meanings. The author of a 1956 advice book on how to write sermons recounted the embarrassing tale of one minister's well-loved sermon. That sermon, delivered on various occasions, expanded on the "general meaning" of the Apostle Paul's reference to the "effeminate," which the pastor took as warning against "the soft, the pliable, those who take the easy road." The take-away point was that Christians must undertake the difficult path of faith. It was a fine sermon, or so the pastor thought, until he read the RSV. He discovered "to his amazement and chagrin" that "effeminate" was translated "homosexuals."[4] The confusion was a lesson, the author of this advice book chided, on the need to use recent translations. A check through earlier Bible commentaries confirms that outdated reference tools may indeed have contributed to this pastor's error. An earlier edition of *The Interpreter's Bible*, published in 1929, said nothing at all about homosexuality in its commentary on the same verse in 1 Corinthians. It noted that the Apostle Paul was keenly aware of the "idolatry and immorality" of the pagan world. However, the named vice that so perturbed the apostle was "self indulgence of appetite and speech," an interpretation that more readily fit with the pastor's call to a disciplined faith.[5] If Christianity did indeed set itself against homosexuality from the first, then this popular Christian reference text neglected to make that prohibition clear.

Several scholars of American religion have puzzled over the peculiar silences of early twentieth-century Christian texts on the topic of same-sex sexuality. After surveying the published Christian literature of that time, Randall Balmer and Lauren Winner concluded that during those decades, "the safest thing to say about homosexuality was nothing." They note that even the published commentary on "sodomy," which would seem to be the clearest antecedent to later talk about homosexuality, yielded little that would illumine a long tradition of same-sex regulation.[6] Although many Bible reference tools mentioned that damnable "sin of Sodom," the muddled and circular commentary on this "loathsome vice" offered little that clarified its nature.[7] Historian Rebecca Davis, on her own hunt to find Christian teachings about homosexuality, similarly notes the profound absence in early and mid-twentieth-century Protestant literature— and especially in the writing by conservative fundamentalists. "The extant printed record," she observes, "suggests that they avoided discussions of homosexuality almost entirely."[8] Adding further substance to this void are the findings from Alfred Kinsey's study of the sexual behavior of white American men, conducted between 1936 and 1946. The study suggested that Christians, although well acquainted with the sinfulness of masturbation and premarital intercourse, knew very little about what their churches had to say about same-sex acts. "There has not been so frequent or so free discussion of the sinfulness of the homosexual in religious literature," Kinsey wrote. "Consequently, it is not unusual to find even devoutly religious persons who become involved in the homosexual without any clear understanding of the church's attitude on the subject."[9] Before the 1940s, the Bible's seemingly plain condemnation of homosexuality was not plain at all.

Such absence and ambiguity may boggle the mind today. We stand on the further side of nearly a half century of rousing debate over what the Bible has to say about homosexuality, and we have heard the specific references to homosexuals in countless speeches about Christianity's plain teaching. Not everyone agrees that "homosexuals" is the correct translation of the two Greek nouns in that 1 Corinthians text, but few are shocked to see it on the list of possibilities. Nor are many surprised by the cross-linked texts—in Genesis, Leviticus, and Romans—that are reliably discussed for their word on homosexual behavior.[10] The question driving most of these debates concerns not whether these texts reference same-sex behavior but whether that meaning has anything to do with modern-day gays and lesbians. There is, to be sure, a growing scholarship in biblical studies and the history of the ancient world that challenges the idea that these texts prohibit "same-sex acts" in a generic sense. These scholars argue, rather, that their authors were concerned with particular social relationships, like pederasty and cult prostitution, that cannot be compared to modern-day romances between same-sex adults.[11] Still, even these inquiries into the historical and cultural construction of these texts' meanings ineluctably contend with a broad common sense that assumes a same-sex meaning. The starting point, even for the challengers, is that these verses represent both an ancient prohibition and a history of regulation focused specifically on "homosexual acts."

What this book shows is that the broad common sense about the Bible's specifically same-sex meaning was an invention of the twentieth century. Today's antihomosexual animus, that is, is not the singular residue of an ancient damnation. Rather, it is the product of a more complex modern synthesis. To find the influential generators of that synthesis, moreover, we should look not to fundamentalist preachers but to their counterparts. Religious liberals, urbane modernizers of the twentieth century, studiously un-muddled the confused category of "sodomitical sin" and assigned to it a singular same-sex meaning. The ideas informing this shift germinated out of the therapeutic sciences of psychiatry and psychology, an emerging field of the late nineteenth century that promised scientific frameworks for measuring and studying human sexual behavior. Liberal Protestants were early adopters of these scientific insights, which percolated through various early twentieth-century projects of moral reform. Among the yields from the convivial pairing of medicine and morality was the midcentury translation of the RSV. The newly focused homosexual prohibitions evidenced the grafting of new therapeutic terms onto ancient roots. The scores of subsequent Bible translations produced in later decades adopted and sharpened the RSV's durable precedent. In the shelves of late twentieth-century translations and commentaries—none more influential than the 1978 New International Version, which quickly displaced the King James as America's best-selling Bible—American Christians read what might be called a "homosexualized" Bible. Instead of the archaic sinners and enigmatic sodomy talk found in the King James, these modern Bibles spoke clearly and plainly about the tradition's prohibition against same-sex behavior. The subsequent debate about the implications of these self-evident meanings overlooked a nearly invisible truth: the Bible's plain speech about homosexuality issued from a newly implanted therapeutic tongue.

Most chroniclers of the history of religion and homosexuality, however, have taken the Bible's new meanings as age-old testimony. As a consequence, stock narratives about the emergence of a gay identity movement assume an oppositional tug between the conservative forces of religious condemnation and the progressive momentum of modern change. What we hear, as a result, is about a transition "from abomination to disease," by which the therapeutic sciences superseded centuries-old religious prohibitions. We hear about how an emerging identity movement gradually emancipated itself from the vestiges of an antihomosexual religious past. We hear of progress forestalled by a religious backlash that resurrected ancient strictures. These narratives, to be sure, capture the felt sense of history told by partisans who understood their labor in terms of progressing modernity, emancipating sex, or defending tradition. When we take them as neutral descriptions of historical change, however, we miss their situated knowledge: they echo with the hidden influences of Protestant modernism.

What this book makes visible, thus, are the complex ways that a liberal Protestant legacy has shaped all sides of the oppositional politics over gay rights. This story begins in the early decades of the twentieth century, with a set of liberal Protestant leaders' eager engagement with the therapeutic sciences. These efforts reached an apex in the heralded psychiatry boom that followed World War II, when the hybrid field of pastoral counseling put institutional muscle into disseminating a self-help mode of spiritual living. A fleet of advice texts for Christian families, circulated by pastoral counseling experts, embedded psychological insights into everyday Christians' faith, relationships, and knowledge about sex. Christian experts on sexuality thus spurred a gradual sexual reformation in churches, which prized sexual health and normalcy as an expression of actualized spirituality. This emergent therapeutic orthodoxy also yielded unintended offspring. The liberal Protestant therapeutic synthesis, I show, also circulated within two social movements taking shape during the 1960s: a nascent gay identity movement and a consolidating network of conservative Protestant evangelicals were direct heirs to this set of therapeutic ideas and practices, and this book traces out those influences. It tells of the collaboration between clergy activists and early gay rights organizers and shows how a liberal therapeutic orthodoxy also came to influence the sexual teachings of evangelicals. The political battles between gay rights activists and religious conservatives that made newspaper headlines in the late 1970s may have looked like a dual jack-in-the-box encroachment from the political fringe: gays roared out of the closet and evangelicals awakened from their self-imposed exile in the cultural hinterlands. The depictions of barnstorming political outsiders, however, overlooked the earlier influence of liberal and moderate Protestants on both sides of a debate that seemed to take place across a religious-versus-secular divide. However, the oppositional forces of the emerging culture wars had more in common than it seemed. The certainties about religious orthodoxy and sexual identity defended on the Right and the Left carried forward assumptions already influenced by liberal Protestants. Both the emancipatory aims of queer activists and the anchors for conservatives' antigay Bible traditions drew from modern therapeutic understandings of sexuality that leaned against an invented religious past.

A key part of that influence was the idea that religion was the taproot source for antigay prejudice, a conviction illustrated by the Bible's newly plain prohibitions. Over the course of the postwar decades, that doughy innovation ossified into hardened bedrock. This sense of the past also had a normative gravity that extended well beyond communities of church attenders. It mattered to many people—religious and not—that taboos against homosexuality had been conceived and nurtured through two millennia of a "Judeo-Christian tradition." It is only recently that this sense of the distant past has come under challenge, and that challenge is still largely confined to the specialized discourses of academic scholarship. What that scholarship shows is that the mechanisms for understanding and regulating sexual behavior have changed markedly over time. Historians of sexuality have interrogated and unraveled the formation of modern therapeutic categories like homosexuality and heterosexuality, as scholars in the history of Christianity have also unpacked the layered inventions and reinventions of Christian sodomy discourses to illuminate the changing behaviors and characters associated with this category of theological invective.[12] To be clear, this research does not discount that Christians of the past—and especially Christian leaders—at times fiercely condemned same-sex sexual behavior. What this body of research shows, rather, is the distinct configuration of modern sexual regulation and subjectivity. The notorious "sin of Sodom" (and of those seen to be guilty of committing it) involved capacious kinds of deviance that do not align with the medical ideas and identity categories that became ascendant in the second half of the twentieth century. Taken together, this scholarship challenges the fallacious picture of an unbroken past of Christian antihomosexual regulation; it shows that neither same-sex behavior nor the religious terms that seem to speak of it have monolithic and transhistorical meanings.

And yet this scholarship still contends with popular assumptions—embedded in politics, law, and identity narratives—that take the contemporary configurations of bodies, sexes, desires, and identity as a durable map of the past. A key contribution of this book, thus, is to suggest that attention to religion, and especially to the Protestant biblicism dominant in the United States, helps account for how and why this idea of the past took up durable explanatory weight. Its power as perceived fact and its real effects on the world can be credited not to its timeless truth but to the ongoing avowals of human actors—from Bible translators and gay activists to Christian traditionalists and secular judiciaries—who have taken commonsense understandings of "what the Bible says" about homosexuality as a reliable measure of a religious past.

Untangling the historical production of that religious past also challenges a narrative about secularism as a driving force of twentieth-century changes in sexuality. This secularist narrative takes for granted that religion, conceived broadly, is the cultural taproot of moral and sexual regulation. The plot tells of the embattled achievement of sexual and gender rights over and against old religious regulation: scientific and medical inquiries shook earlier moral foundations, and political movements challenged the residues of moral taboo that remained in civil law. These changes, we are told, are rightly understood in terms of secularization and liberalization—the decline of religion and the loosening of regulation. Together, they progressively emancipated sexuality to be a matter of personal, individual choice. This narrative, of course, saturates the explanatory accounts of the culture war conflicts of the 1980s and 1990s. The Christian Right—the constitutive face of religion in sexuality politics—seemed to represent the last gasps, the fated "return," of an archaic morality in a secular age. Any insightful commentator on these conflicts, of course, acknowledges that the dividing lines over morality split religious institutions, too—certainly there are religious progressives who take sides with the secularizers. However, the exceptions often reinforce the rule: commentators persistently cast progressive faith as something like a defanged beast, either a lightly christened version of secularism or a watered-down blend of the old gospel. If religion is by nature conservative and progressive sexual politics are presumptively secular, than liberal faith will always seem to be a diluted byproduct of either the one or the other.

This narrative about the secular and the religious, I would suggest, relies on a Protestant metric to measure the relative strength of religiosity. True, "religious" seems to be an ill-fitting term to describe the modern, synthetic approach of Protestant progressives. Notice, however, the earnest ways that many liberal Protestants, then as now, elide "religion" for talk about "faith" and "spirituality." For many of these progressives, "religion" names the excessive, fallible, and temporal residue that has gummed up the search for genuine spirituality and prophetic justice making. They see their conservative counterparts as mistakenly attached to a hidebound dogma—a fallible set of cultural preconceptions—rather than committed to a lively faith. Religious progressives, thus, repeat an account of religion as a backwards drag on the emancipatory *telos* of modern change. Liberal Protestants, in other words, share in what anthropologist Webb Keane calls "the moral narrative of modernity" as a story about "human liberation from a host of false beliefs and fetishisms that undermined freedom in the past."[13] This way of telling religion and modern change is the constitutive tale of secularism, and it obscures the particularities of liberal Protestant influence.

The narratives about religion as backwards and conservative obscure liberal Protestant involvement for the same reasons that a photograph leaves few traces of the person behind the camera. This invisibility speaks to influence. Liberal Protestants, cosmopolitan and left-leaning wing of the venerable mainline Protestant denominations, are perhaps the most influential of modern religious subjects; for this very reason, they are also perpetually one of the most invisible. On their own terms, of course, they constantly slough off their own religiosity in pursuit of a truer faith. Excess, fallibility, and temporality—what Keane calls "semiotic form"— have been ongoing objects of reform in liberal Protestants' quest for transcendence.[14] These purifying aims make them reliable advocates for many of the modern changes often regarded as the force behind secularism. At the same time, their narratives about the role of "religion" in these changes perpetually obscure their own influence. Making that influence legible and visible in the history of twentieth-century sexuality, then, requires a kind of trace dye. In one sense, the history of changing discussions of homosexuality is just that: the messy records of liberal Protestants' disavowed religiosity found in outdated Bible commentaries, old committee minutes, and forgotten correspondence. Tracing these narratives reveals an account of change elided by liberal Protestants' own accounts of progress. As Pamela Klassen notes in her study of Protestants and medicalization, the attention to changing practice challenges worn tropes about liberal religion (or its lack) and opens up "the messiness of how those who have claimed to be liberal have actually practiced their ideals."[15] In this archive of Protestant practice, we find a story of change that pushes back against common assumptions about the role of religion, the nature of the therapeutic, and the particular changes in sexuality—all themes ordinarily plotted along a secular, teleological march toward progress. It shows liberals' own efforts—uneven, stumbling, and misguided—to reform religion in order to emancipate healthy sexuality. Liberal Protestants, as influential "agents of medicalization," to use Klassen's terms, have played an active part in the therapeutic reinvention of sexuality.[16]

Looking at a history of Protestant modernism unravels stock narratives about secularism, and it also challenges the contingent notion that the rise of therapy and self-help have unhinged the jaws of moral regulation. The axiomatic take on religion and therapy has long been summed up by the subtitle of E. Brooks Holifield's classic history of pastoral counseling: "from salvation to self-realization."[17] It is a nutshell lament about how the self-help mode replaced the anchors of traditional faith to set the culture adrift toward narcissism. This shopworn maxim, however, has been put to rest in recent scholarship. "Believers harnessed therapy to their own purposes," notes historian Stephanie Muravchik, whose work on the history of psychology traces the ways that Protestants moved therapeutic ideas from the offices of professional analysts and into the American mainstream. Even Protestant conservatives, though initially resistant to the way that liberals seemed to approach spiritual health with lopsided priorities—"man's wisdom" over "God's truth"—also found that the self-help mode was an amicable aid to conversionary faith.[18] Rather than see therapy as a diluting agent on the strictures of piety, we should notice the ways that twentieth-century religious practitioners have contributed to the dissemination of a self-help gospel. What we might observe, as well, is how the story of solipsistic release misses the ways that this self-help mode is still profoundly regulatory. Cultural theorist Nikolas Rose suggests that the "psy experts" effectively implanted their authority in the deepest interiors of what might seem to be the inchoate, presocialized realms of emotion and desire. "Our feelings, beliefs, desires, hopes and fears," he argues, "are suffused with the descriptions, injunctions, and evaluations of those who claim to know more about what is good for us than we do ourselves."[19] The therapeutic turn to the self, thus, did not supplant piety. Neither did it unpin the self from regulation. Indeed, it brought precisely the opposite: deeply implanted mechanisms and mandates for the ongoing labor of transforming the self.

Sex—and sexual pleasure—took up special importance for that labor of self-transformation. The conventional telling of twentieth-century changes in sex focuses on increasing permissiveness and declining moral regulation. Such accounts, of course, are tied to the perceived trajectories of religious decline and therapeutic ascendance as forces of change that gradually untangled sex from moral regulation and made it increasingly a personal and private matter of pleasure and choice. What we miss in this telling, however, are the ways that twentieth-century Americans put sexual pleasure to work. Certainly, sex in modern America has been unpinned from procreation; however, the non-procreative pleasure of sex has also been freighted with added responsibilities. Rebecca Davis's work

on the history of marriage counseling, for example, traces the rising chorus of sex researchers, advice authors, and relationship counselors who
addressed bourgeoisie heterosexual couples with swelling injunctions to
sexual pleasure.[20] Conservative religious practitioners, no less than their
liberal and secular counterparts, also navigated new mandates to practice sex religiously, as Amy DeRogatis's work on evangelical Christian sex
manuals decisively illustrates.[21] Amid the worries about fragile marriages
and imperiled families, a couple's sex life bore the imperative of holding
things together. Thus, even as many Christians—conservative and liberal—lamented sexual permissiveness and moral decline that they feared
might threaten the stability of the family, they also championed views
about healthy sexuality that rested on the same therapeutic foundations.
Protestant practitioners, even when they positioned themselves in a reac-
tionary role to a changing culture, broadly shared an ideal about sexuality
as core to identity and fundamental to human well-being.

These changes in good sex are critical for understanding the inquiry
at the center of this book, the invention of a Christian tradition of homosexuality. Much of the literature on the history of homosexuality—and
certainly the lion's share of the debate over present-day sexual ethics—
focuses on one aspect of continuity and change in sexuality: the question
of the act/identity distinction. Michel Foucault's famous passage from
The History of Sexuality ("the sodomite had been a temporary aberration;
the homosexual was now a species") is the most frequently cited char-
acterization of this historical shift, and it captures the way that psychiatry animated new ways of relating to sexual desire and attraction. The
medicalization of sex implanted perversions into the self, and Foucault's
work suggests that this therapeutic shift paradoxically established the
conditions of possibility for gay identity.[22] A body of scholarship on the
medicalization of sexuality, however, also adds to and complicates this
singular shift from "act" to "identity." This work points to another crucial change: the concurrent invention of the homosexual's salutary alter
ego, the heterosexual.[23] The twinned oppositions of a sexual binary thus
not only allowed for new ways of imagining selves but also shaped perceptions of sexual behavior. Sexual acts were retroactively sorted into the
binary of the therapeutic grid. Only in the hindsight logic of the medical
paradigm does a singular category for "same-sex acts" make sense. "Sodomy" and "the unnatural vice," two terms that predated the medical neologism of homosexuality, encompassed a broader sweep of perversions.[24]
The split between the "natural" and the "unnatural," rather than dividing

hetero from homo, cleaved productive from unproductive pleasures: the so-called Alexandrian rule in Christian theology held that sex for the sake of pleasure, even within marriage, was contrary to nature.[25] Thus, "sodomy" banned orifices unattached to a womb, penetrating devices that did not dispense seed, and nonhuman partners. But even pinning "sodomy" to non-procreative sex ignores the yet more capacious meanings found in the history of Western Christian theological invective. Sodomy talk also worked as a multipurpose polemic against perceived enemies of the faith; it was a slur that identified Muslim infidels, American Indian pagans, perverse Papists, sodomitical Reformers, and so on with monstrous animality and idolatrous perversity. To name "same-sex acts"— or even simply sex—as a continuous link through this history sloughs off contingent meanings of religious, racial, and colonial alterity.[26] The notion that Christianity has a stable history of condemning a discrete set of behaviors called "homosexual acts" is in large part an invention that stabilized and naturalized modern categories of sexual regulation.

This new past also stabilized and naturalized the expanding embrace of "healthy sexuality," the unmarked category for heterosexuality. By the 1950s a new map of sexuality was firmly in place: it prized the wholesome goodness of heterorelationality, the affectionate bond between husband and wife, and the necessity of sexual pleasure within marriage. Encouraging healthy sexuality, in the reigning terms of developmental psychiatry, required challenging and reforming unhealthy taboo, guilt, and shame that might thwart budding heterosexuals' inclination to desire the kind of sex that came naturally. The expanding encouragement to the fledgling traces of healthy sexuality might have looked like increasing sexual permissiveness, but that trend also coincided with growing worries about a lurking category of deviance. We must see these developments in tandem. Heterosexuality, normal and natural, opened up to encompass various newly sanctioned nonreproductive pleasures in its "charmed circle," to use a phrase coined by sexuality theorist Gayle Rubin.[27] At the same time, a newly consolidated homosexuality increasingly shouldered the discarded burden of sodomitical prohibition.

Religious leaders and institutions played an active part in these shifts, in large part because the therapeutic paradigm problematized religion in new ways. Many religious organizations (as well as other social institutions) of the late nineteenth century placed primary moral scrutiny on male-female social interactions. A gender ideology of separate spheres divided the social realms of women and men, and various single-sex religious organizations, like the Young Women's Christian Association and the Young Men's Christian Association, offered havens from the tempting vices brought by sex mingling. In contrast to the scrutiny on male-female interactions, these gender-segregated spheres celebrated the moral purity and wholesome goodness of same-sex affection and relationships. The ideals of spiritual kinship between brothers and between sisters, several scholars suggest, often allowed for erotic and even sexual relationships to pass without notice.[28] However, those close same-sex bonds, so prized during the Victorian era, increasingly came under scrutiny through the early decades of the twentieth century. They lost their unexamined innocence and spiritual primacy as Christians and others began to more actively privilege hetero-relationality as a primary spiritual good. The new gospel of sex that emerged in the twentieth century also shaped projects of biblical interpretation and Christian teaching, which consecrated the erotic configuration of heterosexual desire and identity as part of God's divinely created order. Thus, the religious project of valorizing heterosexual pleasure as natural, right, and godly, especially within marriage, was intimately connected to the formation of an antihomosexual tradition. The Bible's newly plain meanings consecrated and naturalized the emergent ideology of a homosexual/heterosexual binary.

Reforming Sodom traces what is in many ways a particular story—how American Protestants formed and then reformed religious teachings about homosexuality. My focus on mainline Protestants and their collaborators addresses a site that is limited in scope. The set of clergy, medical specialists, and activists in this frame are mostly (although certainly not exclusively) the proverbial WASPs—white, middle- and upper-class Protestants. We would be right to question, as a consequence, how the narratives offered from this vantage point about religion and homosexual identity reflect a specific and relatively privileged subjectivity even as they purport to characterize the historical relationship between religion and sexuality broadly, generically, and universally. My aim in tracing this history is certainly not to reinstate the cultural dominance of this sectarian story but rather to make visible the distinct Protestantism of a narrative that passes for a neutral, secular account. To use an analogy, we might approach the formation of heteronormative religious teaching as a social and historical process comparable to the ways in which European ethnic communities in the United States became "white." This approach would also suggest that sexuality has been important to the making of twentieth-century ideals of pluralism, as communities marginalized from a white Protestant norm achieved religious normativity by effectively "straightening" their religious practices and teachings. If this project makes one point, it is to turn the observations about antihomosexual religious prohibition into questions rather than answers. Rather than seeing present-day religious certainties—like antihomosexual traditions—as a seamless extension from the past, we need to trace and unpack those dynamics that produce new religious configurations that then pass as timeless and natural.

Where I begin, in this labor, is to examine the changes in the United States that made possible the first version of the Bible to specifically condemn homosexuals. Chapter 1 explores the midcentury invention of the liberal Protestant "therapeutic orthodoxy" and the flourishing of its strangely intertwined fruits: a newly prohibited biblical category of "homosexual acts" and a practice of faith-based counseling that offered a nonjudgmental method for achieving healthy sexuality. I turn in chapter 2 to the subjects of this discourse about homosexuality—homosexuals themselves—to examine the ways that a nascent identity movement of the 1950s strategically negotiated the therapeutic orthodoxy. There, the biblical condemnation and therapeutic self-actualization took up different meaning, as a surfacing identity movement articulated identity with liberal Protestantism's emancipatory logic and against its condemning past. The terms of the therapeutic orthodoxy also contributed to its own unraveling, and chapter 3 shows how liberal Protestants became influential allies and advocates of the emerging identity movement. Over the course of the 1960s, however, the logic of that support changed as clergy activists and allies moved from viewing homosexuals as victims of a medical condition to seeing them as victims of political injustice. Chapter 4 turns from the emerging gay identity movement to a series of theological skirmishes taking place in the late 1960s within mainline Protestant denominations. In the seething conflicts between liberals and conservatives, I trace the emergence of what might be called a heterosexual consensus, where Protestants across the theological and political spectrum adopted modern paradigms for sexuality into both conservative and liberal theological frameworks. Chapter 5 returns to gay activists and reflects on the symbolic moment that stands in for the movement's heralded birth, the 1969 Stonewall riots. Stonewall also served as inspiration for an invented tradition, and the chapter examines the continued influence of religion—and most particularly the continued influence of Christianity—within the ritual commemoration of a street riot in New

York. The epilogue to the book reflects on the peculiar invisibility of this history of religious and sexual change in the post-1970s culture wars.

Even into the twenty-first century, the Bible (and often a distinctly Protestant version of it) continues to serve as a touchstone for debate over a spectrum of political questions around sexuality. *Reforming Sodom* helps explain why. If the persistent debates over "what the Bible has to say about homosexuality" confound the commonsense notion that American politics is or should be secular, then this book suggests that Protestantism tangles—even more than we thought—across all sides of the oppositional politics over gay rights.

1

THE THERAPEUTIC ORTHODOXY

There is no better way to trace the convergence of morality and medicine than through one of the most renowned advocates of that trend. Harry Emerson Fosdick, longtime senior pastor of the ecumenical Riverside Church, was best known as a champion of liberal Protestant theology. His 1922 sermon "Shall the Fundamentalists Win?" earned him both fame and infamy as "Modernism's Moses."[1] Fosdick's eager engagement with the new modern sciences of psychology and psychiatry followed thoroughly from his theological leaning. His best-selling *On Being a Real Person* presented insights from the therapist's office as useful guides for Christian spiritual living. Published during the fraught years of American involvement in World War II, the text circulated across a broad American readership and even into the trenches. Thanks to an Armed Services edition of the book, soldiers too perused its life lessons about religion and successful living. The book recounted Fosdick's stumbling first steps into an experimental ministry—the field of pastoral counseling, a theological-therapeutic hybrid that adapted the new sciences of psychology and psychiatry for use in religious counseling.[2] It was also the first text in a burgeoning new genre of spiritual self-help to speak of homosexuality.

The reference was brief but formative. In his introductory remarks to the book, Fosdick recalled an encounter that took place in 1919 and first spurred his interest in psychiatry. It was three years before the sermon that brought his modernist fame (and, indirectly, the post at Riverside Church). Newly appointed as the pastor of New York's First Presbyterian Church, Fosdick had announced from the pulpit that he was beginning a new kind of ministry. It would be a Protestant answer to the Catholic confessional, where laity could confess their sins and troubles to an attentive pastor. He invited anyone who wished to speak to him individually to show up for his consultation hours the following Saturday. Fosdick arrived that day to find fourteen people waiting in the anteroom. The first conversation, with a "humiliated youth," brought the realization

Harry Emerson Fosdick, 1926. Photograph by Underwood & Underwood, The New York Public Library.

that he needed additional expertise for this practice of pastoral counseling to work. "Doubtless I had heard that there was such a disease as homosexuality," Fosdick recalled, "but never knowingly had I met a homosexual."[3] He contacted an expert, a psychiatrist and sex researcher appointed at Columbia University, whom Fosdick gratefully credited for introducing him to "the new knowledge and the new methods of psychotherapy."[4] Thus, it was the anguished confession of a youth struggling with his homosexuality—according to this recollection—that propelled Fosdick into the pastoral psychology ministry that would define much of his life's work.

When Fosdick published this memory in 1943, his early innovations in religious counseling were rapidly becoming a mainstream practice. The much heralded psychology boom of the postwar decades had a vigorous counterpart in mainline Protestant institutions. In the aftermath of World War II, as historian E. Brooks Holifield notes, pastoral theologians' earlier efforts to encourage mental health quickly became a "veritable flood."[5] In a surge of new publications and educational opportunities, an effort begun in the 1920s to encourage clinical pastoral education quickly became a mainstream part of Protestant ministerial training and practice. Two new professional journals tied the enterprise together—the *Journal of Pastoral Care* began publication in the mid-1940s, and *Pastoral Psychology* was founded in 1950. By the 1950s, 80 percent of Protestant seminaries offered courses in psychology and psychiatry, and a growing number of independent institutes and seminars, such as the Institute for Advanced Pastoral Studies and the Program in Religion and Psychiatry, also provided training beyond the formal ministerial degree.[6] The resources for pastors and professionals were also supplemented by an increasing number of popular how-to books by leaders in the field. It was the popular authors from this field, like Fosdick, argues historian Matthew Hedstrom, who "helped bring depth psychology into the cultural mainstream . . . by placing psychological concepts into a religious framework."[7] The pastoral counseling movement not only embedded psychological insights into the parish ministry but also ensured that for many Americans the turn to therapy was couched in a spiritual idiom.

This fusion of religion and the therapeutic sciences also circulated new understandings of sexuality. When the first pastoral counseling efforts formed in the 1920s, the term "homosexuality" was a medical neologism largely confined to medical journals. By the postwar era, the term appeared not only in newspapers and popular journals but also in the Bible itself, thanks to the 1946 translation of the Revised Standard Version (RSV). The dissemination of this knowledge about homosexuality occurred in the midst of heightened scrutiny and surveillance. Cold War rhetoric positioned so-called sex deviance as a threat to American national security, and new federal policies and policing practices worked to root out hidden homosexuals. Historian John D'Emilio describes a tripartite opprobrium that reigned during these years: "In the Judeo-Christian tradition, homosexual behavior was excoriated as a heinous sin, the law branded it a serious crime, and the medical profession diagnosed homosexuals and lesbians as diseased."[8] From the vantage point of the midcentury, the intertwined discourses of sin, crime, and perversion seemed to represent the vestiges of an age-old, unchanging taboo against homosexuality. The assumed cultural taproot for such views was a "Judeo-Christian tradition" that castigated homosexual behavior from its very beginnings.[9] That perception, however, had a history. The religious, medical, and legal stigmas against homosexuality that so preoccupied Americans of the postwar era were not the archaic remains of a religious past. Rather, they reflected the surfacing of a new synthesis, which knitted together disease theories and religious teaching into an emergent therapeutic orthodoxy.

The conjoined religious condemnation and disease diagnosis so prominent during the postwar era came not from the hellfire preaching of conservatives but from the crucible of a liberal Protestant quest for self-actualization. This chapter traces the invention of that new tradition through the emerging field of Protestant pastoral counseling, which influentially circulated a synthesis of religion and the therapeutic sciences. Theological modernism served as the broker for this meeting of spirituality and science. Modernism as a theological outlook, propelled a capacious quest for truth from ostensibly secular sources. This eager engagement with new scientific discoveries and insights stood in marked challenge to the defensive posture of self-defined "fundamentalists," who rejected their counterparts' cozy relationships with theories and knowledge grounded in overtly naturalistic foundations. Both fundamentalists and their postwar evangelical inheritors instead anchored their teachings to biblical authority and saving faith, seen as the unmovable rock of truth in a rapidly changing modern world.[10] Modernists, on the other hand, gravitated instead toward a notion of God's immanent presence in human culture: God, as sovereign creator, could be illuminated through even the naturalistic inquiries of the so-called secular sciences. Theological modernism, oriented toward the new as a source of revelation and reformation, positioned liberal Protestants as early adopters of the therapeutic paradigm.[11]

Thus, it is in pastoral counselors' optimistic hopes for therapeutic transformation that we must look in order to understand the distinct contours of the biblical tradition of antihomosexual condemnation. Here, we find how the fusion of religion and therapy also brought about the sodomite's transformation into the homosexual. That account admittedly challenges what is often imagined as the relationship between morality and medicine. "From abomination to disease" is the axiomatic description of the perceived shift from an older regime of moral regulation to the emergent discourses of the therapeutic sciences.[12] However, that account overlooks the sustained engagement between therapeutic professionals and religious leaders in the decades following the so-called medical invention of the homosexual. Rather than a unidirectional shift *from* theology *to* medicine, specialists from both fields collaborated in what they saw as a healing mission for the mind and soul. The theological-therapeutic hybrid produced by these collaborations is likely not what first comes to mind as an influence on a Christian tradition of homosexual condemnation. The Protestant therapeutic paradigm, progenitor of self-help spirituality, has been analyzed, in contrast, as a solvent on the strictures of Christian traditionalism. "From salvation to self-actualization," the subtitle of Holifield's landmark history, tells the well-rehearsed lament about how tradition withered in the turn to therapy.[13] Attention to homosexuality in this discourse thus opens up new ways to see the regulatory discipline of the therapeutic endeavor. It shows that the effort to help, to emancipate the self from entangling taboo, did not end regulation and discipline. Rather, it relocated them. As a consequence, this project also yielded two strangely intertwined fruit: alongside the procedures for self-actualization that promised to extricate the self from a condemning past was also found a newly barbed religious tradition of antihomosexual regulation.

Inventing the Homosexual

In 1919, the year of Fosdick's meeting with the troubled young man, the term "homosexuality" and the attached disease diagnosis would have been foreign to most pastors. It is possible that Fosdick himself did not possess at the time the knowledge he recalled in hindsight. Indeed, the sources of information readily available to a minister were notable in their marked absence of commentary about same-sex sexuality. Thus, it is not surprising that a Protestant minister, even a well-educated New Yorker like Fosdick, would have found, in 1919, that the most direct route to information about same-sex attraction was to make contact with a psychiatrist. The Bible commentaries and reference tools that lined pastors' offices at that time offered a very different set of terms and associations from those that governed the medical discussions of homosexuality.

The term "sodomy," notably, was a theological and legal term rather than a biblical one.[14] What actually appears in the Bible is a city named Sodom, referenced in various passages throughout both Hebrew and Greek testaments. The subsequent interpretive commentary focused on a particular account, found in Genesis 19, of God's punishment of Sodom and the adjoining Gomorrah because of the loathsome sin of its denizens. Although the Genesis account does not directly identify the nature of the sin, later readers, who understood that sin to be same-sex behavior, interpreted the city's male residents' demand "to know" two visiting angels as a euphemism for homosexuality.[15] Bible commentaries of the late nineteenth and early twentieth centuries, however, rarely referenced same-sex meanings for that sin. A 1929 commentary offered a typical definition, which was taken directly from a passage in Ezekiel: "Sodom's sin," explained here, was "arrogant prosperity and callousness."[16] Indeed, Sodom, like the biblical Babylon, was frequently invoked in the early twentieth century as a symbolic site of sin—but that sin was not necessarily same-sex behavior. The historical geographer George Adam Smith penned in 1902 the often-quoted reference to Sodom's unique importance as a symbol of God's wrath against human depravity. "The glare of Sodom and Gomorrah," he wrote, "is flung down the whole length of Scripture history. It is the popular and standard judgment of sin."[17] However, Smith made no reference to sexuality. His controversial finding in respect to Sodom was to suggest that the city's famed destruction was a matter of myth rather than history. Sodom, while readily discussed in the biblical reference books available to a pastor like Fosdick, was not yet notorious for specifically same-sex sin.

So too the biblical "sodomites." These figures were referenced in five passages of the King James, all in the Old Testament. The term itself was a much earlier neologism, used by the seventeenth-century translators of the KJV for a particular Hebrew word that in the original text implied no connection to the Sodom story. Bible readers of the early twentieth century could seek explication on these elusive figures by turning to commentaries or Bible dictionaries, which parsed through biblical meanings with reference to the original language and to recent theological and historical scholarship. The standard answer found in these references explained that "sodomites" bore this name because they were guilty of the same loathsome vice for which the residents of the city Sodom were punished. Here, too, commentaries offered different explanations—if they offered one at all—about the nature of this vice. Any commentaries that suggested that this sin was sexual also emphasized an ancient context: the biblical "sodomites" were pagan idol worshippers "consecrated . . . to impure heathen worship," who committed an "offence against nature frequently connected with idolatrous practices."[18] Reference tools influenced by early twentieth-century scholarship in comparative religion offered yet more specific ideas about these idolatrous sexual practices—according to these texts, they were part of primitive fertility rituals practiced by the Canaanite worshippers of Baal.[19] What seems clear across these references was that the vicious acts in question were part of ancient and exotic cults, well removed from the pedestrian philandering of immoral Christians.[20]

The psychiatrist with whom Fosdick consulted likely had a very different idea about what the minister's Christian faith taught about same-sex behavior. It was an axiom of the medical literature on homosexuality that Christian and Jewish scriptures had a long history of ferocious condemnation of homosexuality. The earliest medical books to discuss and theorize homosexuality also parsed through the biblical and theological references to "Sodom" and to "sodomy" as a precursor to the medical theories. Written during the late nineteenth century, those new theories were part of a specialized field of Western European medicine that inquired into the causes of abnormal sexual behavior, including same-sex behavior. Although experts offered various etiological theories, a reigning assumption in most of this writing was that same-sex desire and behavior stemmed from a kind of interior pathology—what Viennese psychiatrist Richard von Krafft-Ebing called *paresthesia*, or perversion. The sex offender, as Krafft-Ebing put it, was "an automaton, the slave of what makes him act."[21] On their own terms, these experts challenged moralizing approaches to human behavior and insisted that the neutral, empirical inquiries of modern medicine offered a more effective way to understand—and possibly remediate—sexual abnormalities.

Havelock Ellis, a British sex researcher writing at the turn of the twentieth century, was one of the first to write about the European medical theories in the English language, and his work also heavily influenced American physicians. Ellis's influential study on homosexuality, titled *Sexual Inversion*, was published in the United States in 1901, and it captured the emic terms of this discourse as a shift from abomination to disease.[22] Ellis made reference to religious prohibitions in order to distinguish the medical inquiries as a break from the misguided moralism of the past. "Sexual inversion," as Ellis theorized it, was distinct from the "theological and legal term, 'sodomy.'" Sodomy, he explained, referenced a "sexual act of intercourse *per anum*, even when carried out heterosexually."[23] It was not anal penetration in general that interested him but the set of erotic and sexual practices that took place specifically between people of the same sex. There was also a second important distinction in Ellis's approach. His work did not look merely at behavior but at something more deeply lodged in the human consciousness: a "psychic sexual proclivity" that was characterized by the "turning in of the sexual instinct toward persons of the same sex."[24] Thus, in Ellis's work, the medical approach differed from the theological in both a distinct focus on same-sex behavior and an attention to the interior condition that motivated same-sex affection and desire.

The person who most influenced American understandings of homosexuality, however, was the Viennese psychiatrist Sigmund Freud. Where a number of earlier sexologists, including Ellis, entertained the idea that durable same-sex desire and behavior—fixed homosexuality—might be an inborn trait, Freud championed a developmental model. All human sexuality, in the Freudian approach, was formed through infantile sexuality and psychosexual maturation. Thus, homosexuality, rather than a hereditary or congenital defect, was caused by early childhood development. Freud's *Three Essays on the Theory of Sexuality* gave an account of the developmental processes that resulted in homosexuality as well as those that yielded a fully mature and "adjusted" individual, whose sexual instinct was directed to members of the opposite sex. In Freud's assessment, adult homosexuality was the result of thwarted maturity; it was an immature stage of psychosexual development with infantile and primitive fixations. Freud, notably, did not see adult homosexuality as a condition that could be changed. However, homosexuality and other sexual perversions could be prevented, an idea that placed renewed scrutiny on practices of socialization and child rearing that might jeopardize the development of healthy heterosexuality.[25]

Freud briefly traveled to the United States in 1909 to give a series of lectures, which began a critical transfer of psychoanalytic ideas to American medical practitioners and intellectual elites. It was in the 1920s that an organized group of liberal Protestants interested in mental health began to systematically engage his ideas. Many of those early pastoral counselors initially responded warily to Freudian theories, which seemed to interpret all of human behavior as a consequence of inchoate sexual urges.[26] It was reasonable to be squeamish, one Christian writer admitted, when "science thrusts her dissecting-knife in among his vitals, and proposes to deal with all his inmost motives, hopes, and aspirations as coolly as she deals with frogs and worms in the zoological laboratory."[27] The early liberal Protestant advocates of these new perspectives, however, insisted that they were valuable for rethinking exactly the question of the motivating causes of human sinfulness. Of particular concern was the suggestion in Freudian theory that religious regulation might actually foster sexual perversion, which would suggest that the conventional ways of teaching Christian morality might have the unintended effect of inhibiting healthy sexuality. Anton Boisen, another influential advocate of pastoral counseling in the 1920s and afterward, was among those to criticize the "uncompromising" Christian views of sex as a cause of sexual abnormality. Many people "have difficulty making adjustments in the sexual realm," he argued, as a result of "the taboos to which sex is subject and the resulting inhibitions and prudishness." Boisen and others worked to develop programs in both Christian counseling and sexual education that replaced "the old 'thou shalt nots'" with "a true understanding of . . . positive values."[28] Thus, liberal Christians' interventions into sexuality followed the logic of a developmental approach.

Even though pastoral counselors of the late 1920s and 1930s did not have much to say directly about homosexuality, it was still the case that a lurking worry about maladjustment fueled new efforts to encourage healthy sexuality. The good news taken from developmental theories of sexuality, as put by the authors of a sex education book for the Young Men's Christian Association, was that "modern science is reinforcing religion at no point more strongly than in its present insistence that no harm need be irrevocable, that there is redemption for qualities that have been warped or thwarted, that it is possible to overcome practically every handicap."[29] The perfectionist tone of this treatise captured the approach of religious and political progressives of the late 1920s and 1930s, who developed educational and personal counseling methods designed to point children and young people toward future heterosexual marriage. A wave of Christian sex education manuals exhibited these deliberate strategies. Authors inveighed against taboos and legalism. They pressed education, rather than prohibition, as the antidote to immorality. They warned against intense same-sex friendships. They encouraged the "comradeship" of mixed-gender friendships and celebrated boys' and girls' "normal" attractions to the opposite sex. These counselors and educators endeavored to inoculate Christian young people from unnatural attractions by making sure that they did not regard "the opposite sex" through fraught prohibitions.[30]

Before the 1940s, even these devoted Protestant students of the therapeutic sciences had little to say about homosexuality in their published writing. Their advice about sex, marriage, and child rearing instead focused on encouraging healthy sexuality. In the years just following the Second World War, however, their few elusive references to homosexuality quickly became a flood.[31] Christian authors' earlier evasiveness was replaced by an urgent call to directly address a long-ignored problem.

The Problem of Homosexuality

Certainly, the war itself contributed to the new focus on homosexuality. The military employed more than fifteen hundred psychologists, and the cultural prominence achieved by these new doctors during the war spurred the demand for their expertise in the years that followed. Funding from foundations, universities, and the federal government provided material support for the therapeutic turn of the postwar decades.[32] Military regulations, for the first time in American history, also barred homosexuals from the service. Enlisted staff psychiatrists were tasked with diagnosing and reporting any cases of homosexuality to the disciplinary boards that discharged military personnel. Military chaplains also played an important role in these procedures and were expected to cooperate closely with staff psychiatrists in ensuring the general mental health of enlisted men and women. "The chaplain should be capable of recognizing serious mental ailments," advised a sociologist who studied the role of the army chaplain, "and of explaining clearly to the medical officer just what he has found."[33] Homosexual desires and behaviors were among these "serious mental ailments," and guidelines circulated to military chaplains instructed them to refer individuals to a psychiatrist at the earliest possible moment.[34]

This wartime cooperation expanded American ministers' awareness of and experience with professional methods for treating mental illness, and it also acquainted them with medical theories and treatments for homosexuality.[35] The account of one chaplain, a Congregationalist minister named Bertrand Crocker, tells of how his wartime service introduced him to the "sex problems" of enlisted men and the psychiatric methods for addressing them. Crocker blamed the military's sex-segregated conditions for inflaming homosexual proclivities. "Many of them had not seen a woman for a year or more," he recalled of soldiers who came to him for counseling, and he surmised that the absence of women had driven them to "practices considered abnormal." Crocker also did not entirely trust the approaches of staff psychiatrists, who he thought were "too definitely Freudian." After repeated—and frustrating—encounters with staff psychiatrists, who seemed to believe that "those kind" were beyond help, Crocker decided to invent his own methods for healing. His innovated practices drew from a smattering of psychological training gleaned from college courses in psychology. He knew that he needed to show a "tolerant attitude," but beyond that, he made it up. He encouraged one soldier to stop by the chaplain's office at any point to talk, with "the assurance that his confidence would never, under any circumstances, be betrayed." He exhorted another man to pray when he felt tempted and encouraged another to meditate on scripture. Crocker concluded from these experiences that Christian counselors needed to develop alternative therapeutic methods, different from those practiced by Freudian psychoanalysis. "That Carpenter Man," he argued, "is still aeons ahead of Freud."[36] In this particular pastor's mind, Christianity went a step beyond the psychiatric diagnosis by promising a cure.

Crocker's article about wartime sex problems was published amid a chorus of warnings about the mental health of returning soldiers. His reporting was directed to clergy and religious leaders, and it urged them to prepare themselves to understand and address the sex issues that psychologically troubled enlistees were bringing back with them to the home front. "Many of these boys are coming back home," Crocker wrote. "They are going to need your help in problems that will amaze you."[37] This pastor's warning echoed amid broader concerns about mental health—and deviant sexuality in particular—as soldiers returned home.[38]

Another development also influenced pastoral counselors' postwar discussions of homosexuality: the medical theories of diagnosis and cure were changing. Most psychiatrists of earlier decades, following Freud's own views, regarded homosexuality as a condition that resisted clinical treatment. During the 1940s, a group of New York–based psychiatrists began to reinterpret developmental theories of sexuality as the key to a cure. These efforts were led by Sandor Rado, a Hungarian-born psychiatrist and a founder of the Psychoanalytic Institute of Columbia University. Rado and his colleagues theorized a model for healing homosexuality through psychoanalytic therapy. If homosexuality was caused by thwarted maturation, they thought, the proper analysis should help homosexuals work through the emotional conflicts that blocked the natural progression of their heterosexual desire.[39] Margaretta Bowers, a psychiatrist in this milieu who also provided services for the New York City diocese of the Episcopal Church, succinctly assessed the destinies of her patients with same-sex attraction: "I consider all homosexuals as latent heterosexuals," she appraised.[40] Pastoral counselors looking for therapeutic resources on homosexuality finally had an authoritative resource that promised the hoped-for healing.

Clergy counselors also had an urgent motive to put those resources to use, thanks to a gall wasp specialist turned sex researcher named Alfred Kinsey. In 1948, Kinsey and a team from Indiana University published the results of their decade of research on the sexual behavior of white American men. The groundbreaking findings in *Sexual Behavior in the Human Male* were followed five years later by *Sexual Behavior in the Human Female*. The studies supplied controversial evidence of what looked like

Americans' sexual hypocrisy: the findings showed that actual practice diverged markedly from espoused sexual mores.[41] The reports of male homosexual behavior were especially shocking. According to the Kinsey study, 37 percent of white American men had at least one homosexual experience at some point in their lives; 4 percent were exclusively homosexual. The loudest reaction to these studies from Christian clergy was outrage—one conservative pastor denounced them as "a moral Hell-bomb" that threatened American's spiritual lives as surely as the threat of communist attack.[42]

Most liberal Christian leaders, however, interpreted Kinsey's findings as a call to action. A rapid succession of articles in the new pastoral counseling journals challenged church leaders to change their "ostrich-like attitude" toward homosexuality.[43] It was an urgent problem that had been neglected too long. The Kinsey report, argued one psychiatrist contributor, made it impossible for pastors to dodge the hard fact that "the ramifications of homosexuality were much more widespread than anyone cared to admit."[44] These authors also interpreted the Kinsey studies through the lens of psychoanalytic theory. Kinsey himself viewed the large numbers of homosexual experience as evidence of benign natural variation (like gall wasps, human sexuality came in many varieties). Pastoral counselors disagreed with Kinsey's naturalistic assumptions. One critic commended the Kinsey reports for bringing attention to the widespread "variety of sexual activities among American males." However, he assessed the variety as a problem—caused, in part, by "ignorance and individual and social pathology."[45] Seward Hiltner, a leader in the field who published a monograph that evaluated the Kinsey studies from a Christian perspective, exemplified pastoral counselors' psychoanalytic interpretation. The statistics, he determined, indicated that "impulses toward homosexual experiences at certain earlier stages of development are within a normal and natural pattern of development." However, Hiltner also maintained that adult homosexuality was another matter: "If this is taken to mean an evaluation of naturalness, normality, or rightness [of homosexual behavior] at a human mature and adult interpersonal level, then that is quite different."[46] For leaders in the field of pastoral counseling, Kinsey's findings, combined with their awareness of psychoanalytic therapies, propelled a mission to address, prevent, and, they hoped, cure a newly urgent problem of homosexuality.[47]

Swirling through liberal Christians' worries about homosexuality was also a larger set of cultural concerns. Sex deviance was a unique preoccupation during this postwar "Age of Anxiety," as it was popularly termed. A widely circulating Cold War rhetoric positioned homosexuality as a surreptitious insider threat to American national security. In an editorial published in 1950, Senator Joseph McCarthy, one of the most notorious trumpeters of these conspiracies, warned Americans that moral toleration might spell national ruin. "Once the people of a nation become complacent about morals, then that nation has not long to live," he declared. As historical evidence he noted that "the great Roman Empire came to an end when the ruling class became morally perverted and degenerate."[48] Under such fears, as historian David Johnson shows in his *Lavender Scare*, federal policies purged suspected "sex deviants" from governmental positions while state and municipal authorities developed policing practices aimed to root out such hidden figures from their communities.[49] Popular magazines ran salacious articles that portrayed homosexuals as psychotic criminals and warned parents that bad parenting practices could foster the same kind of deviance in their own beloved children.[50] From powerful offices of the government to the seeming sanctuary of the home, this Cold War discourse chided Americans to be attentive to a lurking threat.

Pastoral counselors and their therapeutic allies criticized the punitive approaches to controlling homosexuality, but even these sexual liberals participated in the era's scrutiny of deviant sexuality. Pastoral counseling professionals instead advocated what they saw as a more effective and compassionate approach—not punishment, but therapy. Rather than address homosexuality as a threat to be rooted out and punished, they saw it instead as a condition to be diagnosed and cured. Such an approach also went hand in hand with pastoral counselors' concern for encouraging healthy sexuality. Diagnosing homosexuality as a curable condition, historian Rebecca Davis suggests, helped maintain "faith in the possibility of heterosexual perfection."[51] Pastoral counselors spoke glowingly of the transformational effects of self-discovery and imbued marriage—and couples' intimate sex lives—as the apex of that journey to authenticity. In an article articulating a pastoral theology of sex and marriage, Reuel L. Howe advised, "Marriage, by virtue of the structure it provides, is able to give sex life a continuity and stability that is necessary for the fullest realization of the purposes and meanings of sex." Self-realization was no end in itself; it also led to spiritual growth and fulfillment. Here, too, marital sexual intimacy opened up unique doors to the self as "a means of grace" and an "instrument for the reunion of that which is separated and alienated."[52] This focus on the goodness of the right kind of sex also redoubled inspection and scrutiny of behaviors that might inhibit that ideal.

Thus, sexual emancipation and self-actualization in the therapeutic discourse were foundationally tied to the developmental forces that might foster its unhealthy opposite, homosexuality. Focusing on the advice to pastors about how to address homosexuality therefore serves to make visible those otherwise elusive norms of the therapeutic ethos. The same emancipatory ideals—of finding and realizing a true self—circulated in pastoral counselors' companion advice about homosexuality. In this context, those ideas had more visible disciplinary aims. Self-actualization was not the end, full stop, to regulation. Rather, it was the method for producing the right kind of true self: releasing the self from condemnation, paradoxically, yielded heterosexuality. Thus, what we must also notice in the specialized advice that coached pastors in their responses to troubled homosexuals is that rightly practiced religion was essential to the project of forming healthy sexuality. The advice about homosexuality found in the pastoral counseling journal articles and advice books was directed, first and foremost, to pastors, representatives of Christianity in the nest of sexual troubles that might crop up in their congregations. The advice to pastors about how to address the "problem of homosexuality" repeatedly offered direction about how to respond if and when a troubled parishioner—usually a young man—entered the pastor's office. What this pastor had to learn, if he had any hope of helping the person who sought him out, was how to practice a new kind of faith.

A Therapeutic Approach

A pastor's first task was to entice wordless parishioners to tell their secrets. This was the advice offered by one influential textbook on pastoral counseling, William Northridge's *Psychology and Pastoral Practice*, published in 1953. The book's discussion of homosexuality opens with a vignette about a kindhearted pastor and a conflicted young man. Northridge narrates the account in the second person, thus conscripting the reader to identify with a pastor who must decide how to respond to an unexpected telephone call. "You will hear him sobbing," Northridge describes. "He says, 'I am afraid.'" In this story, "you," the compassionate but perplexed pastor, beg the caller to come over immediately. When the man finally arrives, he is "in a state of intense emotion"—so agitated that he is completely unable to speak. This is a crucial moment of action. "The attitude you adopt at the beginning," Northridge warns, "will decide whether he will be frank with you or keep to himself the very facts that ought to be disclosed."[53] If the pastor responds appropriately, the story of his troubled parishioner might go something like this: "He will probably tell you that homo-eroticism has been his problem for years, that he can never remember having any interest in the opposite sex."[54] Whether this confession ever reaches the light of day, however, crucially depends on the attitude and behavior of the pastor, whose response to skittish clients might either begin a process of healing or consign them to their illicit desires.

The experts writing the articles and advice columns in pastoral counseling journals usually began their instruction to pastors with a repeated refrain. The repetition itself suggests that they viewed pastors' own impulses with suspicion—men accustomed to the authority of the pulpit, pastors would need to reform their own ingrained tendencies in order to help homosexuals overcome theirs. Thus, over and again, the experts pressed ministers to leave behind "moralism" in order to approach the troubled client without judgment. "It is no more the minister's task to condemn than to condone," argued a psychiatrist contributor to *Pastoral Psychology*. "It is folly to tell these people to give up homosexual practices," advised a trained pastoral counselor.[55] But the injunctions against condemnation and didacticism did not mean that pastors should accept homosexuals as they were and leave it at that. The problem with judgment or moral instruction was twofold. First, it focused on acts and behaviors, which depth psychiatry saw as only the outward sign of a deeper problem—a "surface manifestation of deeply rooted psychic conflicts."[56] The second problem with a "moral approach" was that it seemed to assume that men and women who acted out of a homosexual condition had conscious control over their behavior—a view that did not account for the compulsive nature of the condition. Homosexuality, explained one psychiatrist, was "a kind of mental illness and not a willful perversity."[57] To uproot this entrenched illness, ministers needed to take up a different method of intervention—a particular "therapeutic approach" that would begin a process of transformation in their troubled clients.

Counseling methods developed by Carl Rogers, the founder of the humanistic psychology movement, directly influenced the on-the-ground counseling practices encouraged by pastoral counseling experts. It was from Rogers that these experts borrowed the language of "unconditional positive regard" to refer to the interactive rapport between counselor and client. Pastors' attitude of warmth and encouragement toward the client, counselors emphasized, enabled them to honestly and productively address their emotional conflicts. It freed them from the inhibiting pressure to conform and gave the self-regard they needed to move toward the "responsible freedom" that was the hallmark of ethical and psychological maturity.[58] Unconditional positive regard, of course, was not mere permissiveness. David Roberts, a theologian at Union Theological Seminary, describes this stance in language that highlights its transformative potential. More than "assure them willy-nilly that they are 'all right'," the process actually changed a client's deeply rooted psychic conflicts "by releasing a power which removes the *causes* of guilt."[59] Unconditional regard, that is, had soul-saving efficacy.

Such a process was particularly important for homosexuals, because guilt—or so psychiatrists theorized—was tangled up in the developmental roots of sexual maladjustment. Those roots extended back to early childhood. Done right, psychiatrists claimed, parents' relationships with each other and with their children encouraged children's natural inclination toward heterosexuality. "A harmonious relationship between a masculine father and a feminine mother is essential in fostering a feeling of security on the part of the child," declared psychiatrist George W. Henry in his 1955 book, *All the Sexes*. This gendered domesticity provided an atmosphere of "affection and security" that nurtured a child's normal sexual development.[60] On the other hand, children who grew up without this kind of security, psychiatrists warned, often developed the anxieties and neuroses that fueled homosexual behavior. This developmental model added yet another danger to the ill effects of pastors' efforts to reform homosexuals by lecturing them. "Guilt, fear, or anxiety," one pastoral counselor warned, "has the effect of reinforcing the [homosexual] impulse."[61] To respond with condemnation or disapproval not only was ineffective but might actually make the problem worse.

Thus, pastoral counselors turned to the nonjudgmental "therapeutic approach" as a double-edged arsenal against the deeply rooted condition of their homosexual parishioners. The counseling process, they believed, tapped into the transformative power of personally motivated change. For homosexuals, it promised to release their innate capacity for heterosexuality. Carrol Wise, a contributor to *Pastoral Psychology*, expressed this dual faith: an attitude of therapeutic acceptance, he advised, offered parishioners with "sex problems" the self-regard to "work out their fear, guilt, and hate, so that their capacity for love can find expression."[62] The process of self-actualization found in therapy was supposed to help homosexuals retrace the thwarted maturation process, surpass the developmental channels blocked by anxiety, and become their true—heterosexual—selves.

Case study accounts of homosexual therapy present this sexual and spiritual transformation in step-by-step sequence. A book written in 1955 by Israel Gerber, a Reform rabbi, depicts an especially intimate account of transformation. Gerber also offers his effective therapeutic method as a counter to the ineffective condemnation his client had experienced earlier from a Protestant clergyman. The book, *Man on a Pendulum: A Case History of an Invert*, gives the firsthand account of Gerber's client, pseudonymously named John Collins.[63] Like Northridge's skittish client, Collins is presented as a deeply hesitant man whose inner turmoil propelled him to seek professional help. "Noticeably anxious" and barely able to control his speech and emotions, Collins impulsively disclosed his homosexuality to the rabbi, who received the confession with a calm placidity that contrasted with his client's evident agitation. Collins' internal response to the rabbi's nonjudgmental regard was the first step toward healing. In this moment, Collins recalled the very different approach of his former pastor, who "called him a sinner doomed to eternal damnation, with no hope of salvation unless he stopped this practice immediately." How different the rabbi was from his minister, Collins thought. He "accepted him as he was. He even called him a child of God." As an almost immediate response, "some of Collins's tension left him." The minute change effected in this moment—the lessening of a high-strung homosexual's emotional pattern of anxiety—was the first of many changes recounted, over the process of nineteen weeks, to the placid ears of the rabbi-counselor. Collins's nervous impulsiveness, by the book's end, had changed to calm self-confidence, a transformation in affect that evidenced both his newly achieved heterosexual masculinity and his peace with God.[64]

It was not only men whom clergy needed to scrutinize for evidence of maladjustment. A pastor's inquiry, published in *Pastoral Psychology*'s monthly "consultation clinic" with expert replies, showed that women might also suffer from homosexual tendencies. The pastor's question aired gossip among members of his congregation who had confided their concerns about two women in the church—one married, one single, both about forty years old—who "held hands" in church services. "It is believed," he reported, "that their constant association is character-ized by one acting as a man and the other as a woman." He suspected an "unnatural sexual relation" but wanted expert confirmation that the rela-tionship was, indeed, sexual. "Could there be," he asked, "this unnatural affection between women? (I know there is between men.)" He further inquired, as if the idea of the thing were improbable, "Would a small-in-stature maiden lady permit sexual advances from a woman who does not have the charm of a lady, but the strength of a man?" The question asked the experts to help him discern the nature of the relationship, and most of the respondents readily confirmed his suspicions. "There could be and likely is an 'unnatural affection' existing between these two women," averred one psychiatrist, and he and the other respondents emphatically stressed both women's need for psychiatric help.[65]

In addition to confirming that homosexuality might beset women, the respondents also challenged the pastor's assumption that the women could be homosexuals only if they actually had sex. Indeed, the con-cerned pastor did not need evidence of physical relations to confirm the two women's maladjustment. The pathology was already evident in the women's relationship. Seward Hiltner, writing as a contributor to the forum, explained the need for concern. "Sex relations or no sex relations," he insisted, the women's relationship was still homosexual in a "motivation" sense. Their attachment to each other suggested that both women were "fixed at a stage prior to maturity" that inhibited their capacity to gain emotional satisfaction from a "woman-man relation-ship." No matter the physical relationship between them, "these women have been unable to reach the kind of maturity in which the most deeply sought love object is fundamentally different from oneself, of the other sex."[66] The overly close same-sex bond was evidence enough that some-thing was wrong.

This idea—that people could be "motivationally" homosexual without having sex—posed some challenging questions to conventional Chris-tian social practices. Various respondents to the forum encouraged the pastor to pay closer attention to the signs of relationship pathology in behavior that passed for normal. To highlight this issue, Hiltner con-tinued by posing a hypothetical situation. Just suppose, he wrote, "that our maiden lady came to church and held hands, not with the married woman, but with a bachelor from the congregation." The scrutiny and judgment, he suggested, "might be harsher if the hand-holder were the bachelor." Another contributor to the forum, a psychiatrist, similarly warned that "among women display of amative affections is socially more acceptable." Yet another psychiatrist instructed, "Sexual contact between female and female occurs even more frequently than it does between male and male."[67] Hiltner, in summary comments at the end of the forum, extrapolated from these remarks to broach what he acknowledged was "no simple matter": the possibility that Christian social practices unwittingly enabled unhealthy intimacies between women. "It is an open question," he pressed, "whether we do not make homosexuality an easier out than heterosexuality."[68] Neither Hiltner nor the other contributors offered a direct admonition to pastors or to churches about what they should do differently with this understanding that "unnatural relations" might not just be sexual ones. By implication, however, this discussion suggested another practice that ministers should add to the therapeutic toolbox: in addition to cultivating nonjudgmental regard for confessed homosexuals, they also needed to sharpen their attention to the signs of a homosexual condition that might ordinarily pass as innocent friendship.

The "therapeutic approach" advocated by pastoral counseling experts and allied mental health specialists offered, on its own terms, a method of freeing self-actualization. It also seemed to entail a radical challenge to conventional Christian sexual regulations. It is on these overt terms that critics have characterized the midcentury turn to the therapeutic as solipsistic and lacking in the discipline and rigor of traditional Christian theology.[69] Pastoral counselors' remarks about homosexuality, however, highlight the limits to the supposed anything-goes pluralism. In fact, homosexuality served as a paradigmatic example when pastoral counselors themselves discussed this concern. One pastor's comments seized on homosexuality as an example to illustrate the difference between therapeutic nonjudgment and ethical relativism. "If a homosexual is living happily in his little homosexual community," he asked, "[shall we say that] this is the most for which we have the right to hope for him?"[70] It was a rhetorical question that assumed his audience would certainly not say that homosexuals' own seeming happiness should be the measure of their mental health. Elsewhere, Hiltner referenced homosexuality to illustrate the continued salience of "the sin rubric" in Christian teaching about sex. We can "hold out a sustaining therapeutic hand to the unhappy homosexual," Hiltner argued, "if we are clear that homosexuality is, at best, a distorted way of achieving companionship."[71] What therapy offered, that is, was not merely self-acceptance but the power to change.

The disciplinary subject of this regulation was, most evidently, the homosexual, whose "deeply rooted pathology" was the focus of pastoral counseling advice. The reiterated advice, however, also addressed another subject of transformative change: the pastor—and, by extension, Christian teaching. As pastoral counseling experts, psychiatrists, and psychologists administered advice for curing homosexuals, they also insisted that Christian teaching and pastoral practice must also change. Therapeutic specialists suggestively spoke of churches as entities with troubled sexual histories and unhealthy patterns of relating, and they pressed ministers to reform the dogmatic tone of moral teaching that might unwittingly thwart parishioners' growth to spiritual and sexual maturity. That is, just as therapy helped women and men discover who they really were, so the therapeutic approaches provided tools for reforming Christian teachings to make them truly Christian. "I believe we must go back to basic Christian principles, then work out from them in the light of our newer knowledge," Hiltner wrote in a reflection on the ways that therapeutic insights challenged older ways of teaching sexual morality. He admitted that this process would "at times contradict what the tradition has said," but, he contended, "at such points, the traditional inferences are not proper applications of Christian principles, but are themselves fallibly human."[72] This was the therapeutic approach put to work in a modernist theological method: insights gleaned from the new scientific understandings of sex promised to perfect Christian teaching and practice. These practices of reforming the tradition, however, extended even further into the foundation of Christian teaching than these therapeutic experts realized. The project of straightening the sexualities of Christian practitioners went hand in hand with the straightening of the Bible itself.

Reforming Tradition

The new terminology found in the Revised Standard Version of the Bible offered the most visible sign of how therapeutic understandings of sexuality were shaping the interpreted meanings of the Bible. The New Testament of this new translation was published in 1946, and the full Bible came out in 1952. Leading scholars from top universities and seminaries had labored over the past decade on what was billed as "the greatest Bible in 341 years." It promised to match the "timeless beauty" of the King James with "more accurate and easier to read prose."[73] That accessible idiom, for the first time, directly condemned "homosexuals" in 1 Corinthians 6:9. In a list of grievous sinners, where the older KJV referenced the "effeminate" and "abusers of themselves with mankind," the new translation now directly named "homosexuals."[74] The new term foreclosed older meanings, including masturbation ("self-abuse") and non-procreative heterosexual sex, which Protestant authors encouraging healthy sexuality routinely insisted were inaccurate misperceptions of the text's true meanings.[75] Readers of the RSV found clear evidence of that insistent advice: what was condemned in the Bible was now plainly homosexuality.

The insertion of the homosexual into this passage was not the only way that modern sexual ideologies were changing biblical meanings. Just a few years after the RSV publication, Abingdon Press, the theologically moderate Methodist publishing house, issued a twelve-volume comparative commentary in its Interpreter's Bible series. This "veritable 'open sesame'" to the world of the Bible, as its editor acclaimed, parsed through the translation changes from the KJV to the RSV. In bridging old and new translations, the commentary also illuminated how modern translators and commentators were reconfiguring an earlier "Sodom tradition" into what might be a called a new "homosexuality tradition." Only one passage—1 Corinthians 6:9—mentioned "homosexuals" in the biblical text itself, but the commentary on Genesis 19, Leviticus 18 and 20, and Romans 1 also spelled out the passages' homosexual meanings. The language of the explication mirrored psychiatric theories. The Romans passage, the commentator clarified, addressed homosexuality as a "manifestation" of "the root cause of both the sin and corruption in idolatry," phrasing that followed disease diagnosis of homosexuality as the manifestation of a deeply rooted psychological condition. The notes emphasized that the sin referenced in this passage impinged upon the lives of modern-day readers. Those who "refuse to give God any place in their thoughts" might also be abandoned to corrupt desires.[76] The entry of new homosexual meanings for these passages also occurred alongside another subtle textual change. In several Old Testament passages where the KJV named "sodomites," the RSV substituted "cult prostitutes." The changed term offered what translators and commentators alike saw as merely a clarification. This figure, they reiterated, practiced a kind of "sacred prostitution . . . common in the worship of pagan deities."[77] Hinted at in the RSV's textual changes were the interpretive powers of a new sexual ideology: as the homosexual entered the text, the sodomite exited.

This multivolume reference set had an admittedly limited reach, but similar changes could be found in books addressed to a popular audience, which discussed what was in the 1950s still quite a new question: What did the Bible have to say about homosexuality? Few books were as influential as William Graham Cole's *Sex and Love in the Bible*. Cole studied for his doctorate at Union Theological Seminary, where he worked with theological luminaries Reinhold Niebuhr and Paul Tillich. When he published his 1959 book, he was a dean and professor of religion at Williams College. An advance excerpt of the book published in *Ladies' Home Journal* and an interview in the *American Weekly* assured Cole a broad audience. Readers who turned to Cole's work found a readable synthesis of therapeutic values with ancient texts. Americans looking for advice on healthy sexuality could find a surprising resource in the Bible's ancient wisdom. "The Bible makes no bones about the fact that sex is enjoyable," Cole insisted; "but it also emphasizes that sex carries with it responsibility."[78] Between the Ten Commandments and the Song of Solomon, the Bible offered a perfectly balanced message for modern couples.

Alongside the Bible's wholesome advice for women and men, Cole also pointed to its equally relevant word on homosexuality. The biblical view, he noted, "coincides with a growing body of thought in contemporary psychoanalytic circles." The particulars of that wisdom confirmed that the Bible, and the tradition of interpretation carried forward in Christianity and Judaism, did indeed view homosexuality as a grave sin. However, Cole was also very much a liberal Protestant; at every turn, he worked to interpret and synthesize those biblical meanings with contemporary psychoanalysis. As a consequence, his interpretation of biblical texts de-emphasized the so-called letter of the law—"the Old Testament prohibitions and all of Paul's diatribes against immorality"—to emphasize the spirit. A "truly Biblical view of sex," as Cole understood it, communicated a "positive" message of "responsible freedom."[79] Having extracted this eminently healthy-minded biblical interpretation, Cole could easily turn to the views of psychiatrists and discover—"curiously enough"—that the ancient and contemporary perspectives were thoroughly consonant.[80] Cole's approach to homosexuality thus followed an earnestly synthetic path. He reviewed the web of Old and New Testament prohibitions and confirmed that homosexuality was "a sin and a crime" that the ancients associated with pagan idolatry. The association with pagan idolatry, for Cole, only confirmed the link to modern disease theories. He reasoned that both reflected "the failure to know God aright" and therefore entailed a warped sense of self and relation.[81] The ancients' link between homosexuality and idolatry thus confirmed the twentieth-century knowledge of homosexuality as a disease.

Cole also proceeded to deal with the biblical prohibition against homosexual behavior through a classic Protestant emphasis on grace over law. The text established the letter of the law, but Cole argued that Christians should not legalistically condemn homosexuality. Rather, they should help homosexuals find transformative assistance from a psychotherapist able to "trace the malady to its root and cure it." Cole's argument—and his faith in the healing aid of science—reiterated and expanded liberal Christians' long-standing emphasis on the perfectionist possibilities of modern science. In Cole's formulation, psychotherapy offered a modern-day supersession of biblical law: rather than "simply condemn homosexuality as against God and nature," Cole urged Christians to place their hopes in modern medicine, which was "able to heal, to redeem, and to restore without condemnation or judgment."[82] Psychoanalysis, it seemed, provided the means of grace for the healing of deviants. Cole's synthetic interpretation presented the psychoanalytic meanings as if they had always been a latent part of the text itself, only now fully realized with modern insight.

Not every liberal Protestant interpreter viewed the biblical meanings as a seamless fit with modern medicine. Another influential approach came from the British church historian Derrick Sherwin Bailey in 1955. His book *Homosexuality and the Western Christian Tradition* also circulated widely, thanks to Bailey's prominent and controversial advocacy of sodomy law reform in Great Britain. Bailey was a member of the committee that authored the *Wolfenden Report*, a treatise that asked Parliament to repeal the so-called crime against nature statutes that criminalized sodomy and buggery. The *Wolfenden Report* argued that private sexual behavior between consenting adults should be considered a matter of private morality rather than of public law. Bailey's book, a systematic appraisal of Christian scriptures, underscored that political argument. Although Bailey confirmed that the Bible condemned "homosexual acts," he also argued that these prohibitions were no more severe than the biblical strictures against heterosexual sins. Thus, the bottom line was that the Bible did not support the law's disproportionate scrutiny of homosexuality. It was a remarkably progressive argument during a time when many public figures took for granted that religion supported antihomosexual laws and policies. Just as important as the political argument was Bailey's nuanced analysis of the biblical record, which influenced subsequent analysis of biblical teachings about homosexuality written by both liberals and conservatives. Even as Bailey challenged legal penalties and social stigma resulting from homosexuality, his work also gave authoritative weight to the emergent homosexuality tradition in biblical interpretation.

Bailey's work in many ways followed the textual meanings outlined in the series of comparative commentaries published through *The Interpreter's Bible*. His work also further unpinned the texts addressing homosexuality from an earlier interpretive tradition centered on Sodom. Bailey hastened the exit of the "sodomite" from the set of Old Testament texts where this figure linked pagan idolatry to the Genesis Sodom account. The original Hebrew term in these verses, Bailey argued, had no clear connection to the Sodom account and seemed to address instead a kind of cultic practice of the ancient Hebrews' pagan neighbors. This term was important to the earlier understandings of the "sodomite" as a pagan idolater, a meaning that appeared in many early twentieth-century biblical reference tools. In that context, a number of religious studies scholars of the late nineteenth and early twentieth centuries theorized its possible meanings as a kind of primitive religious fertility ritual. To Bailey, these inquiries confirmed the illogic of the term's connection to the Sodom story. "Homosexual coitus would be meaningless in a fertility ritual," he reasoned.[83] Idolatrous perversion might have had a place in earlier discussions of sodomy, but Bailey roundly concluded that these figures, called "sodomites" by mistaken translation, were completely irrelevant to any discussion of homosexuality. More controversially, Bailey also questioned the relevance of the very epicenter of the Sodom tradition, the Genesis story of the city's destruction, to discussions about homosexuality. The homosexual nature of the sin in question rested on the understanding of a single Hebrew verb—literally translated "to know"—as a euphemism for sexual intercourse. After a lengthy analysis of the verb and a rousing survey of historical commentary on the meaning of Sodom's sin, Bailey concluded that any homosexual interpretation of this passage was a mistake to be pitched into the dustbin of bad Bible scholarship.

This left five "definite references," Bailey claimed, where the Bible did indeed address homosexuality: two verses in Leviticus as well as passages in Romans, 1 Corinthians, and 1 Timothy. None of these passages, notably, make reference to Sodom.[84] By jettisoning that formative center to the sodomy tradition, Bailey routed the notion that homosexuality was someone uniquely condemned in the biblical record.[85] Bailey's interpretation also carefully distinguished ancient meanings from modern psychiatric theories. "Strictly speaking," he insisted, "the Bible and Christian tradition know nothing of *homosexuality*; both are concerned solely with the commission of homosexual *acts*."[86] What was important about that distinction had to do with the motivating cause for same-sex behavior. The biblical prohibitions, Bailey insisted, assumed a moral actor with free will. However, modern medicine suggested something else—that those who committed such acts were motivated instead by a "*condition* characterized by an emotional and physico-sexual propensity toward others of the same sex."[87] The crux of the issue for Bailey was whether a person with a psychological condition could be held morally at fault for expressing tendencies linked to a mental illness, a question he addressed in an article published on the heels of his book. There, he offered a careful theological caveat to the Bible's seemingly clear condemnation. A "genuine invert," he argued, could not be held morally responsible for acts committed "in a state of invincible ignorance."[88] Bailey's logic separated the moral value of the act from the moral culpability of the agent. In his judgment, the disease theories supplied a modern amendment to the seemingly clear biblical prohibition.

Bailey and Cole suggested different ways of reconciling modern therapeutic meanings from what they took to be ancient biblical ones. A single similarity proved to be more important than these differences: the work of both scholars established that the Bible did indeed have important things to say about homosexuality. Both Cole and Bailey were cited in the 1962 publication of *The Interpreter's Bible Dictionary*, which replaced the conventional entry on "sodomy" with one on "homosexuality." The entry ignored the hair-splitting over what the Bible might say about a homosexual condition and instead cited both Cole's and Bailey's work as simple confirmation that the Bible condemned homosexuality.[89] The assumptions of these reference tools also reflected the assumptions circulating in the culture at large. A *Time* magazine article in 1963 reported on a brewing controversy among British Anglicans over the nature of "the sins of Sodom." The article presented the controversy as an upset to a long-established orthodoxy. Christians, the journalist averred, had believed "for many centuries" that "homosexuality" was the sin for which God had destroyed Sodom.[90] This homosexual interpretation, notably, did not come from new archeological findings or philological discoveries. It came rather from a new common sense, which took for granted a therapeutic model of sexuality and consequently colored the perceived meanings of the text.

Certainly, the most evident change generated by these readings was the taken-for-granted sense of the Bible's prohibition of homosexuality. Another thing that changed in the shift to new therapeutic meanings was the proximity of the sin in question. Early twentieth-century explications of the biblical "sodomites" emphasized a particular context—ancient pagan idolatry—that removed the sin in question from present-day Christians. The therapeutic turn brought that sin forward in time. Biblical scholar Dale Martin notes the curious ways that recent homosexual interpretations of the Romans passage seem to differ from the preoccupations of its ancient author. "What for Paul functioned as a sign of the boundary separating idolatrous civilization from monotheistic faith," Martin writes, became "a symptom par excellence of what is wrong with 'all of us.'"[91] The sodomites and pagan idolaters were distant enemies of the faith. The newly implanted homosexual perversion threatened Christianity from within. But the most elusive change was to the interpretive tradition itself. The emergent homosexuality tradition focused on a different set of texts from the earlier Sodom tradition. The logic of the therapeutic paradigm worked to reconfigure the number and the interrelation between the Bible verses that seemed to clearly address homosexuality. Bailey's five "definite references" continued to be the central texts in later discussion and debate over homosexuality. The focus on these five verses did not entirely unpin the Genesis Sodom account from debate over the Bible's homosexual meanings. However, that once central passage was no longer at the core of the links to both the idolatrous "sodomites" and to the Bible's own varied answers about the nature of Sodom's sin. The new homosexual meanings were made possible, in part, by reconfiguring the textual tradition.

With the seemingly plain words of the Bible as evidence that these meanings were in the text itself, a neologism that was itself not even a century old—and that had only very recently appeared in theological commentary on the Bible—fit so smoothly into the grooves of older textual prohibitions that it seemed as if it had been there all along. The excess meanings of sodomy disappeared altogether as a new reigning common sense perceived the earlier "sodomites," "effeminate," and "abusers of themselves with mankind" as earlier synonyms for "homosexuality." Pastoral counselors and Christian educators rarely, if ever, theorized their revised assessments of practices like birth control, masturbation, and premarital sex as a consequence of the medical understanding of homosexuality as a condition. However, as they reformed counseling and educational practices to fit with their understandings of human sexual development, they also collated moral and immoral sex acts along the lines of a different kind of epistemological framework, which divided "natural" and "unnatural" sex into two categories: homosexual and heterosexual. The homosexual, through the course of the first half of the twentieth century, came to subsume one side of a therapeutic binary, the sum total of unnatural sex.

Conclusion

In 1960, *Pastoral Psychology* issued a retrospective on the field of pastoral counseling in recognition of the journal's ten-year anniversary. Harry Emerson Fosdick, at nearly eighty-two years of age, reflected on the changes in the field since his first amateur attempts at personal counseling. Much had changed, he noted, since "that first day I faced a case of serious abnormality, with fourteen people waiting in the anteroom."[92] The developments pleased him. "We oldsters," he recalled, "had to get it the hard way by calling our psychiatric . . . friends for help, and then picking up from them as best we could." How different for the current generations of pastors, he observed, who "cannot now escape pastoral counseling; it is in the air."[93] Fosdick and early pastoral counselors had to make a contentious argument for the relevance of psychology and psychiatry to Christian ministry; four decades later, it seemed obvious to most mainline Protestant pastors that the mental health fields provided crucial insights to effective ministry.

Also "in the air" of Christian ministry and teaching was "homosexuality," a term appropriated from the mental health fields and used often and broadly enough that its specific etiology had become invisible. The usage of the new term, in publications that ranged from specialized pastoral counseling journals to popular magazines, reflected the ascendancy of the therapeutic view encouraged by pastoral counseling advocates. Homosexual acts, in this view, had been historically condemned as a heinous sin but should now be understood, with the insight of modern medicine, as the symptom of a developmental condition that could be healed with the proper therapy. Even conservative Protestants, despite their earlier suspicions of the secular bent of "modern psychology," were, by the late 1950s, also beginning to reference homosexuality and psychiatric theories of cure in texts on Christian sexual teachings.[94] So thoroughly had Christians baptized this new term, it had come to take on the time-less feel of long-standing tradition.

This new tradition, however, also facilitated marked innovation in Christian teachings about sex. On their own terms, religious advocates of a therapeutic approach worked to challenge what they saw as old taboos against homosexual acts by encouraging pastors to approach homosexual patients with compassion and unconditional regard. How-ever, this understanding of act and condition still already swallowed in total the idea that homosexuality was the unnatural opposite of a healthy heterosexuality. The homosexual, as object of hoped-for transformation, helped naturalize and consecrate the rightness, goodness, and natu-ralness of healthy—heterosexual—desire and behavior. The method of cultivating heterosexuality was a release from regulation. Uncondi-tional positive regard would free sinners of all kinds from the guilt and anxiety that might pervert that natural sexual instinct. Lurking behind this release, spurring the injunction to heterosexual normalcy, was an unhealthy homosexual, whose threatening influence might be prevented by a salutary emphasis on heterosocial behavior. The sexual regulation previously aimed at preventing immorality between men and women and between boys and girls now turned to inspect with suspicion the previ-ously innocent affections between those of the same sex. These shifts influenced biblical texts as well as social practice. In the newly specific homosexual meanings of the Bible, texts that had previously pointed toward practices of masturbation or non-procreative sex now seemed to self-evidently prohibit same-sex desire and behavior. In religion, as well as in other social institutions, homosexuality crystallized as the opposite of heterosexuality. As a result of this new sexual binary, the culture at large—including religious institutions—began to pay increasing atten-tion to the newly consolidated figure of the homosexual.[95]

The therapeutic orthodoxy of the midcentury represented the conver-gence of liberal Protestant modernism and medical theories of disease and cure. It was an unstable alliance within its own terms, but the most incisive challenge to this synthesis came from the patients themselves. Throughout the 1950s, communicating through self-published and sur-reptitiously circulated newsletters, homosexuals were commenting on the moral and medical ideas to which they were subject. Taking the name "homophile"—a neologism meaning "same-sex loving"—a discrete and hidden movement circulated an increasingly vocal counterdiscourse to the moral and medical assumptions of the dominant therapeutic orthodoxy.

2

WRITING THE HOMOPHILE SELF

Many men and women read the advice written by pastoral counselors and therapists and recognized their own experience in the narratives about homosexuality told by the therapeutic experts. Historian Rebecca Davis tells of 139 archived letters to Norman Vincent Peale, one of the leading lights in the pastoral counseling movement, written by men and women who responded to his published advice on homosexuality with hopeful and desperate confessions. "My homosexuality is getting worse every day," wrote one twenty-nine-year-old man; "I really want to stop and lead a normal life." Another letter writer confessed that his attraction to other men "haunts me continually. . . . Truthfully, I am at my wit's end. Something has to be done."[1] Letter writers expressed frustration and fear over attractions that they felt powerless to change, and many of them also seized with hope upon the promise of a therapeutic cure. This private correspondence captures the fraught and fearful process of inspecting one's own same-sex desires and also highlights the limitations of the dominant therapeutic discourses. Peale's advice, Davis shows, offered little reassurance or direction outside of the kind, but brief, referral to a psychiatric professional. The published advice about homosexuality—including Peale's succinct instruction—largely addressed homosexuals as distant figures spoken *about* but rarely spoken *to*.

Amid this crowded arena of authoritative opinion about the problem of homosexuality, those who experienced homosexuality as their own condition were also beginning to find a limited entry point into the discussion. In 1951, readers of *Pastoral Psychology* would have seen a signpost to a different kind of writing about homosexuality: an advertisement for a book written from a "subjective perspective" by a homosexual. The advertisement was posted in the margins of an article that pronounced homosexuality to be "a symptom of a deep-rooted personality disorder."[2] The notice for Donald Webster Cory's *The Homosexual in America: A Subjective Approach* promised the perspective of the mental case himself:

"Here for the first time," it proclaimed, "is the story of homosexuality, as seen, felt, experienced, and told by a homosexual." It promised that this professed homosexual author offered "keen analytical understanding" of a "little-understood" subject.[3] *The Homosexual in America* was one of the first works of nonfiction to represent a self-consciously homosexual perspective to an American audience. Writing with the authorial "I" about one's own homosexuality was risky business, and "Cory" wisely penned the book under a pseudonym; his real name was Edward Sagarin. A Jewish leftist and an autodidact, Sagarin wrote the book while working as a fragrance expert in the perfume industry. He later went on to pursue a Ph.D. in sociology. His dissertation, defended in 1966 under his own name, examined the secret homosexual societies forming during the postwar era. Unacknowledged in the later professional work was Sagarin's key role in the formation of these organizations.[4] *The Homosexual in America* was in many ways a work of identity politics, and it flipped the conventional therapeutic approach to homosexuality on its ear. Psychological buzzwords—self-knowledge, self-acceptance, and personal integration—appeared in this book with altered meanings. *The Homosexual in America* presented the self-knowledge of homosexuals as a perspective that was "as essential as those of the psychiatrist, the jurist, or the churchman in arriving at any conclusions about homosexuality."[5] Sagarin presented his experience as more than a tidbit to be analyzed and interpreted by a knowing expert; his firsthand account, rather, stood alongside the established authorities as a true source of knowledge about homosexuality.

The experts writing on homosexuality in *Pastoral Psychology*, however, seemed blithely unaware of this text. Other than the paid advertisement, the journal contained no further reference to the book. Still, Sagarin's "subjective approach" starkly challenged the experts' discussions about therapeutic nonjudgment and the client's self-acceptance as a route to normal sexuality. Sagarin proposed an alternative meaning for homosexual self-acceptance—he saw it not as a step toward heterosexual transformation but as a path toward happy homosexuality. "A person who accepts the fact that he cannot change into a heterosexual, and who from that point accepts himself for what he is, will have taken the first important step toward ceasing the struggle against himself," Sagarin wrote. This therapeutic project was grounded in self-actualization and self-acceptance, but to different ends: a homosexual who accepted "his" condition, Sagarin argued, might move toward "enjoying his homosexual relationships rather than fighting them, and toward building his life around a realistic program for the future." This process of therapy would yield a "well-integrated and happy invert"—a phrase that turned the psychological terminology of adjustment upside down.[6] Same-sex attraction could be understood as something other than a maladjusted condition. It could be lived and experienced in happy, healthful ways.

Building on this approach to homosexual self-acceptance, Sagarin also shifted the impetus for change from homosexuals to the society that stigmatized their condition. Borrowing a page from social analyses of discrimination faced by social minorities like "Negroes" and "Jews," Sagarin argued that homosexuals were an "unrecognized minority" that experienced stigma and discrimination because they were different from the majority. Just as racial and religious minorities contended with a long history of oppression and discrimination, so homosexuals contended with the stigma and targeting from "the heterosexual society." For homosexuals, Sagarin argued, the taproot of this problem was religion. Borrowing ideas from sex radicals like the Finnish anthropologist Edward Westermark and from Alfred Kinsey's writing on sexuality, Sagarin diagnosed the present-day intolerance as a legacy of "Judeo-Christian" oppression, which germinated among the ancient Hebrews and later influenced Christianity. The problems faced by homosexuals, Sagarin insisted, could be addressed only by confronting and changing this inherited taboo.[7]

This chapter examines three overlapping endeavors authored and organized by homosexuals during the postwar years. Each of these efforts shows how the project of articulating a homosexual identity contended with twinned narratives of condemnation and self-actualization found in the Protestant therapeutic orthodoxy. The "homophile movement," the most well known of the three efforts, has been traced by numerous scholars of gay and lesbian history.[8] Sagarin was just one of a growing number of gays and lesbians who took up the dominant therapeutic paradigm to turn that quest for authenticity into a project of homosexual self-acceptance. As *The Homosexual in America* made its way up best-seller charts over the course of the 1950s, homosexuals themselves, using various strategies to protect their identities, were writing and circulating their own views about their condition. Sagarin was part of an emerging collective that contended with the intertwined doctrines of sin and sickness from within it—as its homosexual subjects. This collective carved out a social space that recognized and valorized same-sex attraction. Various scholars have mapped out the ways that this identity movement emerged out of and alongside other social institutions, with the homosocial world of the military and the queer urban subculture of bars and street life as important channels for a coalescing homosexual identity.

In addition to the bar culture and the military, however, religion was also important to the new identity consciousness. Thus, this chapter also investigates two additional sites that show how religious institutions—Protestantism in particular—provided practices of homosocial kinship and a set of narratives and beliefs that gave language to a homosexual identity. This history, however, is a hidden one—cloistered in what historian Timothy Jones calls "the stained glass closet."[9] Getting at that history requires reading through and behind the evasions and ruses of authors who carefully hid their sexual lives. I sift through the records of the George W. Henry Foundation, a "church connected" counseling agency led by a closeted Anglican layman, and I examine the 1960 work *Christ and the Homosexual*, a United Church of Christ (UCC) minister's self-published treatise for homosexual acceptance.[10] These sources and the relationships they illuminate suggest that religious beliefs and practices covertly accommodated same-sex desire and gave language for locating homosexual identity.

The authors and organizers I analyze in this chapter mobilized distinct ways of identifying—and living—as a homosexual. This identity, of course, had particular gender, race, and class inflections. Alfred A. Gross, in one of many annual reports about the clients served by the Henry Foundation, informally assessed his population as one dominantly constituted of white men with a middle-class background. The audience for homophile magazines, as Craig Lofton has shown in his analysis of archived letters from readers, was also dominantly white, male, and middle class. Women and people of color did contribute to these forums, but their voices remained distinctly at the margins. One homophile organization—the Daughters of Bilitis and its companion publication, the *Ladder*—was founded by a group of lesbians (and included a few women of color) to emphasize a distinct "feminine perspective." Occasionally, the perspectives of people of color appeared in homophile journals, like the rare letter from a self-identified black lesbian (later identified as playwright Lorraine Hansberry), who acknowledged that her experience joined "more different kinds of oppression in my single being than most people ever even think about consciously in a lifetime."[11] These occasional perspectives were exceptions to the rule, however, and this small number of women and people of color participated in a project that was largely inflected by the interests of white gay men, whose relative privilege in other areas of life oriented them toward homosexuality as a singular status of disenfranchisement. Class and gender presentation were also important to the project of articulating an acceptable homosexual identity. Authors distinguished orderly and acceptable ways of living as a homosexual from the visibly marked practices of a disreputable, effeminate, or promiscuous opposite. The acceptable homosexual was one who could pass through life unnoticed. With unmarked class, gender, and race, this sexually controlled, gender normative homosexual figure passed invisibly for normal.

Becoming an acceptable homosexual, finally, was a project that addressed a central problem of religion. Religion constituted a central knot of condemnation, stigma, and taboo that homosexuals had to unravel in order to accept themselves as they were. When most of these authors spoke generically about "religion," they nearly always meant Christianity—and often Protestantism—in particular, and the problem that they addressed was represented as much by the general moral opprobrium of the postwar decades as it was by particular sectarian spokespersons. The harshest moral condemnation against "sex perverts" and "moral turpitude" often came from public officials rather than preachers. Although these public figures drew support from conservative religious leaders, those religious leaders, on their own, tended to preach against sexual immorality in general rather than against homosexuality in particular.

With this background of overt condemnation, the writing by pastoral counselors and other liberal Protestants presented a comparatively friendly resource. Protestant pastoral counselors, as the previous chapter showed, often accused sexual conservatives of having dogmatic, condemning, and unhealthy views about human sexuality. Like the allied therapeutic professionals, a number of liberal Protestants admonished pastors to respond kindly to homosexuals, assuming, of course, that this nonjudgmental treatment was a path to sexual normalcy. Sympathy was preferable to condemnation, however, and many homosexual authors read and commented extensively on the Protestant therapeutic advice. In many ways, homosexual writers and readers approached the dominant therapeutic advice as an elastic resource, and they pulled and stretched it beyond its heterosexist logic. This counterdiscourse to the Protestant therapeutic advice circulated through various quarters of postwar gay and lesbian life. It provided a malleable resource by which gay and lesbian authors and advocates constructed an upright homosexual self as a citizen worthy of social, civic, and moral acceptance.

Digging out the tangled roots of this alterative therapeutic project, however, takes us back to the seemingly unambiguous disdain of one of the therapeutic articles published in *Pastoral Counseling*—one about the George W. Henry Foundation that claimed psychiatrist George Henry as its author and that adjoined "Cory's" book advertisement. The advertisement pointed to an excluded, off-text perspective written by a homosexual. The article in the center of the page about homosexual pathology, in different ways, also excluded and disguised an author's homosexual subjectivity. Sifting through its ruses reveals hidden connections between the emerging homophile movement and behind-closed-doors developments in Christian institutions.

Therapeutics of the Janitor's Closet

The article attributed to Henry was actually ghostwritten by his longtime research assistant, Alfred Gross, who also wrote the annual reports of the Henry Foundation in Henry's name and with his permission. Gross's authorship of some of Henry's articles and his management of the foundation was the outgrowth of a long professional relationship. Henry invited Gross in 1936 to serve as a research assistant for an ongoing study on homosexuality, published in 1941 as *Sex Variants: A Study of Homosexual Patterns*.[12] The two men also coauthored several shorter studies on homosexuality, and Gross continued as an assistant when Henry was enlisted as a staff psychiatrist during World War II as, one of many specialists tasked with administering the psychiatric screening that weeded out suspected homosexuals from the armed services. This decade-long collaboration led, after the war, to a new project, a counseling initiative located in New York City that in 1948 was formally named the George W. Henry Foundation. Historian Henry Minton, who chronicles a number of instances where sex researchers worked with assistants and informants who were themselves homosexual, argues that the cooperation between Henry and Gross served both men well, a symbiotic relationship that continued in the Henry Foundation. The foundation, with its impressive connections to New York social service agencies, solidified Henry's reputation "as an expert and a humanitarian with regard to the problem of the homosexual in society." At the same time, Henry's name provided "the stamp of authority and the cloak of respectability" for a project essentially organized and operated by Gross.[13]

Gross described the collaboration in similar terms in a letter written many years later—in 1983—to a longtime clergy supporter of the foundation. "We used each other," Gross admitted of his reciprocal relationship with Henry. The psychiatrist's loose supervision allowed him to take the program in a "new and unorthodox direction, perhaps without [Henry] knowing it, or perhaps with his willingness to turn a blind eye." At the same time, Gross reflected, "I think I never left him in a position when he could not repudiate me if the conservatism of the early days put him in an equivocal position."[14] The letter's recipient was Paul Moore, who was then in the tenth year of his tenure as the bishop of the Episcopal diocese of New York. Before he took up this impressive appointment, Moore had served for several years on the foundation's board of directors and was one of its many clergy supporters. Gross wrote this letter a decade after the foundation had closed its doors upon his retirement. Gross was a frail octogenarian in waning health, and Moore was an influential bishop at the center of a churchwide debate sparked in 1977 by his decision to ordain an admitted lesbian to the priesthood. The letter reminisced about the foundation's twenty-five years of operation in a substantially different historical moment. Gross's expression of gratitude for Moore's longtime support was, in part, an effort to remind a now-powerful gay and lesbian advocate of the almost forgotten contributions of a small social services foundation. The Henry Foundation, under Gross's skillful management, had been dedicated to a therapeutic project that, at the time of Gross's retirement in the heyday of gay liberation, already looked like an anachronism.[15] That project was also one that Moore himself knew intimately: Gross's work with the foundation was to coach gay men in the delicate skills required to live a double life.[16]

During its first decade of operation, the Henry Foundation provided services from the ignominious quarters of a renovated janitor's closet in a stairwell of the University Settlement House, which was located on the Lower East Side of Manhattan. The office, however unimpressive it may have seemed, was provided free of charge by Charles Cook, who was the director of the University Settlement, a member of the Henry Foundation's board of directors, and an influential supporter of the foundation's work. The location—a closet—has freighted significance only in hindsight. Gays and lesbians at the midcentury did not speak of closets as cloistered spaces for hiding a sexual identity; they spoke instead of "living a double life" or "wearing the mask."[17] The closet was the metaphor used by a subsequent generation of gay liberationists, and their talk about "coming out of the closet" commented on and critiqued the practices of an earlier generation, who assiduously worked to hide the sexual self that liberationists insisted on revealing. Gross, however, like many men and women of his generation and social class, did not see the cultivated public decorum and the rigorously bounded private life as practices resulting from shame or self-loathing. They were, rather, signal marks of a homosexual's self-respect.

Gross's writing about his work with the Henry Foundation was as layered and double-sided as the decorous self-presentation he encouraged for his clients. Sifting through the multivocal representations of the Henry Foundation's mission yields more than a revelation about the hidden "truth" of Gross's work. Just as insightfully, the labor of sorting through Gross's layered and shifting ways of writing and speaking about the foundation gives insight into precisely the practices of self-cultivation that he enjoined in his clients.

The foundation's official mission was "to give realistic aid to persons in trouble with themselves, the law, or society by reason of sexual maladjustment."[18] Most of the foundation's caseload was, indeed, men in trouble with the law. Through a partnership with the New York Court of General Session, many of the clients were men arrested on sex-related misdemeanors who were referred for court-appointed therapy. Clients also came voluntarily through referrals by clergymen, physicians, social workers, and friends of former patients. A tally of the foundation's first seven years counted the total number of cases at 2,100. About three quarters of these cases came from the courts, and the rest arrived voluntarily.[19] The kind of assistance offered to these clients capitalized on the "realistic aid" mentioned in the foundation's mission. Clients often received legal counsel, job placement, medical advice, and other urgent forms of practical assistance. Those who sought long-term counseling were referred to either friendly psychiatrists or, even more likely, to clinically trained clergymen who often provided counseling free of charge. In addition to his work with clients, Gross also saw his writing and public speaking as important to the work of educating the public about homosexuality, and each year's annual report often mentioned several publications and speaking engagements. Gross's cultivation of socially powerful supporters, his partnerships with the courts and other social service agencies, and his writing and public speaking on behalf of the foundation all helped to endow the Henry Foundation with an influence that well outpaced its humble office and shoestring budget.[20]

Key to the foundation's work was its partnership with clergy. From the outset, Gross worked closely with clergy, but it was not until 1965—after George W. Henry's death—that he described the foundation as "a church-connected enterprise." Most of the earliest supporters, he noted, were Episcopal clergymen, and the chair of the foundation's board was a post occupied by more than one Episcopal bishop.[21] Gross was also a proud Anglican, and his religious affiliation clearly shaped the foundation's connections to clergy, and particularly to Episcopalians. Clergy made up a preponderance of the foundation's board of directors, and they also provided much of the counseling services. The ghostwritten article in *Pastoral Psychology* emphasized the Henry Foundation's close work with clergy. In it, Gross presented one of many versions of the role he envisioned for clergy in the therapeutic treatment of homosexuality.

The article presented a harshly disparaging picture of homosexuals' problems. It was a condition "caused by arrested psychosexual adjustment" and expressed in "exigent" sexual urges. Homosexuals, as this article presented them, struggled with compulsive behavior that drove them "to risk untold humiliation for a moment's fleeting pleasure." Compounding the problem with self-control, one of the few spaces where homosexuals could find companionship was in the "homosexual ghetto," a "bizarre universe . . . whose folkways, if reported by an anthropologist, would astonish even the tolerant . . . and would nauseate a great many people."

As a prophylactic against the "nauseating" ends to which homosexuality could lead, the final pages of the article turned to clergy. In this article and elsewhere, Gross approached clergy as a unique antidote to homosexuals' deep problem of guilt, which Gross blamed for the worst of their sexual excesses. Like first responders in a moment of triage, Gross gave ministers one simple task: they must respond without judgment in order to "make the homosexual see that there are no untouchables in the Kingdom of God, for the homosexual is all too apt to count himself a pariah." Where other advice authors followed the therapeutic emphasis on nonjudgment by hopefully gesturing toward heterosexual adjustment, this article simply stopped. Gross eschewed making any remarks on the "ways and means" of counseling beyond the initial point of unconditional acceptance.[22] His silence on this point interrupted the optimistic march toward heterosexual healing found in many of the journals' other writers, and he positioned ministers as a critical stopgap in a different teleology: homosexuals' self-defeating slide into almost certain disaster.

The annual reports, also ghostwritten by Gross and published each year on April 1, expanded on the role for clergy in the counseling services provided by the foundation. The foundation's clients were actually far more likely to receive counseling from a minister than from a psychiatrist. There was a practical reason for this preference—clinically trained clergy usually provided counseling services pro bono, which made them far more accessible than professionally trained psychiatrists for the foundation's financially indigent clients. But Gross also emphasized that clergy, because of their moral authority, brought a unique contribution that psychiatrists lacked. "Much of the homosexual's difficulty comes out of his guilt and his lack of self-acceptance," Gross wrote in one of the annual reports. "The clergy, traditionally the custodians of public morals, have become increasingly the resource to which the community has had to turn for help with a problem regarded by many as essentially a moral one."[23] Thus, not only were clergy an affordable substitute for psychiatrists, but their religious office actually vested them with a unique power to resolve homosexuals' central struggle with guilt and nonacceptance.

As the annual reports also made clear, the ideal end of this therapeutic process was not heterosexuality or even celibacy but a more ambiguously phrased "partial adjustment," an aim achieved when a client was able to "hold a job successfully . . . and work out a social life which passes unnoticed."[24] Implied in this statement was a rebuke against forms of public sexual expression that Gross saw as both a risk for arrest as well as a sign of a homosexual's lack of self-respect. Sexual encounters in public places, flamboyant or "swishy" behavior, or even associating with men who exhibited their sexual preference in visible ways were all cardinal strikes against the injunction to homosexual men, as Gross put it elsewhere, to "write an effective bill of divorcement between his public and private life."[25] These statements about Gross's aims for his clients omitted any description of just what that private life might entail. Metaphorically divorced and effectively disappeared, it seems that the contents of that life should never be acknowledged. Gross's language of "partial adjustment," however, intriguingly echoed Edward Sagarin's discussion, in *The Homosexual in America*, of the therapeutic aim of a "well-adjusted invert." Gross's published writing about the foundation's work during the 1950s never sanctioned same-sex relationships, nor did he ever directly endorse Sagarin's view that homosexuals should accept their "condition" so that they might enjoy their attractions rather than fight them. However, Gross also never expressed his disapproval of this notion, either.

Gross's correspondence with one of the foundation's clients fills in his coy silences about the nature of those divorced private lives. Robert Wells came to the foundation in 1950 as one of the many court-ordered referrals.[26] His later reminiscences about Gross and their archived correspondence attest to Gross's mentorship and fatherlike relationship with the young man. Wells affectionately addressed the letters to "Papa" and regularly asked Gross for advice about managing his relationships with his family and with other gay men. Twenty-one when he met Gross, Wells was an ex-serviceman with an undesirable discharge. The dreaded "blue slip" barred Wells's eligibility for GI benefits and complicated his efforts to settle into stable civilian life. Gross's case report on the young man, however, attributed the arrest and misdemeanor charge to a current fault in temperament. "Tom" was handicapped by "emotional immaturity, instability and too great willingness to be influenced by the last person to whom he has talked," Gross argued; he needed to learn better self-control and moral judgment to stay out of trouble. Gross's answer to the undue sway of bad influences was to refer the young man to a chaplain at Columbia University for religious counseling, which he predicted would help him "gain stability and a better sense of values." Gross's final assessment of Wells's case approvingly reported his stable employment and educational aspirations as evidence of his self-acceptance. Wells "has been able to hold a job during the whole period of his probation. . . . He talks of going to college, and there is some likelihood that this ambition might be fulfilled."[27] In this assessment of Wells's circumstances, as in many of the case reports, Gross interpreted self-control and stable employment as signal marks of a client's successful achievement of self-respect.

Wells's own account of his therapy suggests that his treatment introduced him to a framework for understanding and accepting his homosexual desires. Shortly after coming under the care of the Henry Foundation, Wells wrote a letter to his brother explaining the circumstances of his discharge from the armed services and his recent arrest. The reason for these difficulties, Wells explained, was his struggle with the condition of homosexuality. Here, Wells turned to medical theories learned from Gross to explain that homosexuality was "not a disease and [was] therefore not curable." His account offered a colloquial mash-up of developmental and congenitalist frameworks for homosexual etiology. "When

I was born," he explained, "there were a little too many ladylike genes hanging around, causing a basic upset which could have been cured with the right care during childhood. Second, no fatherly love. This left me with the yearning to be loved by a man and as it stands, I will never be able to get enough affection to satisfy me completely because it's a childhood yearning."[28] Even though his homosexual desires were caused in part by family dysfunction, Wells did not present them as pathological. In fact, the etiology he outlined gave ground to press for his brother's acceptance. "Had the circumstances been a bit different," he instructed his brother, "you, instead of I might have been gay, so please don't judge me too harshly."[29] Wells gave an account of his unorthodox desires and forthrightly appealed for family support.

Gross's letters to Wells reflected his continued role as a mentor and father figure, offering guidance on romantic interests, career decisions, and family matters. Gross also continued to instruct his charge in the necessity of decorous living. He tolerated Wells's "moderately indiscreet" sexual behavior, but he chided the young man about activities that might attract undue attention. During one visit to Gross's apartment, Wells made the mistake of bringing over some "swishy" friends. Afterward, Gross reminded him of "the repercussions of having a whole collection of little boys carrying on noisily around the place" and requested that, in the future, he keep his company "quiet and circumspect."[30] This advice gives an unusual window into the habits and practices that made up the particular kind of "adjustment" that the Henry Foundation, under Gross's direction, worked to bring about in the lives and habits of his clients. In many ways, Gross instructed his charges in the habits of a double life. That life required, first of all, an acceptance of oneself as "gay" and a resolution of feelings of guilt or shame that, left unreconciled, motivated the indecorous behavior that got homosexuals into trouble. The "partial adjustment" offered by the Henry Foundation was a project of self-containment, of carefully curtailing effeminate mannerisms and limiting sexual encounters to men of a similarly masculine comportment. These learned skills in self-presentation and sexual discipline, Gross believed, were a product of self-acceptance. By accepting one's homosexuality and resolving guilt feelings about attractions to others of the same sex, the homosexuals might cultivate a morally upright life—or at least the appearance of one.

Underneath this surface appearance of outward conformity, however, men with same-sex attractions were free to indulge in discreet affairs, and Gross's letters to Wells divulge gossipy tidbits about the various men connected to the Henry Foundation, including some of the affiliated clergy. Gross wrote about an uncomfortable car ride to Vermont with one newly coupled pair, a minister who worked with the foundation and his lover, also a minister, who "didn't particularly relish having a third wheel on the particular buggy ride."[31] Just how many of Gross's associates were men with hidden homosexual lives is a question that those men worked to make unanswerable. Some of the affiliated clergy later acknowledged their sexual identities—Clinton Jones, an Episcopal priest in Hartford, Connecticut, and Edward Egan, a Methodist minister in New York later active in gay liberation, are two well-known examples. However, many of the clergy successfully hid their homosexuality all of their lives. Paul Moore, the bishop referenced at the beginning of this section, was posthumously "outed" in his daughter's memoir. That we do not know the stories of those other disappeared private lives indicates that the clergy were indeed effective models for how to hide their less than respectable private lives.

The work of the foundation, ironically in keeping with its location in a janitor's closet, was to coach gay men in the delicate art of living a double life. As Gross's correspondence shows, however, this hidden private life was anything but a lonely place. To use the later metaphor of the closet, the foundation offered a Narnia-like portal, which ushered clients—including Robert Wells—into relationship networks with other gay men whose lives and relationships were similarly invisible from public view. Gross's personal correspondence and the rare after-the-fact recollections of men involved with the foundation help to retroactively unlock the otherwise carefully closed door, revealing the foundation's hidden connections to the gay social world that Gross publicly disavowed.

Gross protected the respectability of the Henry Foundation by writing his own "effective bill of divorcement," as he put it, from a visible gay world, and he also distanced the foundation from another simultaneous social development—the homosexual membership societies taking shape in the late 1940s and early 1950s. Gross had personal contact with several of these membership societies. He was an invited speaker for a meeting held in 1950 by Sagarin (whom Gross knew as Cory), presumably to speak about the services provided through the Henry Foundation.[32] No doubt this small group also approached the foundation for official endorsement. Gross, in several annual reports, mentioned requests to support the efforts of "homosexual mutual protective societies." With each request, he declared his adamant refusal. The separatist initiatives, Gross maintained, hindered the foundation's efforts to integrate homosexuals into society and, even worse, "could easily degenerate into places of assignation."[33] Gross's personal correspondence also stressed his opposition to the groups. "Let the Coreys [sic] of this world stir up the waters," he cautioned Wells in 1953. "I'm unalterably opposed to any crusadings of any kind. My advice to all who will consider it is that at the moment the part of wisdom is to keep out of sight. Now is the time for little homosexuals to be seen little and heard much less."[34] The opposition to the ostensible separatism and crusading of identity-based groups was more than ideological. As a publicly chartered organization that enlisted supporters and volunteers who participated under their given names and under their professional credentials, the Henry Foundation needed to ensure that its reputation was preserved by the same means as those of its clients. Gross carefully severed the foundation's respectable work on behalf of homosexuals from the disreputable efforts organized by homosexuals to help each other.

In many ways, however, the membership societies and the Henry Foundation were more connected than Gross publicly acknowledged. If the counseling office in a janitor's closet offered a portal into a hidden social world, the "homophile press," as it came to be called, was a samizdat literature that connected far-flung individuals to a subaltern world of gay and lesbian opinion. With authors hidden by pseudonyms and subscribers protected by surreptitious circulation methods, this underground press provided communication channels for a readership that was largely socially invisible. The hidden meetings and published venues of homophile associations in turn gave gay and lesbian writers the space to develop a distinct counterdiscourse around homosexuality, morality, and religion.[35]

Homophile Self-Help

In 1953, an editorial in the Los Angeles–based magazine ONE angrily called out the Henry Foundation's demeaning portrayal of so-called homosexual benefit societies. The author was Dorr Legg, who served as ONE's business director and wrote this editorial under the pseudonym William Lambert.[36] Legg, based as he was on the West Coast, may have known little about the foundation other than the polemical remarks that appeared in the year's annual report; the editorial was addressed only to Henry.[37] Legg excoriated the psychiatrist in a rhetorical reversal of the power relationship between patronizing medical experts and sick homosexual patients. The title, "The Case of the Well-Meaning Lyncher," turned around this relationship by addressing Henry, the psychiatric expert, as the mental case. After placing the expert on the psychiatrist's couch, Legg proceeded to diagnose his problem: Henry was a "busy bungler" who peddled "speculation, folk-lore, and old-wives tales" rather than scientifically verifiable facts. Had Henry investigated the organizations in question with any level of intellectual rigor, Legg argued, he would have known that they were not at all "places of assignation" but "a moralistic league" that was "well-conducted and orderly." This body of self-respecting homosexuals would further turn the tables on the bungling psychiatrists, Legg predicted. Homosexuals would no longer "grasp with tear-filled eye just any outstretched hand." Experts like Henry, unless they learned to treat homosexuals with dignity and respect, should expect to face "the dire penalty of being laughed out of court by the healthy fearless laughter of an emancipated, free-thinking homosexual public."[38]

This remarkable polemic was typed and printed out of an office that was no more impressive than the Henry Foundation's closet under the stairs. The fledging publishing operation had only recently moved into an office, a ten-by-twelve-foot room rented out of a decrepit building in Los Angeles's downtown sweatshop district. The core team of writers and editors numbered five: in addition to Legg, there was Jim Kepner, Don Slater, and a lesbian couple, Joan Corbin and Irma "Corky" Wolf.[39] A little over a year earlier, this team of participants in the secretive Los Angeles Mattachine Society decided to start a separate magazine that would share with a broader audience of gays and lesbians the kinds of discussions taking place in the organization's guarded meetings. Within two years, two additional publications—*Mattachine Review* and the *Ladder*—joined ONE, which continued to be the largest and most provocative of the three. By 1957, the publications began to speak of themselves collectively as the "homophile press."[40]

The audience or "public" to which the homophile press was addressed was in many ways a community imagined and formed through the journals themselves. The term "homophile" conveyed both an identity and a political project: the term was coined to emphasize the nonsexual solidarity of *phila*, or brotherly love, over the clinical focus on same-sex attraction. It was used both as a euphemism for those attracted to the same sex and as a name for those committed to a political project of

ONE, Inc., editorial staff, circa 1957–58: (*left to right*)
Don Slater, W. Dorr Legg, and Jim Kepner. ONE National Gay
and Lesbian Archives, Los Angeles.

understanding and advocating for homosexuals' fair treatment. Under this political banner, the practices of publication and circulation provided the authorship and readership of these journals an anonymous avenue into a hidden forum of opinion. Most authors published anonymously, and those who were brave enough to subscribe received their monthly issues through the mail, discreetly packaged. Most readers picked up their copies at urban newsstands, where ONE was sold alongside other unobtrusively peddled literature. The commentary in these magazines about the dangers of "swish" and the importance of respectability attests to a "homophile public" that was in many ways committed to the decorous, respectable, and gender normative forms of self-presentation that the Henry Foundation enjoined its clients to observe.[41] Thus, the public these journals addressed was primarily connected through its members' carefully hidden private reading practices. The surreptitiously distributed magazines connected a geographically dispersed audience that was largely socially invisible.[42] These self-published magazines and newsletters circulated ideas about homosexuality that were unprintable in other published forums.

From the outset, the editors and organizers of homophile publications identified religion—and Christianity in particular—as a topic for debate and discussion. Most of the journals' editors and most frequent authors addressed religion with a distinctly secularist critique, an approach strongly influenced by Sagarin's work in *The Homosexual in America*. Sagarin diagnosed present-day homosexual intolerance as a legacy of "Judeo-Christian" oppression, which germinated among the ancient Hebrews and later influenced Christianity. "The Judeo-Christian attitude toward sex," Sagarin concluded, "dominated the prevailing moral code in the centuries to follow."[43] Sagarin (writing as Cory) expanded on these ideas in an article in ONE, which traced the continued legacy of religious condemnation of homosexuality through the beliefs of the Puritan. That legacy's "self-avowedly virtuous ban on all things sexual," Sagarin argued, continued to influence American law and culture.[44] The answer to this problem, for many authors, was to find ways to extricate that damning religious influence. Frequent ONE author James Fugaté (who wrote under the pen name James Barr) insisted that "organized religion" needed to "stay out of politics, business, and art."[45] Alongside these critiques of Christian influence in law and society, quite a number of contributors addressed their intimate struggles to uproot the residue of Christian condemnation lodged in their own sense of self. "For many homosexuals," observed one author, "a rejection of religion seem[s] to be a necessary precondition of self-acceptance." He lamented, "The religion is still festering inside," causing emotional pain and self-doubt.[46] Religion, as these narratives approached it, was a problem to be addressed by somehow extricating its toxic influence from within the broader culture and from within the consciousness of homosexuals themselves.

Such views were admittedly not for everyone, and the editors of ONE positioned the journal as "nonsectarian" in matters of religion. However, most of the discussion of religion in this supposedly neutral forum took place in a Christian dialect. With the notable exception of Sagarin, who was Jewish, most of the contributors to ONE and other homophile journals clearly came from Christian backgrounds. Jim Kepner, the lead editor for ONE and one of its most prolific contributors, was a prominent example. Kepner grew up in a conservative Presbyterian church in Texas and had once been a devout Christian. He left his faith and his youthful aspiration to become a missionary once he moved to Los Angeles and entered the gay social world. An adamant skeptic, Kepner epitomized the brand of post-Christian critique that dominated most of the leading editors' religion writing. That critique, however, often converged and overlapped with Christian viewpoints. When an outside reader disparagingly described ONE as a magazine that "pathetically addresses itself to clergy-men and others begging for sympathetic understanding and deploring the condemnation of homosexuals by organized religion," the editors defensively asserted that the journal was "nonsectarian" but also "pretty rough on the Church."[47] The accusation and defense capture the journal's forum well: even the skeptics exhibited a particular Christian variety of critique.

Alongside the skeptics and atheists, however, homophile journals published quite a number of articles written by Christians. Thus the "nonsectarian" forum also facilitated extensive Christian reflection. Here, the aim was not to extricate or banish Christianity but to recover it and reform it, with authors offering their views on biblical interpretation and Christian ethics. Countering those who claimed that the Bible was the taproot of sexual repression, these authors challenged antihomosexual interpretations of biblical texts. Several authors and letter writers acknowledged the recent Revised Standard Version's translation of 1 Corinthians 6:9 and discussed how to understand the text's prohibition of homosexuality. "One's sexual inclinations do not predetermine one's acceptance or rejection by God," one author insisted in contradiction to the antihomosexual claims of the Corinthians passage. This author claimed that the centrality of the Christian ethic of love moderated the judgment of the Apostle Paul.[48] Another author challenged the Genesis Sodom account and argued that this passage represented a "condition of moral turpitude" that could not be equated to all homosexuality. Indeed, this author argued, the miserable state of so many homosexuals was due not to their homosexuality but to the "soul destroying" effects of the common interpretation—"a lie that begets myriads of other lies"—that equated all homosexuals with the debauched ancient residents of Sodom.[49] Other authors wrote in with reflections on the accounts of Ruth and Naomi and of David and Jonathan as examples of sanctioned same-sex love. A common refrain among these reflections was that Jesus's ethic of love offered a higher law than the narrow sexual regulations found in either the Old Testament or Pauline prohibitions. This kind of love, one author argued, could be revealed only through relationship. If this kind of love could be encountered through "heterosexual spouses," he asked, might not it also be encountered through the "physical love of friends"?[50]

Underscoring these challenges to the biblical prohibitions were articles written by Christian clergy, which criticized current Christian practices toward homosexuals as hypocritical and antithetical to their churches' mission. Ministers shunned and ignored homosexuals, one author wrote, because they were afraid of what their other congregants would think. Homosexuals, he argued, "need understanding, and it can only be given through a direct approach, not by praying that no one will find out such people are in the church."[51] A priest writing to the *Mattachine Review* turned his analysis of human failure in the church into a word of advice for his readers. The church was not God, he reminded; "a conflict with the Church should not lead to a loss of faith."[52] These authors, all the more authoritative because they were clergy, criticized their fellow church leaders' condemnation as a human failure. They insisted that Christianity, when practiced authentically, held a place for homosexuals.[53]

Grateful letters from readers testified to the effects of this forum in helping them to resolve feelings of guilt and to find ways to accept their homosexuality. A reader from Syracuse, New York, admitted that he had "pieced together" a personal moral code that helped him accept that he was gay and that guided his decisions about sex and relationships. He thanked the journal for circulating reflections on these questions "that many of us wrestle with alone."[54] Another letter writer from Hot Springs, Arkansas, expressed his thanks to ONE for helping him "in trying to be a Christian."[55] A "Mr. H" from Baltimore underscored his sense of reassurance that God would not abandon him because of his homosexuality. "Those of us who are Christian," he wrote, "know that Christ is always present and all we have to do is to reach out and He will be there to help us, for regardless of what we are, we are His children."[56] Thus, homophile publications—and perhaps none more influentially than ONE—provided spiritual reflection alongside social and political commentary. Authors and readers addressed Christianity with a sifting method that gleaned spiritual resources that they saw as genuine to the faith while criticizing exclusion and judgment as essentially unchristian. The critique of condemnation found in these pages took up an adamantly anti-institutional tack. The "church," fallible repository of condemnation, remained distinct from the genuine Christianity of homosexual acceptance.

As homophile authors criticized institutional Christianity, they also followed encouraging signs of institutional change and homosexual tolerance in the religious establishment. Homophile journals surpassed other American news outlets with the detail and depth of their coverage of events in Great Britain, where a group of prominent Christian leaders took the helm in advocating for sodomy law repeal. In 1954, the Moral

Welfare Council of the Church of England, led by a clergyman named Derrick Sherwin Bailey, released a controversial report pressing the government to strike down the long-standing laws against sodomy. It argued that private consensual homosexual behavior was a matter of moral conviction best placed in the hands of God and churches rather than of the law. Parliament responded by appointing a committee to study the issues and make policy recommendations. Those recommendations, released in 1956 in the *Wolfenden Report* (named after the committee chair, Sir John Wolfenden), largely concurred with the earlier recommendations issued by the Moral Welfare Council. With prominent churchmen like Bailey and even the archbishop of Canterbury standing behind it, the *Wolfenden Report* urged sodomy law repeal on the grounds that moral reproach against homosexual acts did not justify their legal regulation.[57]

The legal stand of the Anglican clerics enticed even the homophile skeptics into the fine points of biblical exegesis and Christian ethics. Homophile journals gave substantial attention to the Christian rationale for sodomy law repeal presented in Bailey's *Homosexuality and the Western Christian Tradition*. ONE editor Jim Kepner exchanged letters with the cleric and invited Bailey's feedback on the journal's religion articles (to which Bailey replied in length).[58] *Homosexuality and the Western Christian Tradition* was of particular interest to homophile skeptics like Kepner because it addressed and criticized the diagnosis of antihomosexual oppression that placed singular blame on religion. Bailey's careful parsing of biblical meanings contested the homosexual interpretation of the Sodom tradition. While he did see evidence of biblical condemnation of homosexual behavior, Bailey also argued that the meaning of that prohibition needed to be interpreted through modern evidence for a homosexual condition. In a subsequent publication, Bailey presented a careful ethical casuistry, which weighed monogamous same-sex relationships against compulsive promiscuity and admitted the former might have some merit: homosexuals might set up house together in a mutual effort to stave off promiscuity.[59] (Kepner, always the doubter, judged the "quaint" quibbling over levels of sin as, simply, "bad advice.")[60] Even this limited toleration, however, seemed to one contributor to be a liberating promise. The review of the book ended by crediting Bailey's truly Christian outlook. Underlying the whole book, the reviewer assessed, was "the spirit of our Lord who said, 'Ye shall know the truth and the truth shall set you free.'"[61]

In the wake of Bailey's writing and the work of the *Wolfenden Report*, it was no longer self-evidently true that religion was the taproot of homosexual oppression. Kepner himself was a convert on this question, and he published several essays at the end of the decade that reappraised the legacy of Christianity for present-day homosexuals. One of them, a lengthy research article published in 1959, rejected the "common, but oversimple view" that attributed antihomosexual opprobrium to Judeo-Christian prohibition.[62] Bailey, Kepner acknowledged, had refuted those arguments, and the homophile author built on this work with a further assessment of the biblical record. Kepner also added a dimension to the inquiry he saw missing from Bailey's analysis of biblical texts and Christian history. Many of the Bible's most intimate, emotional, and affectionate relationships, Kepner noted, were between people of the same sex. David and Jonathan, Ruth and Naomi, Jesus and John, Paul and Timothy—these relationships of "tender passion," Kepner argued, stood in marked contrast to "the virulent opposition to sex and marriage as expressed in the early Church."[63] Anyone who examined Christianity and homosexuality, Kepner prodded, not only must look at these particular relationships but also must address the "homoerotic tendencies" underlying the entire Christian ideal of universal fellowship.[64] In this broad assessment, Kepner capaciously imagined a very different kind of Christianity from the one he knew most homosexuals experienced in their churches. The essay was an inquiry more than an argument: Could Christianity be a religion that fed homosexuals' spiritual hunger rather than merely supplied a begrudging corner for penitence? Kepner admitted no investment in the answer to this question, but he highlighted the community for whom it was urgent: those who currently felt "unwelcomed, uncomfortable, and condemned in the Churches."[65] Kepner, skeptic that he was, adroitly took searching inquiries into biblical interpretation and Christian theology. Thus, in surprising and paradoxical ways, even the secularists took their hand at urging religious reform. Homophile authors not only argued for keeping Christianity out of politics but also waded into the fray with normative claims about the practice of Christianity itself.[66]

Christ and the Homosexual

In June 1960, another unconventional advertisement appeared in *Pastoral Psychology*. It notified readers of a "courageous" new book, Robert Wood's *Christ and the Homosexual*, which addressed a question repeatedly examined in the journal's pages—"How would you counsel the

Rev. Robert Wood, 1958.
Congregational Library and
Archives, Boston.

homosexual?"[67] The advertising blurb appeared in the margins of an article on masturbation that chided a prevalent "misreading" of 1 Corinthians 6:9. Those who mistakenly understood the "effeminate" in the passage to be masturbators could now rest assured that the prohibition was directed at homosexuals instead.[68] The book advertisement in the margins of this article featured the Bible verse's new regulatory subject, the inheritor of the masturbator's former prohibition—the homosexual. "Without mincing words," the notice announced, "the Rev. Robert W. Wood here becomes the first to offer a way for homosexuals to enter the Christian Community and join the Church, yet remain homosexuals without fear or guilt or apology."[69] The book was available for purchase from Vintage Press—a vanity publisher for self-financed authors—for the amount of $3.95.

Beyond this paid advertisement, *Pastoral Psychology* devoted no more ink in reference to the book. The book's premise, that homosexuals should be accepted as they were "without fear or guilt or apology," ran counter to the disease theories that grounded the discipline of pastoral counseling. The book's lone review, published in a journal circulated by Wood's own United Church of Christ denomination, was decidedly bad. Homosexuality was "an aberration of God's creation," the reviewer insisted, excoriating Wood's notions that homosexuality could be normal and moral.[70] Even the psychiatrist who wrote the book's introduction, ordinarily a genre of warm recommendation, warned readers against Wood's upstart ideas. Psychologist Albert Ellis used both his medical authority and his smattering knowledge of Christian ethics in arguing that Wood's ideas were not only "unscientific" but "unchristian." No matter that Ellis was a notorious freethinker; he, too, had a doctrine to share. "Let there be no compromise," he wrote; "if the doctrine of Jesus is to make any consistent sense, it must be interpreted as meaning that all disturbed, sick, mistaken, sadistic, and even criminal persons are to be forgiven, understood, and helped to overcome their all too human failings."[71] Ellis asserted his own view of how homosexuals should see Jesus: in the way a sick patient sees a doctor. Even more damning than the criticisms, however, were the silences of other journals and periodicals. Wood's upstart claims about morality and homosexuality were so far afield they did not even merit refute.

As mainline presses ignored Wood's case for homosexual morality, however, the homophile press nearly exploded with enthusiasm. "Homosexuals DO have a place in the church!" one reviewer crowed triumphantly; "to say the book is a sympathetic one is an understatement."[72] The book received awards and multiple reviews, and Wood fielded requests for more articles and speaking engagements. In the semi-hidden world of homophile organizations, Wood quickly became a minor celebrity.

The book was also very much indebted to the ideas and the networks of homophile organizations. Wood was an insider in this world, a participant in the New York Mattachine Society and also well acquainted with the gay life of New York. In addition to parsing through matters of the Bible and theology, the book also pontificated about gay male clothing styles, physique magazines, and sadomasochist parties. The detail suggested a firsthand account, but the book's hovering authorial voice moved peripatetically through the various subjects who represented homosexuality: authoritative clergyman, self-loathing gay Christian, perverse sadomasochist. The result, argues Mark Jordan, was a voice that was "at once incoherent and inadvertently, painfully confessional."[73] By avoiding the authorial "I" in reference to homosexuality, Wood maintained a plausible distance between the book's homosexual subjects and his own subjectivity. However, a hypothetical gay clergyman haunted the book, and Wood was—almost transparently—that gay clergyman.

Wood was a young pastor in his thirties, serving at Spring Valley Congregationalist Church, twelve miles from New York City in a suburb on Long Island. He also regularly attended meetings of the New York

Mattachine Society, where he recalled a conversation with Sagarin that inspired him to write *Christ and the Homosexual*. Wood asked Sagarin why *The Homosexual in America* said so little that was positive about religion. Sagarin, from his background as a Jewish atheist, averred that it was a topic he knew little about and encouraged Wood to write a book of his own. The material for Wood's commentary on this subject came from his own experience of gay life, discussions with members of the Matta-chine Society, and conversations with and sources from Alfred Gross at the Henry Foundation. Gross obligingly supplied Wood with copies of the foundation's annual reports and of his own written speeches on the topic. Thus, the book's radical challenge to prevailing views about homo-sexuality and morality drew from an archive of hidden relationships and sources that could only be gleaned firsthand from someone who lived in that world on the other side of the closet door.[74]

Wood steered his approach to homosexuality directly into the claim made in much of pastoral counseling advice to ministers that admonished them to respond "therapeutically" rather than "morally" to homosexual-ity. Wood called for a moral approach. Though social workers, medical doctors, and psychiatrists might each contribute aid, Wood maintained that homosexuality was primarily a moral problem: "The homosexual needs to know that homosexuality in itself is morally neutral," Wood argued.[75] The most important call in Wood's work, however, was for homosexuals themselves to understand their condition as moral. Once homosexuals accepted their condition, Wood pressed (echoing Sagarin and Gross), they could learn to live a spiritually and sexually meaningful life. He ended the book with a colloquial challenge presented directly to a presumed homosexual reader: "O.K. So you didn't ask to be gay; but you *are*, and the chances are you are never going to be straight. This leaves two choices, doesn't it? Either such a person becomes the slave of homo-sexuality, or he lives with it in a rational manner."[76] Self-acceptance, for Wood—as for Sagarin and Gross—broke a cycle of guilt and self-pity that kept homosexuals from a sustainable existence. As Wood conceived it, self-acceptance should also keep homosexuals from promiscuity and risky behavior. A moral homosexual was a responsible homosexual. Rather than the "mad dash from gay bar to gay bar," the homosexual needed to "rededicate himself to improved social living."[77]

The other side of the challenge to homosexuals was a challenge to clergy and churches. If homosexuals were to find self-acceptance and satisfying partnerships, churches would need to stop condemning and excluding them. Here, too, Wood's rambling treatise ranged from the grand and the ideological to the concretely practical. Wood urged pastors to take a view of homosexuality that shared in the same assumptions offered to heterosexuals. Homosexuals, too, need to be liberated from unhealthy emotions and base compulsions through unconditional positive regard. The result of such a therapeutic project would not be heterosexuality but rather a homosexual union that might express the same ideals of intimacy and self-actualization that pastoral counselors placed in heterosexual marriage. In chiding clergy and congregations about how to make such acceptance possible, Wood turned to the practical: hold church weddings for sincere homosexual couples and let same-sex couples dance together at the church social.[78]

At the time of this writing, there were actually a handful of congregations and ministries that intentionally accepted gays and lesbians. Leaders of the Mattachine Society in New York, ONE, Incorporated, in Los Angeles, as well as other homophile organizations kept a list of clergy contacts to refer those who asked about supportive faith resources. Various members of homophile organizations also experimented with religious services and study groups. A member of ONE, Incorporated, named Chuck Rowland spearheaded a short-lived experimental church that he called the First Church of the One Brotherhood, which met for a brief time during 1956 in Los Angeles's First Christian Spiritualist Episcopal Church.[79] The New York Mattachine Society also held a Christian discussion group during the 1950s that was led by Rev. Edward Egan, a Methodist minister who was also a clergy counselor with the George W. Henry Foundation.[80]

There was also a network of independent Catholics, a fragmented and loosely organized denomination of priests and bishops, some of whom held gay-welcoming services during this time. Kepner's correspondence included a letter from George Augustus Hyde. In Atlanta, Georgia, in 1946, Hyde and a small group of Christians formed the Eucharist Catholic Church. Hyde, much later in his life, recounted a ministry that was not publicly advertised at the time. According to Hyde's report, it met in a house in downtown Atlanta and gathered homosexual, heterosexual, black, white, Catholic, and Protestant members.[81] Hyde later became affiliated with an independent Catholic denomination called the American Holy Orthodox Catholic Apostolic Eastern Church and moved to Washington, D.C.[82] In 1954, this group published an advertisement in ONE that announced its ministries.[83] Hyde's letter to Kepner, written in 1961, is the earliest preserved description of the group. "We are different from other churches," Hyde asserted in that letter, "in that we do not condemn the homosexual for his nature any more than we condemn the heterosexual. Frankly, we are no more concerned about your sex life than we are about the color of shirt you wear."[84]

However, most gay and lesbian Christians, in all likelihood, participated in congregations where they felt it necessary to hide their sexual identities. For those Christians, Wood's book circulated a compelling narrative about how to understand their homosexuality and Christian faith. Two letters by homosexual Christians to Wood recounted keenly felt conflicts over the necessity to hide their sexual identities from heterosexual church members. In one letter, a Lutheran candidate for ordination addressed the conflicts he experienced when he acknowledged his same-sex attractions during his senior year in seminary. He confessed to Wood that he desired both "the companionship and love of a partner through life" and "to serve our Lord in ministering to people." He continued, "But—how to reconcile all this and not be a hypocrite. I despise falsity, particularly in myself, but can I dare to be honest or must one always retain this hypocritical mask?"[85] In another letter to Wood, written in 1960, a lesbian couple admitted that their fears of being discovered by members of their family and church community influenced them to move across the country to San Francisco. One of the women confessed, "'Wearing the mask' for me was the most difficult of all the problems. . . . We are both happier in our new home three thousand miles away from our families and church connections." She added, "Although we attend no church here, we continue to belong to and support our church in the East."[86] For these Christians, the most strongly felt incongruity between their personal and spiritual lives was the necessity to hide their sexual interests and romantic partnerships from their church communities by "wearing a mask" of conformity in a straight world.

Conclusion

In various ways over the course of the decade, homosexuals themselves worked to untangle the way their identities and desires were tied to a condemning religious past. They contended with a dominant therapeutic paradigm that presented homosexuality as an obstacle to healthy sexuality and self-actualization, and they wrestled with newly circulating anti-homosexual interpretations of the Bible. In various ways, the authors and organizers examined in this chapter told a new narrative about religion and the self, which also envisioned the homosexual life as one that might not only avoid punishment and regulation but also achieve happiness and intimacy. The good news was that homosexuals did not have to live thwarted, truncated lives; they, too, could become well-adjusted individuals with happy, meaningful relationships.

For some—and notably for many leading homophile organizers—homosexual acceptance was a project of self-cultivation that necessarily rejected religion. Leaving behind religion paved the way for accepting and enjoying one's relationships. Many others, however, drew resources from Christianity that also worked as a powerful solvent on the knot of homosexual condemnation. For Alfred Gross, the therapeutic assistance of clergy held unique power to assuage homosexuals' problems of guilt; for many gay and lesbian contributors to homophile periodicals, Christianity had scriptural and theological resources that critiqued practices of Christian rejection; and for Robert Wood, the liberating ideals of Protestant therapeutic theology served as a rationale for same-sex intimacy.

By circulating a specifically religious answer to the dominant theological and therapeutic regulation of homosexuality, homophile organizers facilitated a distinct moral alternative to existing Christian views of homosexuality. These alternative visions of Christianity were particularly important to gay and lesbian Christians, who used them to suture together faith and sexuality. For both Christians and non-Christians alike, however, they also worked as a foundation for a more expansive project. In challenging the intimate ways that religious rejection was lodged within the self, these authors also cultivated resources for challenging public and civic forms of moral opprobrium. New ways of interpreting Christian teachings about homosexuality—and particularly the work of Derrick Sherwin Bailey—also facilitated avenues for social and political activism. The authors and advocates of a homosexual morality—an individual project of living a moral homosexual life—worked at the same time to position the upright homosexual self as a citizen deserving of social and civic acceptance.

As homophile authors were expressing their challenge to the mainstream with greater brass and certainty, the tenor of mainstream Christian publications was changing. A number of writers—including Gross—began to more vocally advocate homosexual law reform, and they were working to push the logic of pastoral counseling's therapeutic approach in the direction of social and legal reform. Gross, in his own evasive manner, had published some of the most positive assessments found in American Protestant publications about Bailey's work. The political involvement of British Anglicans, unlike the solidarity initiatives by homophile organizers, provided a model for legal reform that fit with Gross's commitments to respectability and decorum. Ever the moderate, Gross's assessment offered none of the clarion calls for reform issued by Wood or other homophile writers, whose radical views were yet unprintable in mainstream publications. Gross's 1962 book, *Strangers in Our Midst*, forwarded the Wolfenden model of legal reform.[87] During the 1960s, as the next chapter shows, a cohort of clergy activists responded to the challenge and the precedent of their Anglican counterparts in Britain. Parallel to this development, those religious leaders also encountered an increasingly visible homophile movement.

3

CHURCHMEN AND HOMOPHILES

The incident in question took place in California Hall, a rented event space in downtown San Francisco, on the evening of New Year's Day, 1965. Fred Bird, a pastor at St. John's Methodist Church in San Francisco, was one of eight ministers questioned as witnesses after police raided a costume ball organized by area homophile organizations. The surprise, in this case, was the that ministers, Bird included, were involved with the event from the beginning—as allies of the homophile organizations, co-organizers of the costume ball, and witnesses to the police harassment and abuse.

At ten o'clock the night of the ball, Bird recalled, his home phone rang. The caller urged him to come downtown immediately and to be sure to put on his clericals. Bird donned the black-and-white-collared shirt that visibly marked him as a man of the cloth and hurried to California Hall. It was half past ten when he arrived at the event billed as a New Year's Day Mardi Gras Ball. The arriving guests had clearly capitalized on the mash-up of holidays—in evidence were drag costumes with glamorous wigs and lavish ball gowns made for an eye-dazzling display. Just as visible as the festive costumes, however, was the problem that prompted the phone call. Cop cars surrounded California Hall and a paddy wagon was parked near the entrance, at the ready for any arrests. Plainclothes police and police photographers stood sentinel outside the building. The event had been planned as a private affair and tickets had been sold in advance to avoid the network of laws regulating decorum and dress at public establishments, which should have ensured the event would be free from police surveillance.[1] Those precautions, however, did nothing to protect the privacy of the guests who were arriving at the dance. A published photo of a person attending a "homosexual ball" could mean eviction, getting fired, or being shunned by family. Every time they entered or exited the building, guests at the ball faced the threat of exposure as they passed through a gauntlet of flashing cameras.

Bird and a group of other local ministers responded to the police action by serving as impromptu physical and moral shields. Some tried to block the police photographers, two attempted (unsuccessfully) to get arrested, and others escorted guests through the police line to ensure that anyone caught by the cameras went on record alongside the respectable figure of a clergyman.[2] Lutheran minister Chuck Lewis returned fire, using his own camera to take photographs of the police. By the end of the evening, however, the police had not only harassed hundreds of the guests attending the dance but also made six arbitrary arrests—four ticket takers were arrested for blocking the entrance to the building, and two men inside the hall were charged with lewd behavior.[3] The entire fiasco, as one homophile leader described it, was a "dramatic, large scale exhibition of the police trying to show that they were going to force their morality on the city."[4] For many of the clergy at the dance, some of whom were accompanied by their wives, it was the first time they had witnessed the levels of arbitrary police harassment directed toward those outside the sexual and gender norm.

The ministers attending the dance had been part of the event's planning from the outset. The ball was intended as both as a fund-raiser and as a publicity maneuver to bring attention to a newly formed homophile organization. The Council on Religion and the Homosexual (CRH), as the organization was called, had been formed a little more than six months earlier as a discussion group that would "facilitate a dialogue" between local clergy and members of homophile organizations. Leaders from each of the city's six homophile organizations served as representatives on its board, including leaders of the Mattachine Society and the Daughters of Bilitis, which had been operating since the mid-1950s, and those of newer groups, including the Tavern Guild and the Society for Individual Rights. The dance was the first collaboration of all of the city's homophile groups, and it was certainly the first to be formally supported by clergy.[5] Mattachine leader Hal Call, in an announcement about the upcoming dance, practically crowed with excitement. "Never before have all six groups united in concert to promote a community project," he declared; "perhaps we may be witness to a result which an established institution like the church and its representatives here has [sic] a unique capacity to achieve."[6]

Under the direction of the clergy, the organizers for the dance boldly decided to address the police department and the Alcoholic Beverage Control Board. With clergymen as the contact persons, the planning committee approached these officials in the hope that having minis-ters as negotiators might resolve any excuses for harassment or arrest.[7] Two ministers took the lead in the negotiations—Ted McIlvenna, a white minister serving as director of the Young Adult Project at Glide Urban Center, and Cecil Williams, an African American pastor recently appointed Glide's director of community involvement. As McIlvenna and Williams reported it, the meetings with the police seemed to eventually bring about some change. The first meeting began badly; the police ini-tially berated the ministers for "getting mixed up with a bunch of queers" and demanded that they explain their bad theology. Ministers, the police seemed to think, should be helping enforce the laws instead of encourag-ing homosexuality.[8] Later meetings, however, ended with what appeared to be a truce. The ministers insisted that the event would be conducted with decorum and discretion, assuring the police that they were attend-ing with their wives and other "normal" members of the community. They even invited the officers to attend as guests.[9] The officers agreed—or so it seemed—to leave the dance alone.

The show of force from the police on the night of the event appeared, to the clergy, to be a direct breach of this agreement. It was this turna-round that was the focus of the press conference called the morning after the police raid. The ministers donned their clerical collars again, and the press coverage—on the front page of the *San Francisco Chronicle*—featured eight stern looking ministers, arms folded, over the headline "Incident at a Homosexual Benefit: Angry Ministers Rip Police." The article presented almost verbatim the complaints expressed in the ministers' prepared press statement. They blasted the police officers for their "intimidation, broken promises, and obvious hostility," outlined the meetings and negotiations that had taken place before the dance, and called out the officers for the blatant violation of their agreement. The ministers' report presented the police as untrustworthy authorities whose determination to display their power resulted in completely unwarranted arrests. Plan-ners for the dance had jumped though every hoop to ensure there was no reason for any police presence. As final evidence of police incompe-tence, the press statement revealed that the first arrests of the night—of the "ticket takers" purportedly blocking the entrance—took into custody the lawyers whose job it was to ensure that everyone attending the dance was properly authorized to enter.[10]

As a number of historians have assessed, the ministers' stand against the police raid led to a remarkable set of short-term and long-term gains

Clergy participants in the Council on Religion and the Homosexual, 1965: (*from left*) Lewis Durham, Cecil Williams, Robert Cromey, Fred Bird, Charles Lewis, Clarence Colwell, and Ted McIlvenna. Courtesy of the Gay, Lesbian, Bisexual, Transgender Historical Society, San Francisco.

for targeted queer populations in San Francisco. The ministers affiliated with the CRH, as San Francisco historian Paul Gabriel argues, provided a "cloak of the cloth" to the homophile cause—meaning that clergy, as authoritative spokespersons, brought respectability and credibility to gays' unheeded efforts to challenge police repression and social injustice.[11] In the assessment of a number of historians of queer history, including San Francisco queer historian Nan Alamilla Boyd, the event sparked grassroots activism comparable to the aftermath of New York's more famous Stonewall riots.[12] The comparison points to the successes of the CRH, but it also invites a question: Why has historical memory crowned one event as the "birthplace of gay rights" while relegating the other to local history? Among the many answers is Boyd's succinct response: California Hall, she argues, "did not galvanize a national movement in the way that the Stonewall Riots were able to do."[13] In place of national influence, however, Boyd emphasizes a litany of local gains: the CRH brought attention and redress to discriminatory police practices, helped to jump-start broader grassroots support and cooperation, and inaugurated channels through which queer communities began to exert influence on the city government. In fact, as Boyd notes, queer communities in San Francisco, because of the work of the CRH, had already gained many of the freedoms that New Yorkers sought when they protested at Stonewall. Both Boyd and historian John D'Emilio suggest that these very gains, which made San Francisco a mecca for gay culture, may also have rendered it politically neutral by the time of Stonewall: its achievements facilitated a stable politics of reform that made it less viable as a center for a national movement.[14]

This chapter both expands and contests these assessments of the CRH's historical significance, beginning, first of all, by changing the frame of reference. Stonewall was of course not a reference point for the organizers and activists involved in this event. For them, California Hall was not "San Francisco's Stonewall," it was America's Wolfenden, and it was the homosexual's civil rights movement. These comparisons also shift the markers of the event's significance, foregrounding the notable presence of clerical collars rather than the perplexing absence of angry rioters. Clergy were key to the visual politics of all of these political moments. Looking at the available models of Wolfenden (where British clergy stood at the helm of the movement to repeal sodomy laws) and the black civil rights movement (where pastors, priests, and nuns led many of the freedom marches), homophile activists understood clergy support to be critical to the homophile movement's success. Del Martin and her partner, Phyllis Lyon, both leaders of the Daughters of Bilitis, had been working for several years to cultivate clergy support for proposed legislation to repeal California sodomy laws. In Martin's assessment, California Hall was a watershed moment that ended ministers' "conspiracy of silence" on the subject of homosexuality.[15] Finally, pastors translated the sympathies offered in their counseling ministries into a statement of political support made on the front page of the newspaper. The "cloak of the cloth" meant a great deal more than local respectability for San Francisco's queer constituencies; the public alliances with clergy symbolized a new moment for the movement as a whole.

The clergy support did indeed bring important changes to homophile leaders' organizing and activism. Some of those developments invite further reflection on how to understand the social and political meanings of that metaphorical "cloak of the cloth." For instance, it is worth attending more carefully to the rather thin moral cover offered by the axiomatic terms of the British clerics' support for sodomy law repeal, which sought to separate moral sanction from civil law. This tactic offered a secularist politics, to borrow a term used by theorists of religion and the public square. They were endorsing the notion that the law should not enforce religious teaching—personal sin was a minister's business rather than a magistrate's. Spokespersons for African American civil rights, on the other hand, proceeded using very different logic about the relationship between morality and the law. Theirs was most assuredly a moral politics: Martin Luther King Jr.'s repeated reminder that "the arc of the moral universe is long but it bends toward justice" invoked a higher moral law to inspire the struggle against unjust and immoral human ones.[16] Thus it is important, when analyzing the actions and rhetoric of clergy allies of the U.S. homophile movement, to notice the thickness of the cloak. Did ministers extend a thin secularist politics that covered homosexuals' private infelicities, or did they offer the more robust cover of a conviction that a higher moral law mandated justice for homosexuals? As we might expect, the answer to this question changed as clergy evaluated their convictions and as they reflected on the ethical reasons for their involvement with the homophile movement. An important and untold story about the CRH is thus its significance in conversations among church leaders about how to evaluate the morality of homosexual behavior and how those religious convictions should shape political advocacy.

And finally, there is the matter of the CRH's impact on national movement growth. California Hall, Boyd and D'Emilio tell us, did not catalyze the kind of national movement sparked after the Stonewall riots. In many ways, however, the pathways for that later movement were formed by the connections made through the CRH. Here is perhaps the most surprising story uncovered by paying closer attention to the clergy allies of the homophile movements: a story of quiet church-based support that took place amid the bars, nightclubs, coffeehouses, and street culture of urban America's "homosexual ghettos." The untold story of Stonewall is that a movement sparked by a bar raid held most of its meetings in churches. Those spaces were available because of earlier networks developed by CRH-connected clergy who were also plugged in to ecumenical programs geared toward facilitating urban outreach, young adult ministry, and community organizing. Tracing these connections uncovers the little-known history of late-1960s homophile movement growth that took place in church basements and community centers with the behind-the-scenes support of liberal ministers.

None of these involvements sprang forth from ministers' convictions that homosexuality was good, natural, and normal. California Hall was also a turning point in Christian leaders' own ideas about homosexuality and legal reform. The terms of their support, at least initially, formatively drew from disease theories and offered tepid permission, at best, for the circumstances under which homosexual behavior might actually be morally licit. A 1957 editorial in *Christian Century* assessed then-recent efforts in Britain to revoke laws penalizing private homosexual behavior among adults. "Serious churchmen," the author admonished, "may be counted on not to panic at this latest development, assessing it soberly for the suggestions, that there may be in it, for that part of Christian personal ethics that remains in most woeful disarray."[17] A more elliptical endorsement could hardly have been issued, and the title of the article, "Treading Lightly in a Delicate Subject," seemed to indicate that liberal church leaders, if they must address homosexuality and the law, would do it only on tiptoe. A tentative appraisal was better than no appraisal at all, but this editorial was a thin challenge to the zeal of conservative lawmakers and public officials who advanced the surveillance and targeting of "sex perverts" as their moral duty.

Morality and the Law

The actions of the San Francisco police, in harassing and arresting guests at a private event, certainly exceeded the de jure purview of sodomy laws. Sodomy laws, however, were only one strand of a sticky web of jurisprudence and enforcement practices that targeted gender deviance and sexual perversity during the 1950s and 1960s. Historian David Johnson uses the term "lavender scare" to identify the Cold War–era hysteria over the specter of hidden sex deviates. Public officials in cities from Atlanta to Boise to Washington, D.C., stepped up practices of surveillance against so-called moral perverts, and law enforcement officials used tactics of entrapment and arbitrary arrest that targeted such perceived figures. Lawmakers and public officials often invoked biblical authority for these policies. The destruction of Sodom and the perversity of the Roman Empire, referenced in the biblical accounts in Genesis 19 and Romans 1, were frequently invoked as examples of civilizational ruin brought about by sexual permissiveness.[18] "The Biblical description of homosexuality as an 'abomination' has well stood the test of time," announced a Florida legislative committee in a 1964 brief that advocated for a statewide purge of homosexuals employed in public schools and in the civil service.[19] In various cities and municipalities, conservative clergy lent support to antivice campaigns that targeted homosexuals as moral perverts. "The political structure was religious to the core," John Howard argues in his history of public policing in Atlanta.[20] The Cold Warriors, as they hunted for hidden sex deviants, remixed biblical references with communist conspiracy and moral horror.

The laws and practices that targeted homosexuals, however, were not simply the remains of long-standing religious taboos. Both the laws and the religious narratives had been recently reconfigured in ways that targeted homosexuality—and sex deviance more broadly—as part of amplified worries about psychiatric disease. The work of legal historian William Eskridge shows how the shifting meanings of old sodomy laws, combined with a web of new laws, resulted in the legal targeting of same-sex behavior and gender deviance to an extent unprecedented in American history. The purview of sodomy laws shifted over the course of the twentieth century; by 1961, Eskridge argues, sodomy was "a thoroughly homosexualized term."[21] Not only did sodomy laws have more narrow same-sex meanings; various laws and policies also expanded the kinds of same-sex physical contact that could be prosecuted. As a further component to the legal stew, nearly a third of U.S. states, between 1935 and 1950, also added nebulously defined "sexual psychopath" laws. Initially justified as a net for violent sex predators, the laws in practice resulted in broad targeting of gender and sexual behavior thought to result from psychological maladjustments.[22] The laws in force drew authority from religious censure against homosexuality—a notion of the past that was itself a modern invention—but surveyed and targeted same-sex behavior and gender deviance in uniquely modern ways.

Liberal Christians, along with sexual liberals, took issue with the fevered talk of conspiracy and the punitive targeting of homosexuals. To sexual liberals—and particularly those in the fields of mental health—the harsh laws seemed to represent a kind of sexual deviance of their own. The pervert-hunting conservatives exhibited a taboo-laden prurience and a morbid obsession with abnormal sexuality; sexual liberals deployed psychiatric theories and hypothesized about the latent perversions of the conspiracy-mongering Cold Warriors. But even as sexual liberals began to advocate for legal reform—and particularly for an end to sodomy laws—they drew from perspectives that were still thoroughly informed by psychiatric disease theories. In the early 1960s, three developments brought this logic into the foreground of American discussions about the law: the American Law Institute in 1962 issued broad recommendations for a model penal code, which listed sodomy law repeal among the recommended reforms, and the following year saw the publication of the American edition of the *Wolfenden Report* and also the release of a study by a group of British Quakers titled *Towards a Quaker View of Sex*. Both of these publications advocated an end to laws penalizing homosexuality. These developments placed sodomy law reform on the priority list for American sexual liberals.[23]

A 1963 essay by Union Theological Seminary professor and Christian theologian Tom Driver encapsulated the logic of this liberal intervention. Driver published a review of the Quaker study in the progressive *Christianity and Crisis* in which he largely supported the set of legal changes advocated by this study but also added his own spin about its merits. "All sex is odd," he wrote; "but homo-sex is odder than most. And funnier. The homosexual doesn't know what he's missing. Bigger joke: for emotional reasons, he *can't* know. The guy is trapped." Driver's tone was part and parcel of his argument: he was tired of the Christian pussyfooting around sexual problems. If Christians wanted to challenge society's skewed relationship to sex, they needed to straighten their talk. "The first step to healthy sexuality," he insisted, "is to remove [homosexuality] from the aura of forbidden (therefore exalted) mystery. And I submit that homosexuality brought fully into the light of day and stripped of its exotic defenses will appeal to only a fraction of the people now swept along by it."[24] Driver's rationale for sexual reform assumed that homosexuality and other unhealthy expressions of sexuality were actively caused by prevailing silence, taboo, and punishment. He prescribed a dose of straight talk—as well as legal reforms that would remove the prurient inspection of the law—as a kind of social medicine for curing both homosexuality and a broader culture of sexual unhealthiness. Thus, for many sexual liberals of that time, it made perfect sense: ending laws that targeted homosexual behavior would keep the country straight.

The terms in which sexual liberals advocated ending sodomy laws also took for granted that the particular force and fervor of the laws stemmed from a religious past. The axiomatic rationale separated morality from civil law. Episcopal bishop James Pike received substantial press attention in 1964 when, in an address to the graduating class of Duke University's law school, he derided the assumption "that if something is naughty there should be a law against it."[25] The separation of religion and law also connected to the logic of disease and treatment. Liberal reformers spoke of repealing sodomy laws in order to address the problem of homosexuality in more rational and enlightened ways.

Such reforms, they emphasized, not only ended ineffective and punitive treatment of homosexuals but also helped foster a more sexually healthy society. In these pragmatic terms, American sexual liberals insisted that the tangled opprobrium of antihomosexual legal censure needed to be unbraided and parceled out in new ways. The law needed to be separate from religion, a sentiment endorsed in the repeated call to separate sin from crime. This appeal for separating religion and law also granted important authority to the field of medicine, as therapeutic treatment seemed to hold the only "effective" method of addressing a pathological condition. The result was a new delegation of authority among religion, law, and medicine: clergy should compassionately dispense private moral instruction; lawmakers should regulate to the common good; and both religion and law should defer to the healing powers of doctors and psychiatrists.

Thus, liberals, as they criticized the invasive moral reach of the law, had certainly not entirely given up on regulating sex. Their project of legal and moral reform focused on practices and policies that they believed would help straighten Americans' skewed sexual desires, an effort that placed them in opposition to conservatives' project of moral regulation through the law. Their "rational" and "efficient" program for reforming homosexuality laws took direct aim at a perceived Christian past of archaic antihomosexual regulation that they believed tacitly bred sexual perversions. Liberal clergy cast their lot against the moralists and with the secularizers with the understanding that they were advocating effective modern reforms over bygone taboos and dogmas. Of course, the religious traditions that they discussed, and the laws entangled with those moral viewpoints, were certainly not remnants of a distant past. Both religious and legal understandings of same-sex deviance had already been reshaped within notions of homosexuality as the pathological opposite to normal sexuality, and both liberals and conservatives drew from newly consolidated understandings of homosexuality as a pathological condition.

The conflict between conservative legal moralists and liberal secularists thus was, in many ways, a disagreement shaped by a fundamental ruse: the false notion that the crux of their disagreement was over whether or not the law should enforce religious morality. In truth, reformers on both sides of this issue were concerned with specters of deviant sexuality, which they in different ways connected to the sexual health of normal Americans. A critical difference in their approaches was the mechanism of influence. For conservatives, overt regulation was the only way to curb the sordid world of sex perversion. Liberals, on the other hand, vested acceptance and inclusion with disciplinary power and bemoaned the perverse consequences of arbitrary punishment.

The particular religious liberals in this chapter's story—the clergy who formally allied with the homophile movement—markedly changed their minds about homosexuality through their encounters with members of the homophile movement. At the outset, however, most, if not all, of the ministers stepped to the prevailing tune of early 1960s sexual liberalism. Their initial motivations for ministering to homosexuals, for challenging the laws that targeted them, and even for talking and writing about homosexuality were firmly anchored in the disease theories that informed other sexual liberals of their era. They pressed for change with the conviction that homosexuality, as a pathological condition, had too long festered in the shadow of taboo, intolerance, and evasion. Drawing it into the light would change both the sick culture and even, perhaps, the sick homosexuals.

Confronting Taboo

In September 1963, at the second service at Grace Cathedral, the towering Episcopal church that crowned Nob Hill, the exclusive site of impressive residences for former nabobs and railroad barons, Robert Cromey—newcomer priest to San Francisco via the New York Bronx and invited as the guest preacher that Sunday—decided to discuss the hushed issue of homosexuality. We can only guess how many of the well-dressed congregants listening to Cromey's sermon about homosexuality were themselves gay. Grace's Gothic aesthetic and high liturgy easily fit the type of congregation that Laud Humphreys, Episcopal priest turned sociologist turned gay revolutionary, later termed a "queen parish"—a reference to churches that attracted more than their share of gay men.[26] Patronizing as it might seem for homosexuality to be addressed from the pulpit as a mental condition, it is quite possible that some of those gay church members welcomed Cromey's words as a healing balm. "Homosexuality must be taken out of the limbo of life," he urged. "It must be given the same public understanding and opportunity for treatment now given other human ailments once kept only in the cages of our mind—such ailments as venereal disease or mental retardation." Cromey's message of inclusion drew from a familiar narrative of Jesus's relationship to the sick and the outcast. The sermon ended with a reference to the Eucharist, and Cromey encouraged the congregation to consider Jesus's example as they participated in the ritual meal. "Let us ask God to open us to receive our sinful and troubled neighbors."[27]

There may have been homosexual neighbors roaming the streets around Grace Cathedral, but the closest venues for spotting San Francisco's queer sorts were either half a mile south in the Tenderloin or a mile in the opposite direction in North Beach. There, in the bars, clubs, and streets, were the denizens who gave San Francisco pride of place as America's "gay capital," a moniker bestowed by *Life* magazine's 1964 article on "homosexuality in America." Among San Franciscans, a local argot parsed through the city's diverse queer communities—there were "gays" and "lesbians," transgender women derogatively identified as "hair-fairies" and "street queens," male sex workers called "butch hustlers," and tough-presenting members of the "leather crowd."[28] The outside world peering in at these strange figures through the *Life* article read about the visible signs of queer life in America's largest cities as a new and troubling phenomenon. Homosexuals, no longer content to quietly hide their condition, were part of a newly emergent social problem. The reporting on these seedy "homosexual ghettos" warned that normal Americans everywhere could not ignore these developments for long. "A secret world grows open and bolder," the *Life* article warned; Americans soon would be "forced to look at it."[29]

City ministers like Cromey, by virtue of geography, were on the front lines of this urban trend. In the early 1960s, various Protestant denominations were working to revitalize their work in cities, and Cromey was one of a "new breed" of clergy leading this current. He was appointed director of an experimental outreach program for urban churches located south of Market Street. The Episcopal Mission Presbytery, as it was termed, gathered two Episcopal and two Presbyterian churches that were all struggling to keep pace with the neighborhood's changing demographic. The parish pastors of these downtown churches once ministered to congregations full of white families, but the dwindling numbers in the pews bore witness to their grown children's flight out to the city suburbs. The surrounding neighborhoods of African Americans, Latinos, white hippies, artists, and homosexuals had little interest in the staid white Protestant liturgies preserved in those churches' Sunday services.[30] Cromey, in other words, was braving the urban wilderness depicted by a 1963 article on inner-city ministry as he faced those "certain parts of the inner cities . . .

full of homosexuals, perverts, slaves to dope and drink, and other strange and lost individuals of the Tennessee Williams types."[31]

A cohort of mainline Protestant leaders of this era faced the "urban crisis," as it was often called, with the conviction that status quo ministry was not an option. They approached the demographic challenge of emptying pews as a problem connected to broader social and political developments in American cities. Those churches, along with the neighborhoods around them, were being slowly drained of resources as postwar urban development catered to the rising economy of the city periphery at the expense of the city center. A generation of left-leaning clergy cast their lot with urban churches as a sign of God's preferential option for the poor and disenfranchised over the "comfortable pews" of suburban churches. Their mission, to quote Harvey Cox's encapsulation of these trends in 1965's *The Secular City*, urged Christians to practice an "ascetic disaffiliation" or "holy worldliness" that involved leaving their "palaces" to step into "God's permanent revolution in history."[32]

In developing these revolutionary new ministries, urban ministers traded in Bible dictionaries for *Reveille for Radicals*, a 1946 manual for grassroots organizing written by Chicago activist Saul Alinsky.[33] In a network of emerging urban training centers—foremost among them the Chicago Urban Training Center, founded in 1964—ministers gained skills in grassroots organizing and political advocacy. The rhetoric and strategy taught in these centers challenged the conventions of parish ministry and urged pastors to effectively turn their congregations inside out—to develop experimental programs that focused on the circumstances and needs of communities around the church. Those programs would not offer "handouts" or "charity" but should enable disenfranchised communities to identify and challenge systemic injustice. Thus, the method of ministry was activism; the concurrent struggles for peace and justice—African American civil rights, migrant workers' rights, antiwar, housing inequality, integrated public schools, and so on—were not a backdrop to the work of urban ministry but its very heart. In cities from St. Louis to Seattle, New York to Dallas, Boston to Kansas City, Chicago to Los Angeles, and so on, a cohort of clergy activists worked to develop ministries that responded to a Christian imperative to work for justice.[34]

In San Francisco, perhaps more than in any other city, urban ministers faced the question of queer disenfranchisement as a front-and-center issue. And perhaps more than any other minister in San Francisco, a young Methodist named Ted McIlvenna was at the front lines. In 1963,

McIlvenna was invited to direct a young adult program at Glide Urban Center, a newly formed community organizing foundation that operated alongside Glide Memorial Methodist Church. McIlvenna's job was very different from that of a conventional youth or young adult minister. He was hired, essentially, to start up an experimental program to address the needs of youth and young adults in the neighborhood around Glide, and his institutional home in a foundation for community organizing rather than a traditional congregation gave him freedom to take that ministry in new directions.[35] Because of Glide's location in the heart of the Tenderloin—notorious as a vice district and homosexual ghetto— the job also put McIlvenna "right in the middle of the gay question in a hurry," as one of his colleagues later put it.[36] McIlvenna's mission gave him a front-row seat to the blatant harassment and violence targeting the queer subculture, often at the hands of the police. It was that brutality, he recalled later, that provoked him to develop a ministry that would some-how address this injustice.[37]

McIlvenna soon discovered that San Francisco's homophile organizations were his best resources for understanding the city's queer communities. The Mattachine Society and the Daughters of Bilitis were the city's oldest homophile groups, but the early 1960s saw the founding of a number of new groups that more directly addressed local politics. The League for Civil Education was formed in 1961 to promote an openly gay candidate, José Sarria, in the election for city supervisor. When that failed, the organization continued to publish a local gay newspaper. The Tavern Guild formed in 1962 as a mutual protection society that helped insulate bartenders, bar owners, and patrons from harassment by the police and the Alcoholic Beverage Control Board. In May 1964, the Society for Individual Rights formed as the most politically active of the groups up to that point. It met initially in Glide Church and quickly attracted a membership of around three hundred people, which also made it the largest homophile organization to date.[38] In the spring of 1964, McIlvenna invited representatives from all of the existing organizations to participate in a consultation that would gather ministers and homophile leaders for an extended dialogue. The notice from Mattachine president Hal Call to other homophile leaders expressed his excitement about the opportunity. "The interest in this conference has been unprecedented from the representatives of the Protestant churches concerned," he noted, and he urged fellow homophile community representatives to "match this interest."[39]

The event they planned was a four-day Consultation on the Church and the Homosexual held May 31 through June 2, organized to initiate a sustained discussion about "the relationship between the church and the homosexual."[40] The participant list and the agenda for the meeting facilitated a strategic experiment in interpersonal dynamics: this was a "confrontation" between opposing groups of "clergy" and "homophiles" designed to break down the stereotypes and stigmas that prevented them from working together.[41] The balanced guest list included fifteen clergy and fifteen homophile representatives, with added participants from the Daughters of Bilitis to redress the gender imbalance. The clergy participants included about a half-dozen urban ministers from San Francisco, several national Methodist leaders, a staff person from the National Council of Churches (NCC), and an urban ministry specialist from the Chicago Urban Training Center.[42] The record of this interpersonal experiment was later published in a short booklet circulated by Glide Urban Center that served as an exemplary how-to model for future clergy-homosexual consultations. The subtext for this little book was the awkward transformation of the clergy, who were led through a series of bewildering encounters—a kind of queer Pilgrim's Progress—that ultimately brought them into a true relationship with their homosexual dialogue partners.

The encounter began in the bowels of San Francisco's nightlife, as the newly arrived clergy were treated to a late-night immersion in the city's queer subcultures. They met preppy professionals, leather daddies, and drag queens in a blurry succession of barhopping. The "footsore clergymen" returned to their hotels rooms in the wee hours of the morning, only to be awakened "bleary-eyed" the next day for a picnic with members of the League for Civil Education.[43] Following the lunch, the clergy and homophile participants drove out of the city to a secluded retreat center in nearby Marin County, where the discussions for the next two days focused on their feelings and stereotypes about each other. In those sessions, honesty and directness were prized. Homophile leaders came prepared with hard-hitting presentations that expressed angry disappointment with religious institutions for their neglect and condemnation of homosexuals. Don Lucas, a member of the Mattachine Society, presented the results of a survey completed by gay men about religion that highlighted their weariness with organized religion, while Billie Talmij, a member of the Daughters of Bilitis, offered "demolition fuses for four-walled thinking" that challenged both the participating gay men and the ministers on their sexist and antihomosexual ways of thinking. The retreat began with awkward conversations around the coffeepot—with participants "struggling to use words with only one meaning"—but it settled by the last day into an informal dynamic that one minister described as a "religious gay bar."[44]

For gays and lesbians often on the receiving end of clergy speeches, the retreat offered a novel dynamic: it situated homosexuals as experts of their own experiences and placed clergy in a listening role. Daughters of Bilitis member Del Martin, in an article for the *Ladder*, excitedly described the "new rapport" between clergy and homosexuals. Neither she nor other homophile participants had attended the consultation as an effort to reconcile with Christianity; their interests were primarily political rather than theological. Still, Martin described the consultation as the occasion for "the re-birth of Christian fellowship in the United States to include all human beings regardless of sexual proclivity."[45] This new rapport, she reported, had also created a new agenda for clergy-homophile cooperation. A number of the clergy had pledged to organize similar consultations in other cities, to form a committee on homosexuality within the NCC, and to publish sympathetic articles on homosexuality in Christian publications.[46] In one fell swoop, the clergy allies of the homophile movement had multiplied to include a list of impressive names in ecumenical Protestant justice work.

A few days after the retreat, the San Francisco clergy and homophile representatives formalized their partnership, creating a new organization called the Council on Religion and the Homosexual. Its stated goals were to promote a "continuing dialogue between the church and the homosexual" and to develop programs for further education and advocacy in churches and other social institutions.[47] By November, the council had added forty local ministers to its roster of clergy participants and also gathered stable representation from all of San Francisco's homophile groups. In December, the group received its first public recognition—a human interest article in the *San Francisco Chronicle* and an announcement in the *Christian Century*.[48]

The police raid on California Hall occurred only a few weeks after this public debut, and the CRH effectively channeled the conflict with the police into a springboard for social change. The confrontation with the authorities highlighted systemic injustice, and the clergy allies used the raid as a platform to garner sympathetic press coverage that humiliated the police. The press attention, in turn, gave the CRH both a public forum and grassroots support for further advocacy. The incident, in short, was a textbook model of the strategies for community organizing and social change outlined in Alinsky's *Reveille for Radicals*. In fact, so "textbook" was this case that it seems entirely possible that the confrontation with the police resulted from a strategy devised to deliberately provoke such a confrontation. McIlvenna, in interviews decades after the event, repeatedly averred that the organizers "set up" the conflict with the police. They planned in advance that the ministers and their wives would be present, and they stationed the lawyers as ticket takers—even, McIlvenna claims, putting "a little rouge" on the cheeks of the lawyers so that the police would be more likely to arrest them.[49]

Such a strategy, if it was indeed preplanned, certainly took on incredible risks. Most vulnerable were the arrested lawyers, two of whom—Herb Donaldson and Evander Smith—were gay. Their recollections about the police raid, recorded in 1989, say nothing about trying to entice the police to arrest them, although they were aware of the risks when they took their place as ticket takers. They were standing side by side at the entrance to the hall (with plenty of room on either side, they recall) when the police arrested them for blocking access to the building. Donaldson recalled returning home, where his partner was waiting for him, after he was released from the police station late that night. "I was feeling kind of low," he remembered; "I was thinking, 'There goes my legal career.'"[50] The next morning's newspaper reported the lawyers' names and addresses in connection with the police raid—publicity that for many other gay suspects resulted in getting fired from their jobs.[51] Fortunately, the American Civil Liberties Union volunteered to represent the case, and when it went to trial in February, the judge summarily dismissed the case on the grounds that the arrests had been fraudulent.

Just as important, however, the ministers' involvement as activists and allies required them to trust the critical insights of the gays and lesbians they worked with, and these encounters changed the way many ministers understood the so-called problem of homosexuality. The first glimmers of this reformed view of homosexuality came just a few weeks after the police raid when John Moore, who was then serving as senior pastor of Glide, announced a three-week sermon series on sexuality. The task gave him the uncomfortable responsibility of synthesizing and reflecting on the inchoate convictions that shaped CRH ministers' activism. Many years later, Moore admitted how difficult it was to write those sermons. "I didn't know if I was right or wrong," he admitted. The sermons he offered, in his own reflection, were in a vacuum: "What I was saying wasn't what my parents said, wasn't what my church said, it wasn't what my culture said, and it wasn't what anybody said except a very few people."[52] The sermons also offered little by way of answers to the questions they raised about morality and biblical interpretation. As Moore addressed the people gathered in the pews at Glide, he frankly admitted that he did not have answers about how to understand homosexuality. His one certainty was that "no good can come from rejecting persons," and that meant that Christians needed "to live" in the middle of a messy solidarity with those around them. "It's not for us to proclaim 'the Way' from this monastery in the Tenderloin," he offered. "Rather it is for us to stand with our brothers in the city as they seek 'The Way.'"[53] Rather than answers, Moore offered a method—a practice of solidarity with the marginalized in the midst of moral uncertainty.

In the months and years that followed, the CRH, with the energizing support of Glide Urban Center, began to influentially circulate a new discourse about religion, homosexuality, and the law. In the series of publication, speeches, and pamphlets issued through the CRH and Glide Urban Center, a cohort of San Francisco clergy added a thicker "cloak of the cloth" to the thin secularist arguments for separating crime and sin. One publication that influentially presented this new moral politics was a slim treatise titled *A Brief of Injustices*. Published by Glide Urban Center as a clergy manifesto for homosexual rights, the brief succinctly identified the laws, policies, and practices that targeted homosexuals and expressed the ministers' moral outrage against those injustices. It circulated widely among homophile leaders and their sympathizers as one of the most systematic appraisals to date of the entire web of surveillance, harassment, and violence faced by homosexuals. Just as important as the brief's analysis, however, was its ethical mandate—in the authoritative voice of clergy, it defended homosexuals' rights as an essential part of the "Judeo-Christian commandment" to love the neighbor.[54]

Historians have commented extensively on the moral authority granted by the CRH's clergy allies. They rightly note that the ministers' moral privilege gave San Francisco's queer communities a respectable platform to voice their concern and also helped them gain access to concrete channels for political reform. That support, however, really went beyond symbolic moral cover. Their role, as Glide ministers termed it, was to serve as "enablers," a word that aptly encompassed a broader philosophy and practice of channeling resources for community-based justice work.[55] This included funding, meeting and office space, access to communication and publishing resources, and support for direct action advocacy. Cecil Williams took a lead role in forming Citizen Alert, a call-in center that responded to complaints of police abuse modeled on similar program Williams had organized in Kansas City. Largely because of his leadership, the San Francisco initiative successfully recruited support from pastors of black churches in the city who were also concerned with problems of police brutality.[56] Ministers affiliated with Glide Urban Center were also influential in supporting activism that might have otherwise been marginalized from the homophile organizations. Susan Stryker's work on transgender history recounts the significant role of Glide clergy in supporting the organizing and activist work of the gay hustlers, transgender women, and queer youth in San Francisco. Glide was a meeting place for Vanguard, a support group for street youth that included gay hustlers and transgender youth. It also hosted the meetings of Conversion Our Goal, a transsexual support group that started in 1967.[57] Glide was a venue that provided assistance and space for the formation of a remarkably diverse coalition of activists and organizations.

In the years following the California Hall incident, clergy played an important role in an emerging national network of homophile activists. The most concrete channels for movement growth came through homophile organizations themselves, where a cohort of gay and lesbian militants began to challenge the respectability politics of their founders and to adopt confrontational practices of political advocacy. Many of these homophile militants, following the example of the San Francisco CRH, turned to clergy as important allies in the struggle for justice. The CRH never formally organized a national network, but a number of homophile groups in other cities formed similar councils. Homophile organizations, however, were not the only channels of influence. Urban ministers like the group of clergy in San Francisco played significant roles in supporting gay and lesbian organizing in other cities. The instigating—or perhaps *enabling* is a better word—for that proliferation came out of the Glide Urban Center, which was the closest things the homophile movement had to a national advocacy organization, and other urban training programs and ecumenical initiatives also actively reached out to gays and lesbians. Thus, the channels for an emerging movement ran through Protestant urban ministry programs and ecumenical outreach programs as well as through homophile organizations. Through these connections, a cohort of homophile militants linked arms with a vanguard group of clergy activists to voice a new moral imperative for homosexual rights.

Militancy did not come easily to homophile organizations. Even in the early 1960s, the dominant strategy for bringing around changing attitudes about homosexuality was to cultivate support from experts and cultural authorities, invite these leaders to meetings and conferences, and hope that those spokespersons' views on homosexuality would be positively influenced by the orderly decorum they encountered in the groups of mostly white, middle-class gays and lesbians. Indeed, the Consultation on the Church and the Homosexual that met in San Francisco had been as much an extension of homophile practices of engaging experts as it was liberal ministers' frameworks for encountering outsiders. By the mid-1960s, however, a number of homophile leaders on the East Coast had grown tired of pandering to experts. Their impatience was inspired in large part by the increasing visibility and militancy of the African American civil rights movement taking place around them. An important catalyst for galvanizing homophile activism came from members of the newly formed Mattachine Society of Washington, D.C., and a number of this group—mostly white men—attended the 1963 March on Washington. These homophile activists in the nation's capital, along with a handful of sympathizers in other East Coast homophile organizations, recognized in the civil rights language of minority rights and the strategies of civil protest an ideal template for the kind of rhetoric and tactics needed to bring attention to homosexual rights.[58]

Leading these organizers was Frank Kameny, a Harvard-educated secular Jew whose educational background made him a cultural equal to many of the homophile organizations' expert speakers. After graduating from Harvard in 1956, Kameny taught for a year at Georgetown University before being hired by the U.S. Army Map Service. Less than a year into the job, his employment was abruptly terminated when federal officers uncovered a past arrest on charges of lewd conduct. Kameny fought for his right to equal employment all the way to the U.S. Supreme Court—and lost. Cultural capital and academic credentials were no protection from being targeted and fired as a security risk.[59] In 1961, he and Jack Nichols, a D.C. native and gay man, gathered a group of likeminded women and men to form the Mattachine Society of Washington. Under Kameny's leadership, the new organization had a confrontation-minded spirit, geared from the outset toward political advocacy. Kameny and other members of the Washington-based group were at the helm of efforts to gather East Coast homosexual organizations into a working coalition to push for political change. In 1963, homophile leaders in Washington, Philadelphia, and New York formally organized a collective body, the East Coast Homophile Organizations (ECHO), to coordinate a political agenda. There were certainly outspoken dissenters among the homophile leadership to the activist aims of the new organization. Still, ECHO helped spur on a new militancy. An important outcome of the collective organizing was a picket demonstration held July 4, 1965, at Philadelphia's Constitution Hall. ECHO subsequently agreed to make July 4 the date for continued protests—an "Annual Reminder," as they termed it, of homosexuals' rights.[60]

These protests could not have looked more staid and respectable. Thirty-nine people participated in the first protest, marching in single file before Constitution Hall. The protest's location and message strategically identified homosexuals with America's highest ideals of freedom and democratic rights. The neatly lettered text on the protest placards drove home the point that homosexuals, too, were American citizens with rights.[61] The dignified protest epitomized what historian Marc Stein has termed a "strategy of militant respectability." Kameny, as one of the organizers for the protest, insisted that the men wear suits and ties and women wear dresses. Participants had to appear nothing like the deviant "swishes" of homosexual stereotypes but instead had to physically present as an otherwise invisible minority of patriotic, gender normative, middle-class American citizens.[62]

The homophile organizers involved in these protests quickly seized upon San Francisco's model of partnering with clergy. The CRH in San Francisco sent five representatives to the September 1965 meeting of ECHO to offer guidance about forming partnerships with clergy. Neale Secor, an Episcopal priest and former intern at Glide, reported back that homophile groups in Washington, Philadelphia, and New York already had the tentative beginnings of formal clergy-homophile partnerships. The Mattachine Society of Washington stepped to the plate first and had a formally established Washington-area Council on Religion and the Homosexual by May 1965.[63] In Philadelphia, homophile groups met with the Philadelphia Council of Churches.[64] Secor also noted that the Mattachine Society of New York had an active Religious Affairs Committee that worked closely with sympathetic ministers.[65]

Los Angeles's homophile organizers were also quickly prodded into action by their counterparts in San Francisco. Board members from the

Annual Reminder demonstration, 1969. Photograph by Nancy Tucker
© Lesbian Herstory Archives Photo Collection, Brooklyn.

San Francisco CRH flew down for a meeting with Los Angeles–area clergy and homophile representatives on June 1, 1965. The meeting led to the founding of the Southern California Council on Religion and the Homophile (SCCRH). Jim Kepner, one of the founding editors of ONE, helped to organize this new group, and the leadership also included two local Methodist ministers, Alex Smith and Ken Wahrenbrock, and UCC minister Clarence Colwell, who had recently moved to L.A. from San Francisco for a church appointment. A small but dedicated number of clergy and homophile leaders continued to meet regularly for study and discussion. When L.A. police raided the Black Cat, an area gay bar, on New Year's Eve 1967, the SCCRH responded by holding informational meetings that met at clergy members' churches. However, it was the not the SCCRH but an even newer organization called Personal Rights in Defense and Education (PRIDE) that took the helm in pushing for a more activist politics among L.A. gay communities—an effort joined, a year later, by yet another organization formed in the aftermath of a bar raid, the Metropolitan Community Church. The SCCRH continued to meet into the mid-1970s.[66]

Letters to the San Francisco CRH told of additional consultations and councils organized in Denver, Chicago, Dallas, Kansas City, Boston, Honolulu, and Ottawa, Ontario.[67] The letters about the new councils on religion arrived as the homophile movement expanded rapidly; between 1965 and 1968, the number of local organizations devoted to gay and lesbian rights more than doubled. Some of these were new activist organizations, like PRIDE, in cities that had long been home to homophile associations. Many, however, were entirely new groups located outside the larger gay urban centers on the East Coast and in California. In smaller cities in the South, the Midwest, and the Pacific Northwest, new gay and lesbian organizations were on the rise.[68] For many of these groups, the critical connection to start them came through urban ministry programs. At the center of the fledging organizing efforts were urban ministers working on outreach in "homosexual ghettos." The search for resources for this kind of ministry inevitably drew those ministers to the Glide Urban Center.

In Kansas City, Methodist ministers Paul Jones and Vann Anderson were both involved with the Young Adult Project. They visited Glide Urban Center, and many of their programs replicated practices used by the ministers in San Francisco. They also started a night ministry, which meant putting on the clerical collar and going into bars and nightclubs to simply be available to patrons who wanted to talk. On one night, Jones recalled, a patron brought him to the Arabian Nights, a hidden bar that catered to gays and lesbians. "It was totally strange to me," he recalled, but he stayed and did what he usually did—simply listen to what people had to tell him about their experiences and feelings about religion. Out of these encounters, Jones and Anderson agreed to help a group of gays and lesbians organize the Phoenix Society for Individual Rights in 1966. The group met initially at Westport Methodist Church and then moved to a rented house. The Phoenix Society, with the support of Jones and Anderson, developed programing to educate area clergy, faculty, and students at the Methodist-affiliated Saint Paul Theological Seminary.[69]

There are similar accounts of gay and lesbian groups formed with the support of urban ministers in nearly a dozen other small cities. In Dallas, Methodist minister Doug McLean, who was also connected to the Young Adult Project, became interested in helping support homophile organizing after attending a program at Glide Urban Center. He and a gay man named Phil Johnson gathered contacts—four additional gay men and three ministers—to form a group they called the Circle of

Friends, which met at a house owned by one of the minister's churches.[70] In Seattle, a Japanese American UCC minister named Mineo Katagiri, who was active in an urban street ministry, had similar kinds of encounters with Seattle's queer communities in his ministry. Katagiri's office in St. Mark's Cathedral was the meeting place for Seattle's first homophile organization, which took the name the Dorian Society.[71] In Portland, Oregon, Harper Richardson arrived in 1966 to Centenary-Wilbur United Methodist Church with programming ideas for young adult ministry gleaned from attending a training session at Glide. Richardson started a coffeehouse and welcomed community action groups, including those of gays and lesbians. Both the church and an ecumenically supported house near Portland State University called Koinonia House served as hubs for gay and lesbian organizing in the late 1960s.[72] In Hartford, Connecticut, Episcopal minister Clinton Jones had already begun holding dialogue sessions about homosexuality with the city's council of churches. For Jones, the closest example of a clergy-homophile collaboration was actually the George W. Henry Foundation in New York. Jones first established a counseling ministry for homosexuals as an affiliate of the Henry Foundation. Unlike Alfred Gross, however, he was more than willing to support organizing efforts by his clients, and his church provided meeting space in 1968 for the Kalos Society, Hartford's first homophile organization.[73] Other sources reported on new gay and lesbian groups founded through the support of liberal ministers in Lincoln-Omaha, Nebraska; St. Louis, Missouri; and New York City—where both the Gay Liberation Front and the Gay Activist Alliance met in the basements and community centers of churches.

Clergy also played a central role in the emerging national coalition among homophile groups. In February 1966, about forty representatives from fifteen different homophile groups attended the first national planning conference of homophile organizations in Kansas City. Clarence Colwell, a UCC minister and one of the founding CRH clergy, was elected to chair the Kansas City meeting, and he was also given the task of coordinating the second conference, scheduled to take place in San Francisco the following August.[74] These efforts to organize nationally hardly produced a coherent national agenda—in fact, the gatherings highlighted deep disagreements among the various organizations in attendance. One delegate from Los Angeles joking described Colwell's role as moderator as "similar to the German embassy in helping warring groups communicate."[75] With Colwell again serving as moderator, the second meeting of

Gay Liberation Front meeting at Washington Square United
Methodist Church, 1970. Photograph by Diana Davies, Manuscript and
Archives Division, The New York Public Library.

the North American Conference of Homophile Organizations (NACHO)
took place in San Francisco the following August with an overlapping
pre-conference Consultation on Theology and the Homosexual, which
gathered homophile representatives and ministers for the task of discussing biblical and theological resources on homosexuality.[76]

Robert Cromey took over Colwell's seat as moderator for the 1968
NACHO meeting in Chicago. The triumphant product of that conference
was the unanimously approved statement "Gay is Good." The statement
was a deliberate analogy to the Black Power chant "Black is Beautiful!"
Frank Kameny, the author of the gay statement, reported that his inspiration came from watching Stokely Carmichael lead a Black Power rally
on television. The chant, he noted, repudiated the cultural logic of white
supremacy by challenging a "society in which 'white,' 'snow,' 'purity,'
and 'good' are all equated together." Homosexuals, he mused, "need
the same kind of thing," a way to insist that "homosexuality is GOOD—
positively and without reservation."[77] Kameny's answer borrowed the
common slang term "gay" to reference that new positive identity. The
phrase, he argued, would help "establish in the homosexual community

and its members feelings of pride, self-esteem, self-confidence, and self worth." The statement was the one item endorsed unanimously in an otherwise fractious meeting.[78]

The process of coming to agreement on the question of homosexual morality was not at all a seamless route even within the homophile organizations. The statement was less an observation of fact than an effort to invoke a new and different kind of self for homosexuals who might otherwise doubt the goodness of their sexuality. Cromey, from his role as moderator, shook his head over the infighting that characterized almost every other part of the meeting. In an address to San Francisco members of the CRH, delivered a few months later, he reflected on the work they needed to do to make that statement true. "If 'gay is good' is to mean anything," he commented to that gathering, "we have to deal with each other at the gut level."[79] Homophile activists, he implied, needed to internalize the symbolic language they voted on.

For clergy, too, changing the moral logic of homosexuality also required more than simply invoking a statement. It took work. The context of activism and organizing that informed the movement's statement of identity pride also informed the language used by the clergy allies of the homophile movement. The church basements, community centers, and bar encounters that shaped clergy-homophile partnerships also worked to reshape those ministers' theological and biblical understandings of sexuality. The published accounts of that rethinking began to appear in print in the late 1960s.

Toward a Theology of Homosexuality

Robert Wood, persistent thorn in the side of his UCC colleagues, knew well the uphill battle to push Christian periodicals to address homosexuality. He kept a file of rejection letters from editors dating back to 1959, when he first started pressing Christian journals to publish short essay sections from his forthcoming *Christ and the Homosexual*. Among that pile of rejections was the polite letter from the editor of *Social Action*. The publishing arm of the UCC's Council for Christian Social Action (CCSA)—its social justice office—seemed like the most amenable home for a discussion about the discrimination faced by homosexuals. The publishing committee thought otherwise. "I know you will not be satisfied with the decision," the letter read, but "we will not be doing an issue of *Social Action* magazine on homosexuality in the near future."[80] A year and a half later, however, brought surprising news of the board's change of heart. That letter in January 1967 reported an "important breakthrough." Staff members of the CCSA had taken part in a three-day seminar on homosexuality held by the NCC. Following the seminar, the publications committee voted unanimously to devote an entire issue of the journal to the "long-neglected problem" of homosexuality. Alongside this path-breaking issue, the Presbyterian social justice office would also commit a companion volume of its *Social Progress* journal to a full discussion of homosexuality.[81] Wood's reply, typical of his impatient letters to other church leaders, was alternatively excoriating and commendatory. The much-heralded publication, he reminded them, "will come too late to save several thousand of homosexuals from blighted spiritual lives, sui-cide, heartache, and the brunt of injustices. But if done with understand-ing and light it can yet save other lives."[82] Wood was not about to extend gratitude when editors made the right decision years behind schedule.

Controversial perspectives did not appear in print just because an edi-tor had a change of heart. The slow-moving gears that eventually influ-enced this decision started not with Wood but with the 1964 Consultation on the Church and the Homosexual in San Francisco. Among the partici-pants was Keith Wright, a UCC minister and staff member at the NCC. He returned to New York and organized a study committee on homosexuality organized under the "Special Needs" division of the NCC's Department of Ministry, Vocation and Pastoral Services. The Pastoral Services Com-mission's Concern for Sexual Variation, as it was called, began meeting in 1965.[83] Its committee members included Ed Egan, New York Methodist minister, and Clinton Jones, an Episcopal priest in Hartford. Both, not incidentally, were clergy counselors working with the Henry Foundation. Both were also gay.[84]

Clergy who were gay themselves, however, were in no position to speak frankly about their sexuality. The reports of the meetings of the NCC's Pastoral Services Commission capture the irony—and necessity— of inviting homophile representatives to present a firsthand perspective on homosexuality. This principle of representation followed an insistent politics of inclusion shaped by white liberal churches' discussions of race. Ministers, however, were hardly lining up to volunteer as the token homosexuals; the practical solution to that vacuum was to outsource first-hand representation to homophile organizations. Egan's records from one clergy/homophile consultation make note of a lecture delivered by Barbara Gittings, who commenced with a forthright acknowledgment of her expertise. "My credential for being at this seminar," she announced, "is that I am homosexual."[85] In truth, her unique credential was that she was the one homosexual in the room willing and able to make such a statement out loud.[86]

The guarded line that separated clergy and homosexuals must surely have felt all the more tenuous during the three-day seminar that sparked the twin issues of *Social Action* and *Social Progress*. Just ten days before the seminar took place, a tragic murder in Columbus, Ohio, made it clear that even the cloak of the cloth was no protection for suspected homosexuals. The murder victim was Robert Spike, former director of the NCC's Commission on Religion and Race and a familiar figure to the staff members working in the NCC and in Protestant social justice offices. His body, brutally bludgeoned, was found in the guesthouse of a campus center he had helped dedicate the day before. Almost as terrible as the murder, however, was its aftermath: investigating officers in Columbus brazenly released information to the press that suggested Spike had been murdered in some kind of deviant sexual encounter. He was wearing only a green raincoat, newspapers reported, and among his possessions were "nudist magazines" and a list of bars "frequented by deviants."[87] Investigating police followed up on those initial "leads" by phoning people in Spike's address book. "Did you know that Rev. Spike was a homosexual?" they asked in the process of questioning each contact.[88] Their suspicions that the crime was homosexually motivated turned the victim—and his contacts—into incriminated suspects.

Some of these contacts may well have been in attendance at the seminar on homosexuality; participation was drawn from the NCC and denominational social justice offices, both institutions in which Spike concentrated his efforts to encourage white mainline Protestant involvement in African American civil rights. A few of those leaders might also have known that Spike had a history of hidden affairs with men, despite the fact that he was married and had two teenage sons. And some of them probably knew that leaders in the UCC were doing everything they could to stanch the homosexual-hunting zeal of the investigating officers in Ohio, perhaps in fear that the recent bent of the investigation would add fuel to the populist conspiracies, current among conservative wings of Protestant denominations, that godless, pinko communists were running the NCC.[89] Records from the seminar offer no hints about how Spike's death might have been addressed, if it was addressed at all. However, the hushed rumors surrounding the violent death of a well-loved colleague must surely have haunted the discussions, held just ten days after Spike's murder, about how churches might effectively address the discrimination faced by homosexuals.

The two companion publications, Social Action and Social Progress, appeared in print in November and December 1967. They were the year's final bookends to a series of progressive Protestant articles about homosexual rights. The year had begun with a hard-hitting editorial by Robert Cromey in the Episcopal journal Living Church, maintaining that Christians should "lead the way in insisting that homosexuals be given their rights as citizens and be treated as human beings."[90] Over the next several months, the Christian Century and Christianity and Crisis had also published articles that pushed for homosexual rights, and Religion and Health, a pastoral counseling journal, printed a speech about the homophile movement that had originally been delivered to ONE, Inc., in Los Angeles. Together with Social Action and Social Progress, these publications marked an important shift in progressive Protestant discussions of religion and law, and the voices at the fore were clergy allies of the homophile movement.

Social Action was the most radical publication on this list; the articles included in its focus on "homosexual civil liberties" gave bold attention to the rights claims of the homophile movement. Less than a year and a half later, the CCSA, the office that published the journal, issued a "Resolution on Homosexuals and the Law" that added formal endorsement to the support expressed in the journal.[91] The cover featured protest placards from the Annual Reminder demonstration, and the anchor article, by CCSA director Lewis Maddocks, systematically appraised the laws, policies, and practices that targeted homosexuals and issued a clarion call for change. Maddocks insisted that the Christian church—"the institution most vehement in its opposition to the homosexual"—should be responsible for leading political change. Change not only meant systemic reform to civil laws and policies but also meant reforming the systemic discrimination practiced in his own denomination. He urged fellow Christians to cease "exhorting homosexuals to 'give up their sinful ways'" and to end discrimination against homosexuals in seminary admission, ordination, and employment. The terms for the churches' moral evaluation of homosexuality, he concluded, should be no different than for any other sex act; "the same criteria" should apply "whether a relationship is heterosexual or homosexual."[92] Maddocks offered little biblical or theological rationales to support these arguments for reform, but it was clear nonetheless that a righteous commitment to equality entailed nothing less than thorough change in the denomination's teachings and practices.

This housecleaning, however, did leave some things undisturbed—most especially, the fact that homosexuals were already quietly present in many pulpits and pews. The Presbyterians' *Social Progress* carefully addressed this possibility, even though it treated other issues in many ways more conservatively than did the companion *Social Action*. Rather than taking a clear stand on the question of disease theory and cure, the editors of *Social Progress* published three articles that gave point-counterpoint coverage of opposing viewpoints about whether homosexuality could be cured and, indeed, whether it was a disease at all.[93] Amid the conflicting medical assessments, authors of two other articles addressed homosexuals' presence in churches. Both acknowledged that churches must—and tacitly already did—include homosexuals in their memberships. Southern Baptist minister Carlyle Marney gave a rationale for that acceptance, arguing that churches, as "communities of grace," must welcome homosexuals, even those who did not wish to change. The article nowhere negated the claims that homosexuality was a sickness, but it presented homosexuals' tragic condition as a metaphor for the all-too-human experience of vulnerability and guilt. All Christians shared in homosexuals' condition as "harmed harmers."[94] Rather than a sick exception, homosexuals were the quintessential metaphor for a fallible human condition.

The personification of Marney's metaphor for human vulnerability and guilt was the confession of a "hidden homosexual." By an author pseudonymously named "Marcus Paine," the account revealed the invisible suffering of those "hidden in the congregation." His story was neither a statement of identity pride nor a declaration that homosexuality could be morally good. "I wouldn't recommend homosexuality as a way of life for anyone who had a free choice in the matter," he wrote. It was a "condition," and he had "learned to live with it." He knew very well that homosexual acts were sinful and that Christian teachings mandated celibacy for "confirmed homosexuals" such as he. But he was not celibate; he had a lover of five years and practiced a kind of fidelity "found in many marriages that are presumably happy." He resolved the sinfulness simply: "I lean on the belief that we are all sinners, and if heterosexual sinners can sit in the pews each Sunday, so can I."[95] It was the confession of a person who might feel welcome in Marney's congregation—neither a sick homosexual seeking healing nor a proud gay demanding acceptance as he was but a man whose pained struggle with his sexual limitations merited the kind of grace that could be extended to people who knew they were broken.

Taken together, these essays represented a profound shift in what liberal Protestants were willing to write and publish about homosexuality. They made an argument for Christians' moral obligation both to include homosexuals in their fellowships and to defend their rights as citizens. And yet, this moral argument for homosexual rights did not necessarily declare that gay was good. But in many ways, the goodness of homosexuality was not the point. In classic liberal Protestant logic, these authors made the behavior of those who sinned against homosexuals the focus of their concern. The penalties and prejudices of the culture—and of the churches—were the areas most in need of reform. Homosexuals, in *Social Action*, were a targeted and disenfranchised "invisible minority." In *Social Progress*, the "hidden homosexual" was a person whose name—Paine—marked his condition. The moral politics of homosexual rights rested on a Protestant conviction: Christians had a moral obligation to defend the victimized.

For many of the urban ministers in the trenches of this struggle, however, Christians' solidarity with homosexuals did require facing the question that some of these authors skirted: the moral value of homosexuality. For a number of Christian authors, confronting prejudice and intolerance against homosexuals meant confronting, head-on, the idea that homosexuals were sick. Neale Secor, a former intern at Glide who went on to support homophile groups on the East Coast, published an essay in 1968 that challenged those who grounded an ethics of homosexuality on psychiatric disease theories. Secor argued that the whole debate over sin or disease relied on circular logic that ignored the relationship between the two. Secor saw religious condemnation as the predecessor to the disease theories; thus "the psychiatrist originally received his assumptions (values) from the very ecclesiastical ethical predecessors from whom the ethicists feel he is liberally departing," Secor argued.[96] Liberal Christians who turned to the neutral and empirical studies of the medical sciences to reform their culture-bound taboos, these clergy voices argued, ignored the way the same condemning values were also implanted in the disease theories.

These Christian authors were working to untangle the connection between morality and sickness as a small but persuasive body of new scientific research circulated similar challenges. These studies did not offer new theories of homosexual causation, long the terms on which psychiatrists had debated whether homosexuality could be cured or whether it was an indelible part of a person's psychological makeup. The challengers cut through the congenitalist-developmentalist debates and appraised the foundation for them both: the unexamined assumption that homosexuality was a pathological condition. These challengers took inspiration from the naturalist assumptions of the Kinsey studies, which approached sexual variation as a simple fact of human diversity. By the mid-1960s, a handful of researchers had taken this new thinking directly into the field of psychiatry. Evelyn Hooker, Thomas Szasz, and Judd Marmor—three of the most well known challengers—argued that most of the current assumptions about homosexuality in the mental health field were based on faulty research. Tautological assumptions and sampling bias undermined the claims of most studies, which up to that point were conducted almost entirely on prisoners and mental health patients. Little surprise, the findings showed what researchers expected—that homosexuality coincided with criminal behavior and poor mental health.[97] These iconoclastic thinkers argued that the therapeutic orthodoxy of the mental health fields, as well as the Christian teachings about homosexuality derived from it, were based not on dispassionate inquiry but on the prima facie assumption that homosexuality was inferior.

These studies gave support to many of the Christian authors' arguments for revised moral assessments of homosexuality, but these clergy challengers also turned to other sources. Neale Secor, in the same essay cited above, urged Christians to consult "honest biblical interpretation" as well as new research in the social sciences. He also maintained that Christians must test their convictions against a third important source— "the reality referent of the homosexual himself."[98] Robert Treese, a Methodist minister and professor of practical theology at Boston University, drew from all three of these sources of knowledge in *Homosexuality: A Contemporary View of the Biblical Perspective*, a booklet published through Glide Urban Center.[99] Treese's analysis of the biblical texts "about" homosexuality built on work by Derrick Sherwin Bailey, influential author of *Homosexuality and the Western Christian Tradition*. However, Treese also added textual references that he interpreted as a model for taking into account Secor's third important source—the witness of homosexuals' own lives. Treese argued that his firsthand friendships with homosexuals offered a simple "plumbline of judgment" that was grounded in "my own perception of the capacity of these persons for openness to other human beings, for mature and responsible social involvements, and for love in its fulfilling depths." This observation had roots in biblical teaching, he argued, and was similar to the New Testament account of the Apostle Peter's controversial decision to baptize a gentile into the community of Jewish Christ-followers. Treese's argument for accepting gays' own lives as a witness to their goodness presented Peter's decision as his own: "In the face of the church's 'no,'" Treese wrote, he was compelled to "speak a loud 'yes' to these persons, for I have seen the marks of self-giving Christian love upon their lives."[100] An important source for Christians' ethical evaluations of homosexual behavior, Treese insisted, was the simple testimony of homosexuals themselves.

These new moral frameworks inevitably pried open the gender-based assumptions that structured most contemporaneous thinking about the moral good of sex. For most liberal Protestants (indeed, for most sexual liberals), the rationale for the good of heterosexual behavior relied on gender difference. Only in a complementary union with one's gender opposite could a man or woman truly transcend the self and achieve sexual and spiritual maturity. The prevailing liberal Protestant axiom on this question was repeated by Europeans and Americans alike, from Bailey to German theologian Helmut Thielicke to the synthesis of both of their ideas in American author Kimball Jones's 1966 work, *Toward a Christian Understanding of the Homosexual*. The furthest any of these authors could go in their evaluations of homosexual relationships was the tentative acknowledgment that a "confirmed homosexual," otherwise unable to repress his disease, might licitly seek a stable partnership to keep him from the temptations of promiscuity. Such permission, however, nowhere approached the good of heterosexual marriage, as Jones made clear. "Two homosexuals," he assured, "can never complement one another in the same sense that male and female can." So long as gender complementarity defined the depths and rewards of intimacy, homosexual relationships were always and already incomplete.

And thus, as this cohort of progressive ministers reconsidered the moral value of homosexuality, they also revisited the gendered foundations of marriage. Kansas City minister Paul Jones, who worked with the Phoenix Society, wrote one of the lengthiest assessments of this question. His defense of what he adamantly called "homosexual marriage" first exploded into controversy as an editorial in Kansas City's local ecumenical Christian newspaper, and he expanded the editorial into an article published in 1970 in *Pastoral Psychology*. As Jones saw it, gender difference could not determine a Protestant ethic of sex because Protestant teaching did not hold procreation to be the primary end of marriage. He made this observation in the wake of the 1968 publication of "Humanae Vitae," the papal encyclical that squelched Catholic debate on exactly this question and effectively banned birth control for the faithful. Catholic dogma thus served as a foil for Jones's insistence that Protestants approached sexual ethics from a different framework. Intimacy rather than procreation was the primary end of marriage; sex was a witness to the "the mutual and total interpenetration of lives." Jones grounded this vision of marriage not in the Genesis account of Adam and Eve as one flesh—the usual biblical model for arguments about the importance of heterosexual gender difference. He turned instead to the theological narratives of Jesus's incarnation as fully divine and fully human—"God Himself," he wrote, "wedded himself to man in that marriage called incarnation." Not only was there nothing in this story of divine-human intimacy that precluded homosexuals, but Jones further argued that Christian convictions about the importance of incarnational intimacy should make them active champions of same-sex marriage. Jones put the argument in italics: "*profound relation between two members of the same sex is not only morally permissible but is to be sought, encouraged, supported and enabled with all the powers at our command.*"[101] In contrast to his contemporaries' tepid appraisals of same-sex relationships as a prophylactic against promiscuity, Jones presented them as a vital conduit of human and divine grace, even a sacrament.

A number of other Protestant clergy allies of the homophile movements offered similar arguments for the ethical good of same-sex relationships.[102] But the greatest testament to this newfound conviction about the goodness of homosexual relations was the number of clergy who performed rituals of blessing over same-sex couples. The terms to describe these ceremonies varied. Paul Jones, of course, insistently called them "marriages," and he and Vann Anderson officiated over the marriages of same-sex couples in Kansas City. In San Francisco, the ministers at Glide called them "ceremonies of friendship." Lloyd Wake, a Japanese American pastor appointed an associate minister at Glide Church in 1967, recalled that he and other pastors at Glide officiated at "covenant of friendship" ceremonies between same-sex couples in the late 1960s. One of the ceremonies between two men at which Wake officiated opened up a national scandal in the Methodist Church when journalists reported on it in 1971.[103] For these clergy allies of the homophile movement, "gay is good" was a pastoral conviction as well as a political statement. It was a truth grounded in Christian narratives, texts, and ritual practices.

Urban ministers' encounters with the gay communities around their congregations during the 1960s served as a unique catalyst for a small but passionate surge of clergy activism for and within the homophile movement. As they spoke of the role they played, it was much more than a religious front for a secular movement, even though some of their contemporaries perceived it that way. It was, rather, central to the mission of their churches. Cecil Williams, from his role as newly appointed senior pastor of Glide Memorial Methodist Church, delivered a sermon in 1968 that spoke of the church's unique "word" on homosexuality and encouraged congregants to share that gospel. "We will be silent no longer. We know that homosexuals are not sick, criminal, or sinful," Williams argued. "We must give the word to the professional community—the church must take the lead in showing a way to understanding the homophile world."[104] Paul Jones's comments about his ministry in Kansas City similarly spoke of the church's mission to homosexuals. Recognizing and supporting relationships was only the beginning; he envisioned increasing civil rights, a "homosexual social center," communication and outreach, counseling, and support for homosexual teenagers. "At the foundation of all this should be the church," he argued, which can "provide the moral legitimacy and confirmation without which self-acceptance is so tentative."[105] The clergy envisioned ministries that provided material and ideological support for the homophile struggle, where homosexuals could live into the truth that gay was good.

Conclusion

The history of clergy support for homophile organizing has been told before, but it has been mentioned, up to this point, as an idiosyncrasy of local history. A number of scholars writing community histories have commented with surprise at the discovery that their city's first gay organization met in a church with the support of a local pastor. James Sears, in an article on the gay man who started up the Chicago Mattachine Society in 1965, notes in passing that a minister agreed to host the meetings in his Park Ridge church and also helped to produce the monthly newsletter. Such an arrangement, Sears surmises, was "a rarity in the pre-Stonewall era."[106] As it turns out, however, the instances of clergy support were not local anomalies but part of a larger pattern of church-based support being cultivated and channeled through the activist connections of liberal Protestant clergy. Thus, the surprising and largely untold story of the CRH in San Francisco is the national movement it did catalyze—a movement, however small, that took place in church basements and community centers with urban ministers as behind-the-scenes enablers.

The church-based support continued to be important for gay rights organizing, as chapter 5 shows. However, the left-leaning wing of mainline Protestant denominations was also beginning to face difficult institutional challenges to its ministries. Its place within denominations was tenuous from the outset—it was a radical wing within the liberal-leaning leadership of mainline Protestant churches, but its politics were radically different from the convictions about morality held by most of the denominations' laity. Radical clergy activists received remarkable levels of support during the 1960s from the bureaucratic offices of their denominations. Boards of social justice and domestic missions, in large measure, provided material support for clergy involvement in a variety of urban outreach and social justice efforts. That support made possible their unconventional ministries and facilitated activist efforts that challenged both the social order and the dominant culture of their denominations.

By the late 1960s, however, a number of social analysts studying mainline denominations began to forecast trouble on the horizon. Jeffrey Hadden, a sociologist researching mainline denominations, published a suitably titled book on these trends: *The Gathering Storm in the Churches*. His work warned that the increasing radicalism of Protestant clergy activism was headed on a collision course with denominations' more conservative lay members. Overt political differences were an important friction point, but just as important, Hadden argued, were fundamental differences in what the missions of the churches were to be about. "The clergyman's new theology has moved him beyond the four walls of the church and prompted him to express God's love in concern for the world, particularly the underprivileged," Hadden noted, while "the layman, on the other hand, seeks comfort and escape from the world in the sanctuary of God." The activist ministries of clergy, he predicted, posed an insurmountable challenge to the more conservative laity's nostalgia for sanctuary and comfort.[107]

Mainline Protestant denominations were headed for trouble, and no issue was more controversial than sex and sexual morality. By the late 1960s, a fledging group of progressive clergy and church bodies were working to articulate teachings that supported a politics and a practice of homosexual inclusion. A handful of local Protestant jurisdictions, led largely by clergy/homophile councils, were discussing and publishing new studies on homosexuality that advised church bodies on how Christians should address issues of legal reform, biblical interpretation, and sexual ethics.[108] These efforts were local enough and radical enough to barely catch the attention of larger denominational memberships. However, more centrist versions of denomination-wide studies of sexuality were already underway. In the mid- to late 1960s, a number of mainline denominations appointed denominational committees to make recommendations to the churches about how to better address issues surrounding sexuality and family relationships. The work of the CRH, by forcefully addressing homosexual rights, also influenced mainline denominations to take a stand on these issues. The church statements drafted in the late 1960s and early 1970s, as they addressed issues such as abortion, family planning, and premarital sex, also made recommendations for the teachings on homosexuality. The next chapter examines this process of deliberation and debate.

4

SANCTIFIED HETEROSEXUALITY

On a bright Sunday morning in May 1970, Janet Brunger opened her local Fort Lauderdale newspaper. The headline that caught her eye, "Religious Storm Center: New Sex Code," appeared in *Parade Magazine*, a nationally syndicated addition to local papers that delivered human interest stories, advice columns, and coupons. She read the feature article with growing alarm, as it informed her that leaders in her own denomination, the United Presbyterian Church, were proposing an entirely new approach to sexual morality—one so liberal, the article reported, that it "practically eliminates sin as a major factor in sexual relations." The particulars were located in a new denominational study, titled "Sexuality and the Human Community," from which the newspaper article listed a few key points: "removal of all restrictions against unmarried adults who wish to live together," "wide-open abortion laws," and "removal of any stigma that makes homosexuals feel they are in irresolvable conflict with the Christian fellowship."[1] This "new sex code" would be up for a vote at the end of the month at the General Assembly, the denomination's national legislative meeting. Dismayed by this news, Brunger immediately turned to her typewriter to compose a letter to the national leaders of the Presbyterian Church. She appraised the proposed "sex code" as "a missile of tripe" and expressed her "personal protest against the relaxing of the moral fiber of all Christians."[2]

Scores of similar letters rolled into the Philadelphia-based headquarters of the United Presbyterian Church, and denominational leaders took their turn at dismay. The *Parade* article detailed a report from a task force appointed five years earlier by the Council on Church and Society; the committee had been charged with developing resources for understanding and teaching "the Christian concept of sexuality in the human community."[3] As was customary, the committee report was included in the Presbyterian "blue book"—a compendium of church governance matters circulated in advance of the General Assembly, which rarely drew the attention of lay Presbyterians, much less of national newspapers. The *Parade* article highlighted the study's most controversial recommendations and suggested that the proposal augured churchwide policy. While the issues addressed in the study were certainly controversial—they included contraception, abortion, reproductive technology, nonmarital sex, masturbation, and homosexuality, among other issues—the point was certainly not to license permissiveness. Presbyterian leaders regarded both the newspaper article and the reactions as a grave misunderstanding: they were not at all trying to "eliminate sin" from Christian sexual morality. They wanted, rather, to develop new resources for teaching Christian ideals for sexuality.[4]

This chapter traces what might seem to be an unlikely center of a sex scandal: a thirty-five-page committee report written by Presbyterians. The debate over this document connected to larger concerns about religion and sex in the late 1960s and early 1970s, a moment at which the much-discussed "sexual revolution" seemed to reach a breaking point. A hot-button political issue at this time was sexuality education, and Presbyterians were hardly alone in navigating denomination-wide skirmishes over sexual morality. Similar debates roiled other mainline denominations, and they also surfaced in arguments over local public school sex education curricula. The battle lines, in both denominations and public politics, pitted self-declared defenders of traditional morality against liberals accused of peddling a faithless "new morality." These debates, while significant in their time, figure even larger in hindsight. A number of historians of sexuality have revisited the sex education battles taking place in local public schools, seeing them as skirmishes that led to the later culture wars over issues like abortion, feminism, and gay rights. It was in these early controversies, argues historian Janice Irvine, that "the nascent Christian Right recognized the mobilizing power of sexuality."[5] Conservatives rallied a defense of moral values against what they saw as secular and amoral curricula. Despite this rhetoric, the issue of sex education was hardly absent religion. Leading mainline Protestants—including the people involved with the Presbyterian study committee—had a prominent role in the sex education initiatives that drew conservative fire. The contenders in this battle to govern sex were not Christianity and secularism but two varieties of Protestantism, both of which presented their efforts as an intervention in a permissive, secularizing age. The arguments over a Presbyterian study thus highlight the Protestant ideals shaping both liberal and conservative interventions in sex education and show how their differences took up capacious meaning in this freighted moment of perceived secularization. By investigating the denominational context for the sex education battles, that is, we see how a sectarian idiom came to provide a seemingly neutral, descriptive diagnosis of a religious-versus-secular divide.

The dissension over "Sexuality and the Human Community" also illuminates the obscured story of influence and change taking place across sectarian battle lines. True, the heated terms of the argument addressed a perceived battle between tradition and modernity—liberals worked to reform unhealthy taboos and dogma as their challengers, in turn, stood against the permissive liberalization of old absolutes. The polarizing rhetoric clouded an important symbiotic relationship between liberal mainline leaders and their conservative challengers. This traditionalist resurgence, that is, took place within a moment of modern reinvention as a group of charismatic, conservative Protestants left behind fundamentalist separatism to form new cross-denominational evangelical networks. In this moment of innovation, evangelicals also adopted new resources in their teachings on sex. "Contrary to popular stereotypes" notes religion scholar Amy DeRogatis, "evangelicals did not turn away from the sexual liberation moment begun in the 1960s, they simply made it their own."[6] The sex education controversies shed light on the cultural transmission taking place in this moment: conservative Protestants embraced many of the liberals' sex-positive ideals, even as they adapted them to a different religious idiom.

Indeed, Protestants of all theological stripes answered the perceived perils of the sexual revolution by engaging in a revolution of their own, one that decisively ratified new visions of Christian sexuality. For partisans on all sides, the polarizing debates over how to teach sexuality worked to naturalize and consecrate the attraction between women and men as fundamental to God's created design. Their debates in this moment focused on how to foster that kind of good sex, with heated disagreement about how to point Christians toward marriage as the rightful—and natural—context for sexual pleasure. These debates over the boundaries of heterosexuality took for granted that healthy sexuality had an unnatural opposite. What this chapter shows, thus, is how the dynamics of a sexual binary—an assumed opposition between heterosexuality and its unnatural opposite—tacitly aided the project of valorizing the gendered mechanisms of male and female desire as an intrinsic, natural, and good part of the self.

Both mainline Protestant leaders and their conservative challengers presented their interventions in sexuality in religious terms, and they both understood their efforts as supporting marriage and family in an era of rapid secularization and religious decline. However, only one side would emerge from this battle over sex education with participants' professed religious and moral commitments represented as such in the mainstream press. Fundamentalist Protestants had long accused mainline liberals of being traitors to the core principles of Christianity. By the late 1960s, however, many mainstream journalists and commentators echoed this perception of establishment Protestantism as a hollowed-out faith, a cultural institution rather than a religious one. When the news of "Sexuality and the Human Community" circulated in 1970, it seemed emblematic of a larger crisis in the nation's values, a sign of establishment churches' accommodation to secular culture. Understanding these shifts in public religious authority requires turning, first of all, to media narratives about America's sexual and religious decline during the 1960s.

A Crisis in Sex

For the executive leaders of the Presbyterian Church, the *Parade* article was a press disaster. The lament from the Philadelphia headquarters of the denomination was that the purported "storm center" was produced by salacious press coverage, which misrepresented the content and the aims of the study. A form letter to local pastors from the executive office of the Council on Church and Society, the office that commissioned the study, offered a belated attempt to present that board's own talking points about "Sexuality and the Human Community." The letter told of a careful five-year study of sexuality, an earnest effort to retool Christian moral teaching to effectively counter a crisis in sex. As a "study paper," it was by no means a "code" or a statement of policy. It was, rather, drafted to "speak *to* rather than *for* the church," and the pending vote of approval would merely allow the board to circulate the document for further discussion.[7]

The actual storm center that surfaced in the late May meeting of the General Assembly only further muddied the nature and purpose of this study document on sexuality. The committee authors of the study watched in dismay as the parliamentary deliberation resulted in changes to the carefully written document. Presbyterians are famously committed to a practice of decision making that proceeds "decently and in order."[8] In churches, no less than in public governance, such orderly processes often yield policies—and documents—that plainly exhibit the divided views of the ratifying body. So it was that Presbyterian delegates voted, narrowly, to publish and circulate the study document on sexuality, even as they also assented to the demand by critics that subsequent publications must note that the denomination by no means endorsed its contents. Further underscoring that the document's ideas were not an official statement of policy, one delegate—Robert Crose, a layman and medical doctor from Yakima, Washington—proposed a more explicit disclaimer. This statement countered the deliberately nonjudgmental tone of the study by affirming that the Presbyterian Church adhered to "the moral law of God as revealed in the Old and New Testament, that adultery, prostitution, fornication, and/or the practice of homosexuality is sin." The proposed amendment also passed by majority vote.[9] The result was a textual monument to Presbyterian heterodoxy, a visible display of deeply rooted differences within the denomination.

In the eye of both the press and the document's critics, the added amendments and caveats only cemented the permissive reputation of the Presbyterian leadership. Case in point was an article by Louis Cassels, senior religious editor of United Press International, whose writing influentially chronicled the religious trends of the 1960s. Cassels was a devout Episcopalian, and his reporting on "Sexuality and the Human Community" chastened denominational executives for their fickleness. Cassels raised an agnostic flag as to the value of the studies. "Whether these reports about sex are consistent with Biblical teachings," he demurred, "are questions on which Christians may sincerely differ." His concern, rather, was the "hypocrisy" of denominational leaders, and the amendments to the sexuality study were proof that those leaders did not even have the backbone to make an honest stand of their tolerance. Presbyterian leaders, through their "sotto-voce disavowal," were "propagating permissive statements about sex without taking official responsibility for them."[10] Cassels presented the internal inconsistencies of the sexuality study as evidence of behind-the-scenes scheming on the part of its authors.

The reported facts about "Sexuality and the Human Community," communicated through various media channels, presented this study as part and parcel of the era's trend toward sexual permissiveness. The liberalism of mainline Protestant leaders, it seemed, led them to sanction moral laxity. Certainly, there were media outlets that cheerfully welcomed this news. The *National Informer*, a tabloid newspaper, reviewed the study under the headline "Presbyterians Give Green Light to Sexual Freedom." A photograph of a buxom and scantily clad model included the caption "There's nothing wrong with sex when it looks like this!"[11] Presbyterian executives, of course, found little to celebrate in this review. It was one of many clippings tucked away in an irksome file of sensational journalism. Just as misleading as the tabloid press were articles like the one on the front page of the *Christian Crusade Weekly*, a newspaper published in Tulsa by fundamentalist minister Billy James Hargis. The content of the article forwarded the same facts found in the *National Informer*. However, the headline replaced jocular congratulations with moral horror. "Presbyterian Church Approves Sex Code That Repudiates Biblical View of Sin," Hargis accused.[12] Enthused hedonists and outraged traditionalists shared the same talking points. Both were persuaded that liberal Protestant clergy were ready to grease the nation's slide into godlessness.

These reports followed larger media trends, which cast a reported decline in religion as symbolic of a breaking point in the nation's moral values. The much-discussed sexual revolution was an important part of this trend. Social scientists, for well over a decade, had reported on a sex revolution indicated by changing norms around divorce, out-of-wedlock birth, nonmarital sex, and homosexual behavior. By the mid-1960s, however, those whispered and rumored behaviors were the subjects of books, plays, and music that frankly celebrated the pleasures of illicit love. It was these changes that experts of the day termed a "second sexual revolution."[13] Changes in sex were also just one part of what seemed to many Americans to be symptoms of a national crisis. The high-profile assassinations of John and Robert Kennedy, of Martin Luther King Jr., and of Malcolm X seemed emblematic of a national malady. At the same time, Black Power advocates, antiwar demonstrators, and free-speech activists staged adamant protests that more insistently pushed against the status quo. In May 1970, newspapers also delivered the story of the killings of four Kent State student protesters by armed National Guardsmen. These issues were of concern across the political spectrum, but conservative politicians and pundits stoked fears of racial, sexual, and gender disorder to push the nation's politics to the right. Richard Nixon, in 1968, won the presidency with a "law and order" platform that galvanized opposition to gender, sexual, and racial disorder through a coded appeal to white middle-class Americans as a "great silent majority." Critical to this moment of the late 1960s, thus, was a circulating political rhetoric that interpreted broad social and political challenges through a narrative of declining morality.[14]

Against this perceived moral breakdown, developments in mainline Protestant institutions took up outsized significance. By the late 1960s, a number of books and studies announced the rapid decline of the venerable denominations that had historically occupied the center of American culture and politics. By nearly every possible way of measuring influence—finances, membership, programming, and decaying physical buildings—it was clear that established Protestant churches had not only stopped growing but were losing ground.[15] The nostalgic narrative found in both popular reporting and sociological analysis identified mainline institutions with the nation itself and interpreted their decline as nothing less than the unraveling of the nation's moral core. In one journalist's woeful report, "the Puritan ethic, so long the dominant moral force in the U.S., is widely considered to be dying, if not already dead."[16] The withering mainline seemed to augur the state of the nation's soul.

Press coverage of "Sexuality and the Human Community" suggested that the liberal-leaning leaders of the Presbyterian Church were ready to toss the nation's morals into that staid Puritan grave. But such reports of Presbyterian permissiveness overlooked the study authors' own descriptions. John Charles Wynn, the lead author and chairman of the study, adamantly insisted that its aim was to "firm up the sagging sexual standards of today."[17] Liberals also worried about the excesses of the decade's sexual revolution and positioned their education efforts as an intervention. However, sexuality education advocates also approached their task through the reigning assumptions of the therapeutic paradigm. Since the early decades of the twentieth century, liberal Protestants reformers had championed educational changes that aimed to challenge moralistic taboos and to foster a positive view of the goodness of sex. The assumptions about sexual development that undergirded these efforts presumed that such a health-based approach would foster the kind of relationships—committed, monogamous, and heterosexual—toward which the gendered natures of men and women gravitated naturally. Certainly, these optimistic assumptions about human sexual nature faced marked opposition at a time in which much of the frank celebration of good sex no longer took heterosexual marriage as either a predestined end or a natural boundary.[18] What the Presbyterian sexuality study shows, however, is that a team of sexual and religious liberals aimed to develop an effective intervention in these cultural excesses, and they were all the more adamant that the old "thou shalt not"s offered no solution.

Liberal Sexual Regulation

Appointed in 1966, the committee that produced "Sexuality and the Human Community" included notable leaders in a broader movement to reform sex education curricula. The assumed ideological parity between progressive religion and sexual health came through clearly in the roster of committee members. These leading lights included Seward Hiltner, founding expert in the field of pastoral counseling and professor of theology and personality at Princeton Theological Seminary; Edward Gallahue, a specialist in religion and psychiatry working with the Menninger Foundation; Clark Blackburn, general director of the Family Service Association of America; and Helen Southard, a executive in the national office of the Young Women's Christian Association.[19] On the list of consultants for the study was William Genné, a recognized leader in various initiatives in sexual health. An American Baptist minister, Genné was a point person for faith-based curricula development in the National Council of Churches and the cofounder (with Mary Calderone, a Quaker) of the Sexuality Information and Education Council of the United States, the organization at the center of the debates over public school sexuality education curricula.[20] The Presbyterian sexuality study was one of various initiatives in sex education, which routinely drew together leaders in mainline Protestant denominations, other religious liberals, and health reformers.[21]

Few participants in the committee exhibited the sustained commitment to religion and health more thoroughly than its chair and lead author, John Charles Wynn. An influential leader in the ecumenical initiative in sex education, Wynn's background helps make sense of the commitments that grounded this endeavor, which were characterized by critics as secular, unchristian, and permissive. That perception, however, nowhere fit Wynn's own biography. Married to the daughter of a minister with whom he had three children, Wynn's personal history added a stereotypical wholesomeness to his vocation as an ordained minister and marriage and family counselor. An article in *Pastoral Counseling* playfully dubbed him "Mr. Family Man Himself."[22] This reputation was known even to some of the critics of the Presbyterian sexuality study. One critic included a duplicated page from Wynn's 1955 book, *How Christian Parents*

John Charles Wynn, date unknown (likely late 1960s). Office of Institutional Advancement, Colgate Rochester Crozer Divinity School.

Face Family Problems. "If the *Parade* article correctly reflects Wynn's present thinking," the letter writer noted with puzzlement, "then he certainly has done an about face."[23] Wynn's place at the helm of "Sexuality and the Human Community," however, was hardly a betrayal of his earlier commitment to support Christian marriage and family. His rise in influence from parish minister to denominational leadership focused centrally on training ministers to adequately counsel families in the church. This expertise was the bread and butter of his work as professor of Christian education at Colgate Rochester Divinity School, and it also brought him into a number of different positions of leadership in the NCC as well as in the United Presbyterian Church.[24] Wynn's repeated passion, in these different appointments, was developing faith-based resources that would help parents, families, and churches effectively guide the sexual decision making of youth and young people.

Wynn's involvement in sex education, like that of many other members of the committee he chaired, was an essential part of a broader ecumenical initiative. Organized through the NCC, this project aimed to develop educational resources for Christian family ministries. Wynn was an organizer and a keynote speaker for the 1961 Green Lakes conference on Christian family policy, a weeklong gathering cosponsored by the NCC and the Canadian Council of Churches that convened ministers, counselors, and medical experts in human sexuality for a discussion focused on the "stresses and strains" facing modern families. The discussion included what organizers delicately called "sex problems"—unmarried pregnancy, masturbation, homosexuality, infidelity, abortion, and so on. The experts gathered for the Green Lakes conference, however, spoke with a confident certainty about the conjoined insights of science and religion as "twin beams" to illumine the troubling challenges that confronted families. The most notable offshoot from this conference was the Sexuality Information and Education Council of the United States. The Presbyterian study on "Sexuality and the Human Community" was also a direct product of the conference. It was precisely the kind of resource that Wynn himself urged in his summary comments at the event; what Christians needed, he pressed, was a "fuller and more explicit literature concerning the hard issues in family life."[25]

The religious and medical experts who met at the Green Lakes conference also bent their efforts toward developing pedagogical models for *how* educators might encourage healthy sexuality. A key concern for clergy and educators in sex education reform was a sense that the moral consensus of earlier decades was breaking down in an anti-authoritarian age. "We have come to the end of a time when morality will be accepted as an edict from a deity," wrote the authors of an article in *Pastoral Psychology*. As youth and young people rejected external moral authorities, liberal sex educators argued for a pedagogical approach to sexual decision making that emphasized "authentic selfhood."[26] Dominant social norms no longer reinforced moral absolutes. Therefore, churches needed to develop ways to talk about sex and sexual decision making that would empower youth and young adults—as well as their parents—to make choices that expressed their own moral commitments. It was to this end that sex educators, and the authors of many of those denominational curricula on sexuality, appropriated a trend in Christian social ethics called "the new morality" or "situation ethics."

For sexual liberals, the conversations among Christian ethicists about the new morality and situation ethics offered pedagogical resources for guiding Christians' decisions about sex during an age where the rules seemed to have lost moral authority. They drew chiefly from two influential authors: John A. T. Robinson, bishop of the Church of England and author of *Honest to God*, published in 1963, and Joseph Fletcher, a social ethicist appointed at Harvard Divinity School and author of *Situation Ethics: The New Morality*, published three years later.[27] Both of these slim best-sellers emphasized honesty and authenticity as a foundation for moral decision making. Drawing from German theologian Paul Tillich, Robinson spoke of Christian faith in existential terms. The human impulse to love the other, Robinson insisted, was a kind of "built-in moral compass" that enabled individuals to "'home' intuitively upon the deepest need of the other." In similar ways, he stressed that the guidelines for living should not be understood as an "alien universal norm" but a moral compass that was found within the deepest recesses of the self.[28] Like Robinson, Fletcher also emphasized that love for the other provided a powerful ethical compass for human decision making. He even went so far as to claim boldly that love was the only ethical norm that Christians should follow. Taken together, these works powerfully challenged an ethic based on abstract rules and norms and imbued the choice-making agent with power to choose the good.

Many of the counselors, ministers, and medical experts who met at the Green Lakes conference were also some of the leading voices in translating the ethical methods of "new morality" into a pedagogical format for counseling and sexuality education. Critics often regarded the phrase "the new morality" itself as a sign of moral permissiveness. For advocates, the clear benefit of this model was the emphasis it placed on moral agency and responsible decision making. William Genné, the American Baptist minister and leading sex education specialist, explained how this framework, put to use in education, provided principles that actually countered loosening morals. "The New Morality," Genné wrote, "is no easy-going, pleasure-seeking, fun morality. It demands a rigorous self-evaluation of every personal act in the sight of God. It cannot accept the rightness of any sexual acts that two mutually consenting adults may do without evaluating this in the light of all we know about the ultimate meaning and purpose of sex as created by God."[29] For Genné and other religious advocates, the new morality provided a pedagogical method that directed students to internalize moral values as their own. In an era in which those values were under scrutiny, this flexible but rigorous self-inventory supplied a method by which students could respond to the pluralism around them by claiming their own values. Against moralistic approaches that expected flat obedience, the new morality worked to instill personal moral agency and skills for ethical deliberation.

Wynn and the committee appointed to draft Presbyterian sexuality education resources drew heavily from this existentialist pedagogy. By this moment in the late 1960s, the terms "situation ethics" and "new morality" were politically toxic. Robinson's and Fletcher's books were both widely publicized and highly controversial, and opponents to sex education used these labels not as descriptions but as slurs that epitomized the lax values of "newsex" teaching.[30] Thus, Presbyterians took up a new name, presenting the ethical methods discussed in their studies as a "covenantal ethic." This method, the study authors stressed, challenged unchristian "taboos and prohibitions" and restored a decision-making process founded upon "careful ethical reflection in light of the gospel."[31] The case-based, nonabsolute system, as these authors conceived it, provided a framework for addressing modern quandaries around sexual morality that the biblical authors and traditional Christian theologians could never have anticipated. It also empowered individuals to make sexual decisions free from guilt-inducing dogmatism, bad information, and base gratification. Following the existentialist leadings of situation ethicists, the authors of "Sexuality and the Human Community" relocated the norms of Christian ethics into the interior recesses of the self.

The Presbyterian study guide took as a given that sexuality was more than mere behavior—it was a central part of the self, conceived in gendered terms. "Sexuality as we understand the term," the authors wrote, "refers to our entire experience as persons who are created male and female."[32] This sexual self, divinely created and innately gendered, also formed the vital conduit for God's salvific work in the world. It was with this foundational assumption that the committee authors eschewed a narrow focus on right or wrong behavior to envision the whole of human relating in a cosmic frame. Rather than rules, they set up goals: human relationships, sexual or otherwise, should enhance spiritual freedom, glorify the Creator, nurture creative potential, and "open up to persons that flow of grace which will enable them to bear their burdens without despair."[33] These grand and laudatory aims placed the minute decisions about a glance or a touch within a metaphysical drama of redemption. Rather than "Is this good or bad?," the question to ask was "Is this 'an instrument of God's reconciling activity'?" The intent, in this framework, was to transcend the twin pitfalls of legalism and licentiousness typical of "act-based" approaches to sexual morality. The guiding rule for sexual decision making could be found instead by focusing on the intrinsic good of a relationship.

This approach typified the two most controversial aspects of "Sexuality and the Human Community." Opponents singled out comments about premarital and extramarital sex as particularly objectionable parts of the study. These comments appeared in a section addressing "courtship and marriage," where the authors reflected on the Presbyterian Church's concern for the "sanctity of the family" and the "permanence of the marriage bond."[34] What offended critics was the report's insistent focus on the value of "intrinsic" meanings over "extrinsic" rules. In line with this ethical approach, the document criticized the "ineffective and widely disregarded standard" of premarital virginity. Rather than try to resurrect that bygone marker of purity, the document encouraged Christians to address "the more significant standard of responsibly appropriate behavior." The authors carefully stipulated that this emphasis did not "give either tacit or explicit approval to premarital sexual intercourse," but their discussion certainly did elliptically acknowledge a trend in American sexual behavior that had long been true—most married couples were not waiting until after marriage to have sex. In light of this fact, the study made two recommendations: Christians should not alienate or judge couples that may have had premarital intercourse, and the Presbyterian Church, as a matter of public advocacy, should encourage the repeal of existing laws that prohibited unmarried couples from having access to contraception. Taking into consideration the failure of chastity, the Presbyterians authors pragmatically urged responsibility.[35]

This section also addressed sex outside of marriage in much the same way as this discussion of virginity. The authors' reflection on the question of sex outside of marriage was included within a much larger section on "courtship within marriage" dominantly focused on the meaning of fidelity within marriage. The thrust of the section was to emphasize an ethic and practice of sexual pleasure and relational intimacy between married couples. "Nothing is forbidden," the authors asserted, "except that which offends the sensibilities of one's partner." The point of sexual fidelity was not merely to chasten sex outside of marriage; it was to nurture "a truly reciprocal and caring relationship between husband and wife which supports each one's unique worth as a child of God." It was within this context that the authors expressed a very cautiously worded acknowledgment that "extramarital sexual activity," under "exceptional circumstances," may at times not be a violation of the marriage vow to fidelity. The given example was indeed exceptional—a partner's "permanent mental or physical incapacity." The illustration served to point to the ways that emotional and material faithfulness to a spouse could not merely be measured by the single rule of "coital exclusivity."[36] Thus, throughout the study, the authors insisted "extrinsic" boundaries could not serve as absolute guides to what was truly good in a relationship. In theory, the ethical framework effectively peeled off the exoskeleton from the rules of sexual morality to reveal the unbounded interior of a relationship to which men and women would gravitate naturally if they oriented themselves toward the other's highest good.

This antilegalistic framework unerringly pointed toward monogamous heterosexual relationships as the ideal of human sexual striving. The authors approached heterosexual intimacy and relationship fidelity as ideals that might allow (at least theoretically) an ethical trespass across the boundaries of marriage and monogamy. These permeable borders stood in marked contrast to a fixed line that divided healthy heterosexuality from the evident pathology of homosexuality. The approach to homosexuality in "Sexuality and the Human Community" was thoroughly centrist for its time. The author for this part of the Presbyterian study—Seward Hiltner, one of the founding architects of the field of pastoral psychology—reinforced the reigning therapeutic orthodoxy and its foundation in psychoanalytic theories of disease and cure. The report's two progressive recommendations—that congregations should not stigmatize homosexuals and that felony laws against "homosexual acts" should be repealed—appealed to theories of disease and treatment as their authoritative foundation.[37] This discussion of homosexuality rested on the assumption that it was a pathological condition that could, with proper treatment and willingness on the part of the homosexual, perhaps even be cured. Indeed, that elusive possibility of a cure was the motivating carrot for progressive reforms in laws and for social tolerance of homosexuality. This state of affairs was on a par with broader discourses in the mental health fields, where prominent psychiatrists continued to endorse the disease/treatment model of homosexuality.

Those disease theories now circulated widely in popular writing, even as they faced increasing challenges within the mental health profession. Psychiatrist Edmund Bergler's best-selling *Homosexuality: Disease or Way of Life?* (1956) gave a popular boost to disease theories. His work brought broad public attention to homosexuality as a terrible, but curable, disease.[38] Bergler's ideas received substantial attention from liberal Protestants, and authors in the field of pastoral psychology continued to reference his work into the 1960s as an important and readable resource on homosexuality.[39] By the late 1960s, however, those theories also faced prominent challengers. Both the discipline of pastoral counseling and the broader field of mental health contended with new research that contested the disease theories. No one was more instrumental to this challenge than Evelyn Hooker, a clinical psychologist who began publishing pathbreaking studies on male homosexuality in the late 1950s.[40] Her work was welcomed in the subcultural fringes of an emerging gay rights movement and among allied clergy supporters. In the less-radical milieu of Protestant-connected initiatives for sexual health, Hooker's work had a hearing but not an endorsement. Hooker was among the invited speakers at the 1961 Green Lakes conference; it was certain that her work was familiar to the marriage and family specialists involved in creating denominational sexuality curricula and study material, like "Sexuality and the Human Community."[41] However, the challenge to disease theories of homosexuality received sparse attention in the Presbyterian study, which only briefly acknowledged that "the state of knowledge about homosexuality is far from fully developed."[42]

Amid these shifting scientific currents, the Presbyterian authors of "Sexuality and the Human Community" used a choice phrase that gave them a way to reiterate dual commitments to mental health and to conventional interpretations of biblical morality. "There is a difference," the authors admonished, "between homosexuality as a condition of personal existence and homosexualism as explicit homosexual behavior."[43] The particular phrasing came from the newly published *Dictionary of Christian Ethics*, which was drawing, in turn, from two other recent works. Derrick Sherwin Bailey's *Homosexuality and the Western Christian Tradition* influentially argued that Christians needed to distinguish between the biblical condemnation of homosexual behavior and the medical sciences' recent discovery of a mental condition, an idea echoed and expanded by succeeding authors.[44] Another important voice in this conversation was German Protestant theologian Helmut Thielicke, whose *Ethics of Sex* circulated widely in English translation. Thielicke also argued for a conceptual and theological distinction between a condition of "endogenous homosexuality" and "concrete acts of libidinous excess."[45] Thus, the study underscored the perspective of a new but influential body of Christian scholarship that distinguished between homosexuality as a condition (a product of recent medical research) and homosexuality as a condemned act (an ancient biblical regulation that predated modern medicine). The authors inveighed against stigma and penalty because such condemnation might have the adverse effect of "inhibiting the possibility of change."[46] Challenging regulation served as a paradoxical strategy for straightening perverse desires.

This hope in homosexuals' malleable natures epitomized the transforming aspirations of sexual liberalism. It also illuminated how the assumed oppositions of a sexual binary informed the way that liberal sex education advocates of this moment navigated the boundaries of heterosexuality. The authors of "Sexuality and the Human Community" understood the study as a model for how to nurture healthy sexuality. The way to do that, religious leaders assessed, was not to repeat the old dictates but to propose a framework that would empower Christians to take responsibility for their own moral choices. This approach expanded the nonjudgmental therapeutic approach developed by pastoral counselors and charted a pedagogical framework for guiding Christian talk about sex. It provided a generation rebelling against absolutes an existentialist approach to internalize the ideals of Christian teachings. However, this "open" and "nonjudgmental" framework for sex education did not jettison normative ideals about sexual relationships. Like the pastoral counseling model that preceded it, it approached the release from taboos and shame as a method for instilling healthy sexuality, which they assumed in terms of an innate and natural heterosexuality. Thus, the situation ethic framework enticed and prodded its readers to internalize—as authentic to the self—the sexual choices that would lead toward a relationship of committed intimacy between gender opposites.

What sex education advocates saw as a method that would produce healthy sexuality was regarded by their critics as simple moral permissiveness. The debate that erupted in the wake of the Presbyterian study focused on the place of moral absolutes in guiding right sexual behavior. Obscured by the back and forth over tradition and modernity, however, was the fact that opposing evangelicals were adopting a modernist method of their own to synthesize sexual teachings with their version of liberals' therapeutic orthodoxy.

Evangelicals and Therapeutic Sexuality

"Christianity without rules of Christian conduct is not Christianity but paganism."[47] This critique of Presbyterian liberalism was penned by L. Nelson Bell and published in the Presbyterian Journal. Bell was a Presbyterian of a different stripe—a conservative member of the Presbyterian Church of the United States, which had origins (like the Southern Baptists) in Protestant denominations' antebellum divisions over slavery. Former medical missionary and father-in-law of Southern Baptist evangelist Billy Graham, Bell was also the founder of the journal in which he published this critique. Bell's dig at those other liberal Presbyterians was a thoroughgoing part of his mission to stand against encroaching theological liberalism both inside and outside of his own denomination. For many white conservative Protestants like Bell, cooperation with the liberal mainliners spelled a deal with the devil.[48] His article warned fellow conservatives against uniting with religious leaders who had clearly lost the faith.

The Presbyterian "sex code" was of concern to a variety of leading conservative Protestants, including many outside of the denomination. A front-page article from the *Denver Post* reported on an address by Billy Graham, perhaps the nation's most famous Southern Baptist. The Presbyterian near-endorsement of "promiscuous sexual relations," Graham warned, was only a short step from "church-supervised brothels" and "the temple prostitution of ancient Corinth." The reference to the sexuality study was part of Graham's larger polemic against liberal clergymen. "Where many of these men get the 'reverend' in front of their names I do not know," he said; "certainly they don't get it from God."[49] Such evangelical critiques of clerical liberalism gained a hearing from conservatives in mainline denominations, who echoed the criticisms coming from evangelical leaders like Graham and Bell. In the United Presbyterian Church, as in other mainline denominations, conservatives were also beginning to organize and publicize this dissent. A Presbyterian pastor from Illinois offered this view in the fledging journal *Presbyterian Layman*: "We are not called to be clinicians, but Christians," he argued, "not followers of Masters and Johnson, but hearers and doers of the Word."[50] The comment drew a line between scientific and biblical authorities and insisted that proper morality was based in the latter. The accusation repeated a sentiment found repeatedly in the journals' pages, which regarded liberals' accommodating views toward worldly authorities as a threat to the purity of the Christian body. The mobilizing rationale in churches, as in public politics, was that a heretofore "silent majority" in the pews was finally speaking up against the permissive denominational leadership.

Letters to the United Presbyterian headquarters in Philadelphia made it clear that its membership was listening to the critical voices from both inside and outside the denomination. Many of these writers included clipped and folded newspaper articles as supporting evidence for their remarks. The complaints voiced by national spokespersons and protesting laity alike linked sexual permissiveness to a compromised faith.

Outraged members of one Waverly United Presbyterian Church sent in a collectively written letter as a formal protest against "the growing moral permissiveness seen in material produced by our church boards and agencies, and dependence upon man's wisdom rather than the teaching of scripture." One layman surmised that "situation ethics" was to blame. "The authors have rejected the Biblical standards in regard to sexual conduct," he accused.[51] The top leaders of the church, wrote a small-town pastor, "are rapidly going off the beam in their heretical determination that men can do a better job on social and moral questions than God has revealed in his Word."[52] Another longtime Presbyterian layman succinctly identified the source of the study: it expressed "the feeling of the world and the Devil."[53] Where the liberal religious authors of the Presbyterian study understood science and morality as "twin beams" to illuminate right living, these conservative critics regarded this mixture of God and Mammon as evidence of worldly compromise. They argued for a different relationship between Christian and non-Christian sources of insight: the faithful needed to draw a strong and uncrossable line between "the church" and "the world," between "God's wisdom" and "man's wisdom," and between biblical truth and the devil. They took issue with the study document's reliance upon the behavioral sciences, its challenge to biblical interpretation, and its trust in human agency over divine edict. The problem with "Sexuality and the Human Community" was not just that it was too theologically liberal but that its overreliance on secular sources of knowledge placed it altogether outside the faith.

These debates were new flame wars in battles that dated back to the late nineteenth century. The contending theological camps of "modernists" and "fundamentalists" diverged over precisely where Christians should draw the line between the church and the world. Liberals, inheritors of early twentieth-century "modernist impulses" in Protestant theology, approached new sources of knowledge as perfecting resources for religious practices that preserved hidebound human foibles rather than relevant truths.[54] Conservatives, on the other hand, gravitated to an ideal of unchanging "fundamentals," with the truth of Christianity revealed in the past and preserved in Christian scripture. These long-standing tensions surfaced with renewed vigor in the late 1960s, as a consolidating network of conservatives from both inside and outside of mainline denominations took aim at what they saw as the modernist apostasy of the mainline leadership. Not only sexual morality but also a whole host of issues channeled enduring tensions like lightning rods. Protestant clergy, according to these accusations, prioritized politics over soul winning; they invested in social justice rather than missionary work; they sought ecumenical unification rather than doctrinal purity. The back and forth rehearsed an axiomatic difference between counterfeit and truth: as liberals perched on the shifting sands of modern culture, their counterparts stood on the rock of God's unchanging revelation.

Scholars of American Protestantism have roundly demonstrated that these ideological divisions had more complex lived histories. From their inception, fundamentalist movements for renewal relied on an operative modernity, a de facto modernist method, which authorized and naturalized religious change.[55] Such innovative practices continued to be important during the postwar decades, as formerly factionalized fundamentalist leaders worked to consolidate a cross-denominational movement organized around a professedly conservative white Protestant identity. The formal structure for this collaboration was organized in 1942, when a group of conservative leaders created the National Association of Evangelicals. They made the key decision to officially slough off the pejorative label "fundamentalist" for the more modern and optimistic-sounding moniker "evangelical." Through the 1950s, charismatic leaders like Graham were important to the continued consolidation of a shared conservative religious identity among the formerly divided ranks of fundamentalist, pentecostal, and conservative mainline denominations. The fruit of this long labor was visible by the late 1960s, as the balance of power in American Protestantism shifted from northern mainline Protestants to the evangelical churches in the South and the Sunbelt.[56]

Indeed, the shared opposition to Protestant liberalism helped to shore up the common cause of defending orthodoxy, even as conservatives adaptively formed their own synthesis with modern culture. Despite the oppositional rhetoric—the labeling of the behavioral sciences as "man's wisdom" and the accusation that liberals relied on "Masters and Johnson" over the Word of God—evangelicals were also reforming their views of sexuality to incorporate insights from the therapeutic sciences. A number of evangelicals in earlier decades had strongly criticized liberal Protestant articulations of therapeutic culture as a "do-it-yourself religion" made up of little more than "self-help baptized with a sprinkling of devout-plus-medical phrases."[57] Yet a number of evangelical leaders also seriously engaged the ideas coming out of psychology and psychiatry and recommended that some books, when read with the critical check of the "inner resources of the Holy Spirit," might supply useful information for "discerning" Christians.[58] The critical key for appropriation: Christians must not take the insights of psychology and psychiatry as a replacement for the certainty of human sin and divine salvation. God, not therapists, saved sinners.[59]

Over the course of the 1960s, conservatives' approaches to sex and gender changed markedly. Conservative Protestants published books and articles that frankly and directly addressed sex and also took up the core principle of sexual liberalism, that sexual pleasure was healthy and good. The shock troops for the evangelical changing views of sex were the handful of conservative Christians with professional training in psychology and psychiatry who actively worked to reconcile the therapeutic sciences with born-again faith. Their efforts helped to form an evangelical variant of therapeutic culture. Like the predecessors in the field of pastoral counseling, the new field of "Christian counseling," as it was termed, focused a great deal of attention on questions of marriage, family, and child rearing.[60] During the 1940s and 1950s, most evangelical writing addressed sex largely as a topic of concern for teenagers, and the dominant tone, to quote one Christian author, was a "two-fisted, straight-shooting, Biblical presentation of stern reality."[61] By the mid-1960s, however, a boom of articles and advice texts offered more nuanced and positive advice to both teenagers and their parents. In this emergent literature, evangelical Christians found new resources for thinking of, talking about, and practicing sex.[62]

Thus, as evangelicals castigated a secular culture for its permissiveness, they also experienced their own version of the sexual revolution. The evangelical variant of therapeutic sexuality, however, maintained a professed commitment to moral boundaries, biblical authority, and Christian conversion.[63] The pleasures of sex had unambiguous boundaries. Rules—clear ones—guided godly men and women toward marriage and blocked off the various detours from the ultimate goal. This did more than reinforce boundaries, however; it also presented rules as something more than divine edicts against sin. God's rules, rather, guided obedient men and women into lives of health, happiness, and spiritual maturity. Some of the most important changes in evangelicals' advice about sex addressed God's permission—indeed, mandate—for sexual pleasure. Marriage advice published by evangelicals, beginning in the late 1950s and expanding through the 1960s, endorsed marital sex for a litany of good effects beyond procreation: it enhanced emotional intimacy and expressed God's will and design for human sexual nature. Two bedrock

Sexuality education tract, published by the Christian Life Commission of the Southern Baptist General Convention (1960s). Archives of the Southern Baptist Church, Nashville.

convictions held sway. Evangelical authors insisted that God created sex—including sexual pleasure—as wholly good. However, the misuse of this divinely created gift could also spell personal ruin. Billy Graham, in an article for Christian youth published in *Moody Monthly*, expressed this view: "Sex is a God-given instinct, just as sacred as anything else he has given us. . . . If we give this energy to Christ it becomes a power, a dynamic, that will drive and carry us to heights undreamed of; but if misused, it will destroy both body and soul."[64] Thus, the flip side of the wholesome pleasure found in the right uses of sex was the destructive consequence of sex used outside of God's plan.

In authorizing this view of good sex, evangelicals led with biblical narratives rather than with appeals to science. In doing so, they also discussed scriptural passages that might mistakenly be read as evidence that sex should be embarrassing or shameful or as biblical prohibitions against non-procreative sex in marriage. Advice authors challenged, for example, the mistaken notion that Adam and Eve's choice to eat the forbidden fruit in the Garden of Eden—the entry point of sin into human nature—was a coded reference to a primordial act of illicit sex. Evangelical authors also revised earlier interpretations of the biblical story of Onan, whose condemned "spilling of seed" had earlier been understood as a prohibition against birth control.[65] Through these and other ways of reinterpreting biblical texts, evangelicals worked to create new meanings for sex. Indeed, biblical authority served as a powerful authorizing narrative for an emergent sex-positive ethic. Their challenges to earlier interpretations did not oppose the meaning of the text itself but emphasized that the text, properly understood, offered a different meaning. Through these new scriptural narratives, conservatives advised husbands and wives that their lovemaking was not merely a pragmatic avenue to procreation but was rather a "one flesh" uniting of gender opposites in marital union—a "sacrament" that expressed God's intrinsic design for husband and wife.[66] These new interpretive practices opened up the possibility of a sex-positive Bible.

Unlike religious liberals, who saw taboo and dogmatism as guilt-inducing obstacles to sexual health, evangelical authors stressed biblical authority and clear rules as guides to happy and fulfilling relationships. Teens needed to follow biblical standards in their choices with their dates; married couples, likewise, were enjoined to follow biblical guidelines for setting their relationships right with God—with the promise that spiritual obedience also provided best practices for relationship health and marital fulfillment. For conservatives as well as liberals, authenticity, happiness, and self-actualization were still key values. Evangelicals articulated an approach to therapeutic culture that placed happiness and self-actualization in a framework that emphasized "rules"—God's moral laws—as the avenues to those ideals. Those rules, they insisted, were anchored in the Bible, which revealed God's expectations for moral living, and they were accessed through a born-again relationship with Jesus Christ.[67] What evangelicals produced, beginning in the 1960s, was a biblically authorized, revelation-bound, born-again sexual gospel.

As evangelicals formed teachings about healthy sexuality, they also begin to speak of its unhealthy opposite. The injunction to sexual pleasure—within the boundaries of marriage—also coincided with subtle changes that worked to single out homosexuality as a distinct category of sexual perversion. These changes began to see specific homosexual meanings within biblical texts and narratives formerly used to reference catchall categories for sexual perversion. The Genesis 19 references to "Sodom's sin," discussions of "the unpardonable sin," and the threat found in Romans 1:28—"God gave them over to a reprobate mind"— gradually shifted meanings. Evangelicals saw them not as general warnings against sexual licentiousness but as specific warnings against homosexuality.[68] In other words, evangelicals began to form their views of sex around the binary logic of therapeutic health. As they created a sex-positive ethic for heterosexuality, they also increasingly specified same-sex attraction as a distinct type of deviance.

This conservative Protestant commentary on homosexuality followed a few steps behind that of liberals. Liberal Protestant pastoral counselors chattered through the 1950s about counseling practices and strategies for curing homosexuals, secure in the conviction that knowledge about a problem was key to its solution. Their conservative counterparts, in the meantime, regarded sexual speech as potential enticement, and they spoke about same-sex behavior in cautious and coded language.[69] During this time, however, a small handful of conservative Protestant authors worked to fuse together the disease theories of the behavioral sciences with the accounts of condemnation that they read in their Bibles. Christian psychologist Clyde Narramore was a leading voice in this synthetic project whose disease/treatment perspectives drew broadly from related views of pastoral counseling. His widely popular *Life and Love: A Christian View of Sex* of 1956 was an advice book on dating that coached young men and women on how to navigate natural (hetero)sexual attractions rather than simply "flee" them. An appendix to the book addressed same-sex attractions. Narramore, like his liberal Protestant counterparts, understood homosexuality to be a pathological condition caused by developmental factors within early childhood, and he stressed psychiatric treatment as a cure for the condition. Unlike most pastoral counseling experts, however, Narramore also emphasized conversion to Christianity as a critical key to sexual healing. "Until they knew Christ," Narramore advised, "many former homosexuals . . . had no desire to change." He concluded, "The greatest dynamic in the rehabilitation of homosexuals is vital Christianity."[70] Where the liberal-leaning pastoral counselors emphasized unconditional positive regard as a healing balm for perverted psyches, Narramore prescribed a saving relationship with Jesus Christ.

Narramore knit together psychology and Christian conversion as complementary practices of healing, but a number of conservative Protestant authors writing around the same time placed them at polar extremes. David Wilkerson, the evangelical pastor whose outreach to New York gang members became well known through the book (and subsequent movie) *The Cross and the Switchblade*, also published a slim treatise on homosexuality. *Hope for Homosexuals* addressed same-sex attraction in a manner analogous to Wilkerson's approaches to gang membership or drug addition—it was yet another kind of spiritual affliction to be overcome by Christian conversion. The book narrated homosexuals' unsatisfying quest for love, gratification, and help from worldly sources—including psychology and psychiatry—and presented in the final pages the one true solution: an invitation to turn a hopeless life over to Christ.[71] For Wilkerson, homosexuality was a spiritual rather than a psychological problem, and as such, it demanded a distinctly spiritual cure.

It was not until the late 1960s that *Christian Life* and *Christianity Today*—two of the most widely circulated evangelical periodicals—addressed same-sex attraction in any length. Here, too, authors grappled with whether homosexuality was a spiritual disease caused by rebellion against God or a mental illness that might even afflict committed Christians. *Christian Life* led the way in 1967 with a forum that aired divergent views. An anchor article by a British social worker described the deep distress of a Christian youth minister struggling with the fact that he was "predominantly homosexual in outlook, even if not practicing." The article presented homosexuality as a completely involuntary medical condition—a problem that might even afflict a sincere spiritual leader—and it challenged readers to reflect on their reactions. The responses by four Christian medical specialists registered a surprising range of opinion. One respondent concurred that the "homosexual condition" might well be unchangeable and tentatively suggested that Christians should be willing to consider "homosexual marriage" as a permissible way to manage homosexuals' compulsive attractions to the same sex. The most reticent to accept this view was the final respondent, William Standish Reed, a medical doctor who challenged the original article and the other respondents by declaring that there could be "no such thing as a Christian homosexual." Listing a litany of bible passages (Genesis 19:1–11, the Leviticus texts, Romans 1, and 1 Corinthians 6:9), the author roundly declared homosexuality to be a sin and argued that any Christian who led a homosexual to believe otherwise stood in the way of the needed process of conviction and repentance. Despite his medical background, Reed's recommendation for a cure was entirely spiritual: any person with homosexual tendencies "can be delivered through the ministry of Christian exorcism, and through contemplating the Word of God and living a righteous, holy, and moral life."[72] While airing a range of views, the editors of *Christian Life* clearly gave Reed the final word.

Even airing the debate, however, opened up a door for those who struggled with this affliction to tell of their experience. Both *Christian Life* and *Christianity Today* published confessional letters from homosexual Christians that responded to earlier published articles. These writers told of their dogged efforts to change unwanted attractions. One of them, a woman, declared that God had given her "full victory" over homosexual desires through a process of rigorous prayer and scripture meditation. The second, a man, wrote in the midst of his struggle. Despite his faith in Jesus, he wrote, "homosexuality has been a problem that has plagued me my whole life. . . . Thank God, he has given me victory and deliverance from overt acts during the past few months," he wrote, "but my nature is unchanged."[73] Such firsthand confessions presented same-sex attraction as a condition that affected even sincere Christians and suggested that it might also be an unchangeable "nature." Later articles published in these journals addressed these claims, which they took as evidence that homosexuality might also be a nonmoral mental health problem. *Christianity Today* gave advice to pastors about "helping the homosexual," with instructions that were reminiscent of the pastoral counseling advice of their liberal counterparts. The article pressed pastors to be "a good listener" and to "offer hope and support in the struggle for a sexual identity." The article made it clear, however, that homosexual behavior was a sin to be resisted and encouraged Christians struggling with these problems to seek the help of a Christian psychiatrist or psychologist.[74]

During this moment in the late 1960s, most evangelical and mainline Protestant views on homosexuality took for granted that homosexuality was pathological, and they embedded this assumption in moral teachings and biblical interpretation. Christian conservatives, no less than their liberal counterparts, were discussing and debating homosexuality within medical frameworks. These conservative Christian authors worked from several certainties. They affirmed the distinction between "acts" and "condition" that were already well rehearsed among moderate and liberal Protestants. Such a distinction connected same-sex attraction to an interior condition. A number of authors surmised that people might be afflicted with a condition for which they were not entirely morally culpable, but conservative Protestants also disagreed about the possibilities for curing such a condition and the role of Christian faith in expediting that cure. Most remarkably, these authors had relatively little to say about the Bible's view on the topic. They seemed content to follow assertions about the Bible's clear condemnation with parenthetical citations, following the common practice of providing self-evident "proof texts" for biblical claims.

Moreover, if the responses to the Presbyterian study of sexuality are any indication, homosexuality was not an important issue of religious and political dissent between liberal and conservative Protestants. This relative consensus, it seems, contributed to an absence of conflict. However, most letter writers said nothing at all about homosexuality. They were more concerned with where to draw the boundaries around heterosexuality, and issues of fornication and adultery, rather than homosexuality, stood at the center of the disagreement. Indeed, quite a number of letter writers, though critical of other aspects of "Sexuality and the Human Community," registered agreement with its views on homosexuality. Although this sample of protest letters provides only a partial glimpse of the opinions within the broader denomination, the study guide's comments on homosexuality seemed to find fairly wide assent—or, at the very least, they did not provoke the same measure of outrage.

Janet Brunger, whose protest letter opened this chapter, discussed her view of homosexuality in her outraged response to the *Parade* coverage of the "new sex code." The newspaper article only briefly mentioned that the study advocated "removal of any stigma that makes homosexuals feel they are in irresolvable conflict with the Christian fellowship." Though she disagreed with nearly everything else presented in that article, Brunger noted her assent on this point. Homosexuals, she concurred, should not be rejected from Christian fellowships. "I daresay that there are few Ministers who would feel qualified to treat or to counsel this type of individual," she remarked. "This is a highly specialized kind of treatment and more harm than good could come from 'unqualified interference.'"[75] These comments underscored a therapeutic axiom: homosexuality should not be condemned but treated. Other letter writers displayed a similar commitment to disease models of homosexuality, even if they presented those views through biblical narratives. Two churches in rural Pennsylvania cooperatively discussed the study, and their members jointly wrote a lengthy review of the entire sexuality study. They were largely critical, and they were among the few responders to take particular issue with the study's presentation of homosexuality. The issue: the study presented medical theories instead of teachings anchored "solely on the basis of Scripture." The review cited 1 Corinthians 6:9 to argue that only a "truly repentant homosexual" should be forgiven and accepted by churches; "practicing homosexuals" should not be.[76] What these authors presented as a biblical view, however, echoed a distinction between condition and act—between "repentant homosexuals" and "practicing" ones—that already suggested a view influenced by medical theories. Another lay Presbyterian, writing from Fillmore, California, voiced a similar opinion. Citing the Genesis narrative of creation, this woman reiterated that "God positioned sex securely: 'male and female created He them.'" The creation of different sexes, this comment implied, grounded heterosexuality in the created order. As a consequence, this writer maintained, there could be "only one attitude about homosexuals . . . not how to accept them but how to go about restoring them from abomination."[77] What this showed was that medical theories were already part of the assumptions that Christians brought to their Bibles. Their interpretations embedded popular understandings of homosexual deviance into the seemingly plain meaning of the text.

Thus, at this moment in the late 1960s, a tenuous consensus held sway. A dominant—but unraveling—approach to homosexuals in liberal Protestantism overlapped with an emerging evangelical therapeutic orthodoxy. Both viewed homosexuality as a condition in need of a cure. Such views, notably, were only just beginning to circulate in conservative Protestant publications, and the synthesis of disease theories and religious teachings left many questions unaddressed. Most especially, what conservative Protestants did not have at this moment was a comprehensive analysis of biblical texts and homosexuality. What they had, rather, were proof texts—brief references to verses that supported propositional statements. By contrast, their liberal counterparts at this moment were drawing from several books and dozens of chapters and articles that systematically appraised the biblical record on homosexuality. The dominant answer to this question rehearsed the familiar principle, which divided act from condition: the Bible condemned homosexual behavior, even if it did not address the modern understanding of homosexuality as a disease. Indeed, notably absent in conservative Protestants' remarks about homosexuality in the late 1960s and even into the early 1970s was the deep sense of tradition that later informed antigay politics. With neither a systematic appraisal of biblical teachings nor a consistent theological response, evangelicals at this moment were still stumbling toward the much later axiomatic formulation of "love the sinner; hate the sin."[78]

Conclusion

The contending arguments over the 1970 Presbyterian sexuality study put a spotlight on the differences between Protestant liberals and conservatives over the place of rules in Christian morality. However, a more subtle and foundational story involved their shared assumptions. From the liberal leadership of mainline churches to the spokespersons of an emerging evangelicalism, leading Protestants worked to circulate new teachings about sexuality. These ideas borrowed in profound ways from the certainties of the therapeutic sciences. They countered false teachings about sex as dirty or shameful and valorized the attraction between men and women as natural, right, and godly. In their respective efforts to quell the excesses of the sexual revolution, Protestants across the theological spectrum participated in a revolution of their own. They put in place a new cultural formation—a Christian sexuality, in effect, that presented sexuality in sacred terms as a good part of God's creation and thus core to the divinely created self.

There was another important dynamic to these debates. In the controversy over "Sexuality and the Human Community" and in the larger discussions about Christian teachings about sex, we see a symbiotic relationship between the eager modernism of liberals and the adamant traditionalism of evangelical and conservative Protestants. The deliberate synthetic method of liberal Protestant reformers provided a ready script for their dissenters. Conservatives adopted much of the substance of a liberal therapeutic model for sexuality even as they synthesized those certainties within their own religious idiom. "Evangelicalism adopted much of the liberal program but integrated it into a different system of authority," writes historian Leonard Sweet, an apt description of the patterns by which conservative Protestants formed their own version of liberals' earlier synthesis of morality and medicine.[79] Thus, even as conservatives chastised their liberal counterparts for privileging science over scripture, they also adopted as their own ideas about sex, marriage, and family developed by an earlier generation of liberal Protestants. However, evangelicals also integrated those certainties into a different system of authority. Vis-à-vis the antilegalism of their liberal Protestant counterparts, evangelicals persuasively claimed tradition and defended it against what they cast as a secular incursion.

What both sides assumed was rightfully Christian, however, was that the natural attraction between women and men was God-given and good. They also assumed, of course, that this good sex required heterosexual monogamous intimacy—the kind of sex that came naturally. While conservatives and liberals largely shared a view of heterosexuality as part of the created order, the fiercest battles between them focused on the rightful boundaries around that good sex. Heated questions about premarital virginity and marital monogamy remained at the center of dueling visions of *how* Christians should teach sexual morality. These disagreements, however, assumed an unhealthy opposite. Homosexuality was the quiet foil against which Christians developed their injunctions to heterosexual pleasure. Inherited therapeutic doctrines that celebrated the goodness of sexuality also seamlessly knit disease models for same-sex behavior into the fabric of Christian authority. Christians, liberal and conservative, understood homosexuality as a lamentable "condition" and cited biblical texts that they took as clear injunctions against the overt "practice" of that inclination. Liberals and conservatives synthesized these certainties in different directions—conservatives discussed the healing power of conversion, while liberals turned to psychiatrists for transformation. However, Protestants of all stripes embedded disease theories in both Christian teachings and biblical texts.

In 1970, conservatives and liberals alike shared in the reigning consensus of an antihomosexual therapeutic orthodoxy. However, the terms of that orthodoxy also singled out same-sex sexuality in new ways and authorized more direct discussion of homosexuality. Among conservatives as well as liberals, this discourse unwittingly opened up a genre of Christian confession. Even conservative Christian publications devoted space to the anguished testimonies of men and women who struggled with unwanted same-sex attractions. Thus, the attention to the opposite of sexual health opened a narrative of confession through which devout Christian believers testified to their own same-sex desires.[80] The frank discussion of homosexuality found in the Presbyterian study guide "Sexuality and the Human Community" also spelled out sexual teachings in a way that invited challenge and response. Mainline Protestants' thin consensus about the ethics of homosexuality would not last for long. Indeed, it was already unraveling. By 1970, a handful of published articles by progressive clergy and by gay and lesbian Christians directly challenged medical theories of disease.[81] These challenges proceeded alongside political challenges to the mental health profession itself—in 1973 gays and lesbians successfully lobbied for the removal of homosexuality from the *Diagnostic and Statistical Manual of Mental Disorders*, a change that signaled the formal end to the disease model.

Thus, as the dissent of conservatives worked to pull mainline Protestant denominations back to their visions of tradition, another movement was already at work to push those same religious bodies toward more radical practices of Christian inclusion. In September 1970, the Methodist mission journal *New World Outlook* devoted the entire issue to the topic of homosexuality and Christianity. The editors reprinted the section of the Presbyterian study that discussed homosexuality. On the facing page, another author—identified as a Christian lesbian—told of her involvement in a growing political movement.[82] A key aim of that movement, as she explained it, was to challenge precisely the teachings on homosexuality spelled out in "Sexuality and the Human Community." This growing movement for gay liberation, in its various activist forms, brought a forceful challenge to the therapeutic orthodoxy that stood in for a long tradition of Christian antihomosexual teaching.

5

BORN AGAIN AT STONEWALL

Dick Leitsch, president of the New York Mattachine Society, chose the title "The Hairpin Drop Heard Round the World" for the last-minute report slipped into the organization's July 1969 newsletter.[1] It announced a street riot that took place just blocks away, at a popular gay bar on Christopher Street called the Stonewall Inn. Bar patrons responded with violence to a police raid, and the brawl spilled out onto the streets, sparking a series of demonstrations that upended Greenwich Village during the last weekend in June. Leitch's description cheekily compared the event to the "shot heard round the world" that reportedly sparked the American Revolution. The hyperbolic prose was a convention of the genre—Leitsch and other homophile authors perpetually trumpeted events of evident importance as historic "firsts" for the movement, and in the coming weeks other homophile organizers in New York turned to their typewriters to analyze, dissect, and predict the significance of the event for a movement that was by then nearly two decades old.[2] The opinions circulated through the alternative news channels of the homophile press, which now reached a rapidly growing national audience. It was in the pages of gay newspapers that most readers learned about both the riots and the two New York–based organizations created in its wake, which claimed the legacy of the riots as a mandate for radical political activism. The Gay Liberation Front (GLF), formed in late July 1969, and the Gay Activist Alliance (GAA), commencing five months later in December, were the new voices for a movement of "gay liberation."

Most Americans, however, missed the sound of that hairpin until the following summer. The mainstream press attention at the time of the riots was limited to the New York dailies and the alternative press—particularly the *Village Voice*, whose reporter was accidently trapped inside the Stonewall Inn with the police during the riots.[3] Readers of the *New York Times* might have easily overlooked two squibs, which focused on injuries sustained by the police.[4] The commemorations of the following year, however, received the kind of press attention later credited to the riots themselves. The front page of the *New York Times*, syndicated national coverage through the Associated Press, and articles in *Time* magazine announced that a new radicalism was "taking to the streets."[5] The marches and demonstrations, tamed and stylized versions of a street raid, brought attention to an increasingly militant movement. The thousands who showed up to march in New York and Los Angeles (and with less fanfare in Chicago and Boston) were part of the largest mass demonstration by homosexuals that had occurred to date in the United States. As those activists told it, the grand show of force pointed backward to the overlooked event of the year before. The organizers and the participants had a ready narrative about the significance of the day they were celebrating: it was the one-year birthday celebration of the gay liberation movement, which had been born in the streets outside the Stonewall Inn.

The statement was the germ of a subsequent popular history, which traced the beginning of the "modern gay rights movement" from the spontaneous resistance on Christopher Street.[6] Popular narratives about the movement's origins at Stonewall have chafed historians as much as they have galvanized activists. The narrative that charted the movement's beginning in 1969 obscured the earlier and ongoing role of the homophile movement, which had provided the organizing muscle and national networks that made possible the coordinated national demonstrations. It took a movement already in place to so effectively announce one that had just been born. Gay and lesbian historiography is peppered with exactly these pointed challenges to the inaccuracy and overstatement of the accounts about the movement's beginnings at Stonewall. "Almost the entire corpus of gay and lesbian history," historian Terence Kissack points out, "can be read as an attempt to deconstruct the Stonewall narrative."[7] Professional historians, however, have proved to be a poor match against the history-making power of commemoration. Quotidian details like chronology and precedent recede from significance in the history of the streets reenacted each summer. Marchers—with sweaty chests, sunburned faces, and sore feet—retrace the steps of the original queer rioters in a collective embodiment of identity pride. These repeated actions, summer after summer, also help to put the event being commemorated into the pages of history books.

Religion is at the same time present and absent in this annual rite of return. There are things strikingly *religion-like* about the pride commemorations, even something distinctly Christian. They remember a Friday night act of violence with a triumphal Sunday ceremony that initiates newly transformed selves into a community of celebrants.[8] And yet, despite these resonances, the historical narrative attached to the commemoration markedly excludes religion from view.[9] New York–based gay liberation groups, the immediate inheritors of the Stonewall legacy, had a well-earned reputation for avowed secularism. In much of the liberationist rhetoric, religion and gay identity took up the aura of a civilizational conflict. One participant in the GAA made his feelings about religion clear in a mock "to do" list for achieving sexual liberation published in one of New York's gay newspapers. "I may attend a dance, a discussion, or even a debauche at some neophytic church or temple," he wrote, "[but] I will never bend the knee or neck except to spit on some low altar, or to mock scripture."[10] There was an element of self-parody in the article, but the sentiment held: sexual liberation required eradication, by whatever means necessary, of gays' oppressive attachments to religion. With this kind of adamant secularism at the center of the movement, gay religious practitioners seemed like a misplaced oddity, at best, in a movement otherwise devoted to uprooting toxic pieties. The new riddle for the post-Stonewall generation: given the evident oppositions between gay and religious identity, how could someone claim both *at the same time*?

This rhetoric of oppositional identities and civilizational conflicts, however, obscures what was almost at the surface of the annual ritual of gay pride: gay liberation, in both ideology and practice, was profoundly shaped by religion, even by specifically Christian beliefs and practices. Indeed, the broader history of movement activism during the 1970s bears out this point. The early 1970s saw the flourishing of a series of new gay-welcoming religious organizations. The central momentum for this growth, and the most well known of the grassroots movement of "gay churches," was the 1968-founded Metropolitan Community Church (MCC), a gay-welcoming congregation founded in Los Angeles by Troy Perry. The MCC was only one of at least a dozen local Christian fellowships that overlapped with gay movement organizing at this time. But the MCC had staying power; organized as a denomination in 1970, the United Fellowship of Metropolitan Community Churches (UFMCC) claimed ninety member bodies by its eighth anniversary.[11] The MCC, in turn, inspired a network of similar religious fellowships in other traditions: the Roman Catholic group Dignity, gay and lesbian synagogues, and a loose network of independent Catholics also advertised their outreach to the gay community. This religious flourishing also brought significant incursions into established religious institutions. Quakers and Unitarian Universalists formed early lesbian and gay fellowships, and Dignity, which began meeting in 1969 as a confidential support group, also had a network of local chapters by the mid-1970s. By 1974, mainline Protestant churches had a coordinated movement of gay caucuses. The "radical turn" in the movement, when we look capaciously at movement developments in the 1970s, hardly threw religion out the window. To the contrary, the 1970s brought queer-identified religious organizing that intersected with every sector of the gay and lesbian social movement and also crossed every major American faith tradition.

This chapter tells a history of this religious organizing and works to situate it within a historiography of early 1970s gay activism that almost entirely overlooks religion. What was centrally important to both this religious flourishing and its historical invisibility, I argue, was the Stonewall narrative itself. The Stonewall explored here is not the actual event of the street riot but the remembered symbol of movement birth that was cultivated and commemorated by diverse movement participants. Religious practitioners were among the most enthusiastic purveyors of the Stonewall narrative, and their participation in the commemorative practices helped to hoist a movement myth to popular prominence. Their telling and retelling of the riots on Christopher Street scripted and performed gay identity in ways that evoked powerful spiritual themes. The story of a late-night bar raid—transposed through collective memory to Friday night instead of Saturday morning—recalled the familiar story of the Crucifixion, while the Sunday ritual of gay pride, in turn, evoked the twinned triumphs of the Exodus and Easter. The linked practice of "coming out" rehearsed a narrative about a transformed self that recalled conversion and testimony. For religious groups—and particularly for gay Christians—the Stonewall narrative and its commemoration were a perfect vehicle for fusing gay and religious identities into a seamless whole. In ways both deliberate and inadvertent, a dominantly Christian and post-Christian collective collaborated in cultivating and celebrating an invented past that evoked the plotlines of a familiar religious—even Christian—story.

To call Stonewall an "invented past" is not to deny the fact of the bar raid and the street protests or to ignore the organizations for gay liberation formed in its wake. It is to attend, rather, to the outsized claims to primacy and uniqueness that granted movement-founding significance to this bar raid and this act of resistance. The durable power of those claims, I suggest, cannot be accounted for without looking more closely at ways that religion—and particularly Christianity—continued to shape and inform the views of movement activists. This attention decidedly challenges the notion that the identity politics mobilized at this proclaimed point of rupture actually left religion behind in a vestigial pile of sloughed off false consciousness. Nor was it the case that gay Christians adopted or appropriated an essentially secular gay identity and refitted its sharp contours into a Christian-shaped self. It is, rather, to show the ways that a politics of identity visibility mobilized through the memory of Stonewall carried on Christian ideals and practices from the very outset. From the moment the embers died in a despised, Mafia-run hole on Christopher Street, Stonewall had already accumulated an excess of signification.

Mobilizing a Memory

Homophile activists had a hand in shaping the meaning of the Stonewall riots from the outset, and no person was more influential in this process than Craig Rodwell. A midwesterner raised in the Christian Science Church, Rodwell was one of many who left behind religious involvement after taking up gay movement work. Rodwell moved to New York in his teens and became involved in the New York Mattachine Society. He also added two new homophile organizations to the New York scene, and both harkened back to his Christian Science roots. The first was an organization called the Homophile Youth Movement in Neighborhoods, or HYMN, a gay youth organization that also published the HYMNAL, a journal devoted to encouraging positive self-esteem with a name selected to imply a crusading mission. Alongside this journal, Rodwell also opened a space where gays and lesbians could read and study. The Oscar Wilde Bookstore opened in Greenwich Village in 1967 as a space devoted as much to perusal as to purchase. Rodwell's faith in the consciousness-transforming power of instructive literature was certainly informed by the tracts and reading rooms of Christian Science. One of the early chroniclers of gay liberation history, sociologist Toby Marotta, emphasizes the profound influence of Christian Science on Rodwell's activism. "The first eastern homophile leader to act like a gay liberationist," Marotta noted, was "an unintended offspring of Mary Baker Eddy."[12]

Rodwell's Greenwich Village location gave him a front-row seat to the riots that erupted in late June 1969, and anecdotal reports credit him for leading the group of angered rioters in the shouts for "gay power," a

Craig Rodwell in the Oscar Wilde Bookstore, 1970. Photograph by Kay Tobin,
© Manuscript and Archives Division, The New York Public Library.

slogan already espoused in the HYMNAL as a critique of Mafia-run bars.[13] Rodwell also posted fliers that encouraged gays riled up by the raid to participate in another demonstration day scheduled by homophile groups for July 4, just a week after the riots subsided. The Annual Reminder demonstration, held every year in front of Philadelphia's Constitution Hall, was now in its fifth year. Rodwell fronted seventy dollars to rent a bus, which brought down a group of androgynous-looking, bell-bottom-wearing activists from New York to the Philadelphia protest.[14]

The generational tensions were immediately visible. Frank Kameny, the organizer for the demonstration, had long insisted that participants exhibit professional decorum and properly gendered attire—men in suits, women in skirts. Kameny turned irate when two women, both wearing blue jeans, marched in the picket line holding hands.[15] Kameny and other so-called homophile militants found themselves alongside newcomers whose participation in organizations of the New Left informed their political commitment to total liberation and a critique of what the new activists saw as veteran homophile organizers' staid respectability politics and integrationist aims. The differences foiled homophile leaders' initial efforts to simply incorporate the new activists into existing organizations. In July, the radicals formed their own organization, with a name—the Gay

Liberation Front—that made it clear that they had rejected proper decorum as a condition of political acceptance.[16] The name itself was electric. In the months after the founding of the New York group, activists in cities and in college towns from Chicago to Tallahassee formed their own local groups.[17] As the movement for gay liberation spread, however, the founding organization in New York suffered from internal dissent. In December, a group that was frustrated with the GLF's chaotic meetings and internal division formed the Gay Activist Alliance to focus on single-issue organizing. These organizations were not the first to embrace gay identity pride or to emphasize direct confrontation as a strategy for change, but they did bring an unabashed militancy that boldly surpassed the more moderate tactics of their homophile predecessors.[18]

Even as a growing number of new organizations took up the banner of gay liberation, it was the veteran homophile leaders who spearheaded the efforts to commemorate the riots. Rodwell, again, took the initiative. In November 1969, he and a small group from the newly formed GLF brought a proposal to the biannual planning meeting of the East Coast Homophile Organizations. The proposal, in effect, requested authorization for an act of ritual supersession: the Philadelphia Annual Reminder demonstration would be scrapped in favor of a new "more relevant" demonstration day to be held in New York to commemorate the riots. The suggested Christopher Street Liberation Day (a name that pointedly avoided crediting the bar itself) would encompass the homophile movement's ongoing commitments by celebrating "the ideas and ideals of the larger struggle in which we are engaged—that of our fundamental human rights."[19] The gathered delegates overwhelmingly approved the plan and agreed to circulate the resolution to contacts in other cities, and Rodwell and a small group of other homophile organizers formed the committee dedicated to making the event happen. An announcement about these plans appeared in the HYMNAL, which urged activists in other cities to help make possible "the largest homophile demonstration in history."[20] For the organizers involved, the commemoration day extended the momentum already underway in the homophile movement by creating what would be another historic first. By April, the committee touted its plans with even grander language—this would be "possibly the biggest affair in the history of the homophile movement."[21]

By June, the descriptions for the commemoration lost the clunky language of "homophile" to refer instead to "gay liberation." The veteran activists adopted the colloquial argot and movement rhetoric preferred by the liberationists. The Gay Liberation, which was by now the largest and most active face of the movement in New York, was heralded as the triumphant product of the riots. Fliers announced a planned mass march through Manhattan with a lead-up of smaller events scheduled during the preceding "Gay Pride Week." The event was no longer an "extension of the ideals" of the homophile movement; it was instead a celebration of "the first year of the Gay Liberation movement, born the last week in June 1969 during the Christopher Street uprising."[22] The plans for commemoration, that is, gave existing activists—homophile and liberationists alike—the opportunity to re-narrate the event's meaning in new symbolic language. The explanatory literature presented the previous year's street riots as a liberating breakthrough into identity pride, which could be reenacted anew through collective remembrance. Those who participated in the commemoration—whether a veteran of the homophile movement, a radical liberationist, or a complete newcomer—were being symbolically inducted into a new movement era and thus a new collective identity. The GLF newsletter, instructively titled *Come Out!*, reiterated the ideological meaning of the commemoration: it was a day "to openly affirm the beauty of our lives and throw wide open the closet doors which will no longer be nailed shut."[23] The fliers from the planning committee similarly instructed participants about the historic importance of the event and the political feelings it embodied. "For the first time in history," the fliers read, "we are together as The Homosexual Community. . . . We are Gay and proud."[24] The commemoration of the previous year's riots staged a collective moment of liberation: by symbolically restaging the riots, activists ritually enacted their collective rebirth into a proud gay identity.

Those who wrote about the experience afterward seemed to turn reflexively to religious metaphor. The organizers of the march plotted the route as a symbolic journey from the closet to freedom.[25] Marchers assembled in the streets outside the Stonewall Inn, which was now shuttered and closed. The alternative dances scheduled by gay and lesbian organizations themselves had put the reviled Mafia-owned bar out of business. The demonstrators exited the symbolic site of shame to proceed northward up Sixth Avenue, the Avenue of the Americas, where the ranks of the marchers swelled as bystanders joined the demonstration. The last leg of the march crested a hill into Central Park, which provided a vista of the participating throngs of marchers. The group of a couple hundred that gathered in the Village had grown to over a thousand, and the participants grew again as the marchers arrived at the final destination, a mass occupation of Central Park's Sheep Meadow for a "Be-in." With the smell of grass "like incense" wafting around them, demonstrators chanted, sang, necked, and celebrated in "a promised land of freedom to be." The event was a "a cup running over," a "sweet morsel of glory," a "celebration of life itself."[26] Gay identity, in these descriptions, was a spiritual arrival at authentic self, an initiation into a new community. Political demonstration merged with spiritual transcendence.

Nothing about this commemoration, of course, celebrated a specific religious inheritance, but religious and spiritual metaphors were an important part of the descriptive language of the event. For some, the analogy worked as a substitution—gay identity and gay movement protests were a replacement and a critique of oppressive religious belonging. Martha Shelley, a Jewish lesbian and GLF member, acknowledged in 1971 that "the gay movement has its own religious aspects." However, she also emphatically separated those aspects from either established faiths or "the re-upholstered Christianity you can find in the newly-created gay churches." The religion-like aspects of the movement, rather, reflected a more natural, earth-centered spirituality. "Gay-Ins in the park," she argued, "are our spring festivals."[27] For Shelley and for many atheist and non-Christian activists, the protest rituals were not an effort to reclaim established traditions. Indeed, they were important for gay pride precisely because they offered a liberating critique—even a primordial alternative— to the oppressive connections to established faiths. However, the insistent declarations of a divorce from religion also hid submerged continuities. Queer theologian Mark Jordan, in his analysis of atheist critiques of religion written by gay liberation Marxists, suggests that the claim to "a new birth without religion" repeated older "religious rhetorics." Even as they claimed a divorce from a religious past—indeed, *especially* in that moment of heralded new birth—gay and lesbian activists rehearsed new versions of the thing they claimed to leave behind.[28]

Adding to Jordan's rhetorical analysis of religious continuity is David Hollinger's historical one. Hollinger, an intellectual historian, suggests that ecumenical Protestantism shaped various movements of the radical Left, including gay liberation. The left-leaning wings of mainline Protestantism, he claims, provided a "commodious halfway house" to the radical critiques of post-Protestant secularism.[29] Exhibit A for this dynamic, Hollinger argues, was the Methodist youth publication *motive*, which in 1972 "came out" with two final issues written and edited by gay and lesbian liberation activists. The journal's own editors facilitated the transfer. The senior editor of *motive* was B. J. Stiles, a Methodist minister previously involved in the 1964-founded Council on Religion and the Homosexual, who also later came out as gay. Assistant editor Charlotte Bunch was a lesbian involved at the time with the Furies, the D.C. lesbian collective that edited the lesbian feminist issue. Hollinger points to the moment as a telling example of a larger dynamic: progressive Protestants were actively engaged in the leftist milieu that included gay and lesbian liberation. When faced with funding cuts and opposition from the more conservative center of the denomination, those in the radical fringes made the choice, as Hollinger puts it, "to detonate the institutional suicide bomb."[30] When asked to choose between social justice ideals and institutional loyalty, many progressives walked their convictions out of the churches. The effect, in countless other instances like this one, was to unpin ideals initially nurtured in liberal religious contexts from their institutional roots.

Hollinger's analysis focuses on how liberal Protestantism gave way to a "post-Protestant secularism," but it additionally points to the ways that the radical Christianity of the *motive* editors overlapped with gay liberation. The connections that led to *motive*'s final lesbian and gay publications in 1972 were also an important backdrop to some of the widely reported incidents of presumed antireligion. In 1971, for example, both the *Christian Century* and the more conservative *Christianity Today* reported on a "zap" in Washington, D.C., where gay activists invaded a conference on religion and homosexuality taking place at the Catholic University of America. Both journals presented the theatrics of the demonstration: radicals bearing pink banners marched around the conference hall, seized the microphone, and demanded that conference participants stop examining homosexuality and begin practicing it instead.[31] In the *Century*, this was a story about the counterproductive tactics of radicals; in *Christianity Today*, it was evidence of the movement's sacrilege. Neither picture, however, offered a full account. Paul Breton, one of those gay activists, recalled that the "zap" ended in dialogue. Conference speakers ceded the floor to the liberationists, who turned the event into a series of dialogue sessions and a tour of local gay bars intended to introduce the religious leaders to real-life gays and lesbians.[32] Breton, at the time, was also leading a religious ministry for gays and lesbians in D.C., which later became an MCC congregation.[33] The dialogue sessions and bar tour were both tactics used in years past by homophile organizations seeking to educate clergy.[34] Another confrontation that ended in cooperation took place in Albany, where Ernest Reaugh, a Methodist layperson and member of the Albany GAA, delivered an ultimatum to lay leaders of his congregation. Welcome gay people, he demanded, or he would lead a "zap" of activists into the church. Those leaders responded positively, and the congregation hosted a memorial service for gay rights that took place around the 1971 rally for gay rights in Albany.[35] The behind-the-scenes collaboration also included facility rentals; in many locations, the meetings and events organized by liberationists took place in churches.[36]

Laud Humphreys, the sociologist and Episcopal priest who later came out as gay himself, wrote with surprise in 1972 about how many gay movement participants had either past or current vocations in Christian ministry.[37] Some of these cases involved former or inactive members of religious institutions, but there were also quite a number of gay activists who organized ministries of religious outreach that overlapped with their activism. A formal proposal for this kind of "gay lib" ministry circulated in an article published in the Union Theological Seminary Quarterly Review in 1970. John Rash, a gay man working as a cataloger at Union Theological Seminary, urged ministers and seminary students to develop outreach ministries to gay communities.[38] In quite a number of places, this was not merely an idea; it was a practice. In Minneapolis, gay liberationists and progressive ministers collaborated to open a community center called "Gay House" in March 1971.[39] In Dallas, Gene Leggett, a Methodist minister without a church appointment, founded the Covenant House, an outreach ministry that involved local participants in the gay liberation groups.[40] In New York, an ordained United Church of Christ minister named Roy Birchard sought out Rash after reading his article. Both men joined the New York GAA in 1971 in the hopes of starting a "gay lib" ministry. Birchard's account of participating in the GAA showed how people of faith found common ground with even adamant atheists. "Religion is a highly controversial subject within GAA," he explained in a letter to a New York pastor. "It is seen as one of the sources of oppression by many of our members." He also admitted, however, that he sympathized with those concerns: "these 'good atheists' echo the critique we 'committed Christians' have to make of the institutional Church," he explained.[41] Activists of various faith (or non-faith) commitments, Birchard's comments show, shared in a common critique of oppressive religious establishments.

Gay liberation thus overlapped in various ways with progressive Protestantism. In the experimental "gay lib" ministries, in various progressive journals, and even in the instrumental provision of meeting space, radical Christianity and gay liberation coexisted, at least for a time, in these left-leaning outliers of the mainline Protestant establishment. The connections, however, were not merely halfway stops toward secularism. They were also seedbeds for other kinds of religious organizing. Some of the "gay lib" ministers become involved with the MCC; others helped initiate movements of reform in mainline Protestant denominations. Some did both. The moment of cooperation between progressive Protestants and gay liberation had offshoots and afterlives—new religious organizations and initiatives for institutional reform—in addition to a broader influence on a post-Protestant secularism.

It was also the case that religious activists were some of the most enthusiastic purveyors of Stonewall commemoration. In New York, the first Gay Freedom Day celebration was also an important day for a new church. Rev. Robert Clement seized upon the march as an opportunity to advertise the first meeting of the newly founded Church of the Beloved Disciple. Clement marched in the parade with clerical robes and a large placard that declared "Gay People this is Your Church!" as his lover passed out fliers with the time and place of the first service.[42] The Beloved Disciple, one of several independent Catholic churches, regularly attracted a congregation in the hundreds. The most influential congregation to welcome gay people during this time, however, actually preceded the gay liberation movement by almost a year: the MCC began meeting in October 1968, a full eight months before the Stonewall riots. As the GLF gained steam in the fall of 1969 in New York, the MCC was already attracting a regular attendance of four hundred for Sunday services that met in a Hollywood theater. The MCC was at the forefront of the rising activism in Los Angeles, and its pastor, Troy Perry, also spearheaded plans for the Los Angeles Stonewall commemoration. Whatever remnants of religion could be found in the mass demonstration in New York were certainly not in the background in Los Angeles. Perry and the Los Angeles MCC traced over the vestigial Christian contours of this origin story and fused it with specifically Christian practices. Fliers for Christopher Street West, billed as "a freedom revival in lavender," urged Angelinos to express "Lavender Unity" with their "homosexual brothers and sisters of Christopher Street, who . . . fought back in rage, resentment, and frustration in their powerlessness."[43] The next year, for the second anniversary, Perry led a "long march" from Oakland to Sacramento that ended on the steps of the state capitol building for a "Gay Power Revival."[44] As the eye of the mainstream press turned to the new radicalism in the gay movement in the early 1970s, it also lingered over the perplexing figure of the gay preacher, whose homespun gospel and fast-growing church seemed to fit as readily with the Southern California "Jesus Movement" as it did with the New York gay liberation movement. These religious groups adopted the liberationist account of Stonewall as their own because they recognized in its plotlines a familiar sacred history.

Freedom Revival in Lavender

Los Angeles was the only city outside of New York to attract significant participation on the first commemoration of the Stonewall riots. Christopher Street West: A Freedom Revival in Lavender gathered an estimated one thousand, with the numbers amplified by the parade format. Clowns, flags, drummers, horses, motorcycles, and floats brought a mash-up of protest theater and camp festival. A float by the Los Angeles GLF staged a mock crucifixion—a bare-chested Jesus expired under the sign "Crucified by the L.A.P.D." Farther down, another float carried a giant replica of a jar of Vaseline, a coded celebration of gay sex. As the parade's final contingent, the MCC church choir marched behind a convertible carrying Perry and his lover while singing an enthusiastic rendition of "Onward Christian Soldiers."[45] The choice to hold a parade rather than merely a march was a point of pride for parade organizers, who boasted of this historic first on the event's fliers. "Never in the history of Western Civilization have homosexuals legally paraded in the streets of their cities," was the jubilant announcement.[46] New York may have claimed the first gay riots, but Los Angeles answered with the first gay parade.

Although the visual spectacle of the parade itself was enough to attract reporters, it was also followed with another attention-getting protest. Perry and a handful of supporters marched directly from the parade to a well-policed corner of Hollywood Boulevard, where they began a planned hunger fast for gay rights. The police, true to expectation, promptly made arrests. Perry spent a night in jail on charges of blocking the sidewalk, while two other activists, both lesbians, were released later the same day. Undaunted, Perry and members of the group reconvened the next day at the Federal Building, where they took advantage of jurisdiction formally outside of the purview of the Los Angeles police to continue a nine-day public hunger fast. The protests gained little more than public visibility, but local organizers counted the press attention as an important victory.

Troy Perry and Steve Jordan (*in rear of car*); Perry's mother, Edith Allen Perry
(*in front passenger seat*); and MCC members at Christopher Street West, 1970. ONE
National Gay and Lesbian Archives, Los Angeles.

Jim Kepner, who had been monitoring news coverage of homosexuality since the 1950s, estimated that Los Angeles activists garnered more press coverage over those ten days than in the previous two decades combined. The credit, in Kepner's assessment, went to Perry: "This young minister's faith, determination and infectious spirit had already worked wonders in the gay community," he reported.[47] From an adamant atheist and a longtime veteran of the homophile movement, this was not small praise. It also pointed to how Perry's faith brought attention to a larger story: the queer novelty of a gay minister hooked journalists into reporting on gay activism.[48]

That oddity, however, meant journalists of all kinds at times struggled for descriptive language for the purported "gay church." One interviewer, during a live radio broadcast, politely informed Perry that he did not regard him as a real minister and so would refer to him as "Mister" instead of "Reverend." Perry promptly hung up and followed up with a demand for a public apology, which the interviewer later provided.[49] A New York Times article on gay churches puzzled over the growth in the "ecclesial gay liberation movement," an unlikely phenomenon, since "homosexuals have generally felt about as comfortable in most local churches as early Christians did in the Coliseum."[50] Evangelical Christians were particular avid chroniclers of the gay church phenomena. The conservative Christian publication Christianity Today kept an attentive eye on the MCC during the early 1970s, and the first published study of that church was conducted by two conservative Protestant sociologists, Ronald Enroth and Gerald Jamison. For this wing of Christianity, Perry's faith was not taken as a sign of shared ground but as evidence of sacrilege. As a result of their study, Enroth and Jamison concluded, essentially, that the Christianity of the MCC was inauthentic cover for a fundamentally secular lifestyle, a "religious or spiritual dimension . . . tacked on in an attempt at securing moral legitimacy for homosexual behavior."[51] Added to the head-scratching of conservative critics, even some nonreligious activists in the gay movement interpreted the church as an oil-and-water mixture. One gay liberation activist, in an article in Gay, a New York–based newspaper, sarcastically asked about Perry, "Can a man who gets down on his knees to suck cock also kneel to worship his god without feeling hypocritical or schizophrenic?"[52] The implied answer was "no." The riddle of homosexuality and Christianity flummoxed observers of all sorts, who regarded a gay church as a contradiction in terms.

To be sure, Perry was one of the gay movement's more unlikely activists. Perry's preparation for leadership came from two institutions widely reviled by gay leftists: conservative Christianity and the U.S. military. Perry was a self-identified "cracker" from northern Florida who arrived in Southern California via the fundamentalist Moody Bible Institute in order to pastor the Santa Ana Church of God in Prophecy, a culturally conservative Pentecostal congregation filled with other white southern migrants to the Sunbelt suburbs. Perry and the congregation, devoted to "plain-folk religion," represented exactly the demographic that was gradually pushing Sunbelt politics rightward in the 1960s and 1970s. In 1963, however, Perry confessed to his presiding bishop that he was attracted to men. He was immediately ousted from the church, his wife and two sons left him to live with extended family, and Perry was drafted to serve in the military. After a two-year conscription in the armed services (in a noncombat role), the former preacher moved to downtown Los Angeles, where he took a job as a retail clerk and found a second family in the urban gay subculture.[53]

The idiom of that plain-folk religion, however, was important to the religious identity of the gay-welcoming church. Perry's particular brew of Christianity was not the justice-leaning wing of liberal Protestantism, where a vanguard of Christian authors worked out an accommodating view of homosexuality through deliberate synthesis with modern science. Perry's sermons and speeches bypassed the self-reflexive modernism of liberal Christians with a direct testimonial style. "The Lord is my Shepherd and He knows I'm gay" was a commonly referenced phrase in Perry's sermons and the title of his 1972 ghostwritten autobiography. In a single sentence, it joined the perceived gap between Christian conviction and gay identity with nothing less than God's intimate knowledge of the human heart. The phrase "and He knows" was perhaps the MCC's most effective suture for fusing gayness and Christianity into a seamless whole.[54] The same confidence in a conversational relationship with God informed the MCC's narrative of origin. Like the Stonewall narrative that came after it, this was a story about a police raid on a gay bar. In August 1968, police raided the Patch, a popular gay nightclub in South Los Angeles. Arrests included Perry's date that night, a Chicano pseudonymously named Carlos. Perry joined an impromptu protest led by the bar's gay owner, but his recollection of the event focused on a conversation with his friend after his release. Perry listened with an awakening sense of presence as his friend complained bitterly that no one—not even God—cared about gay people. A familiar "still small voice" prodded

Perry. "God, when do you want me to start the church?" he found himself asking. "Now!" was the reply. This story appeared in the *Los Angeles Advocate* when the MCC was only a few months old; it was told again in sermons and published on the church's anniversary.[55] Like the Stonewall narrative, the retelling of Perry's encounter with God in the wake of a bar raid provided more than a chronology of the past. It was a story of divine solidarity in homosexuals' most dreaded experience of powerlessness.

The Los Angeles MCC leapfrogged in a matter of months from a small gathering in Perry's living room to a congregation in the hundreds. Sunday services offered a polyglot liturgy: a preservice "Singspiration" of show tunes and favorite hymns, call-and-response preaching, and a weekly service of Eucharist conducted by clergy wearing formal liturgical robes.[56] "That's what happens when people with many varied background get together," Perry acknowledged in the church newsletter; "your turn will come, when something from your background will show up in services and people of other faiths could throw up their hands in horror."[57] The eclecticism drew even atheists like Jim Kepner, whose enthusiastic descriptions of the church in the *Los Angeles Advocate* doubtlessly attracted further followers. The church was "a center of a New Movement," Kepner wrote in October 1969; it welded together "people from different backgrounds, with different prejudices, [and] different expectations . . . into a united community."[58] The congregation did indeed represent an unusual demographic. MCC–Los Angeles in those years was predominantly white and male but also included a visible population of Latinos and a smaller number of African Americans. The greatest diversity represented was religion; participants in the church came from every major American denominational and faith tradition. The church even offered a category of affiliation for non-Christian "friends," which incorporated into the congregation a number of Jews, Buddhists, atheists, and others who did not hold Christian beliefs. The MCC, as a result, was a broadly ecumenical, even a multifaith, congregation.[59]

The church, under Perry's leadership, also demonstrably contributed to the activist energy in Los Angeles. Perry and members of local homophile organizations joined together in October 1969 to form a new activist organization, the Committee for Homosexual Law Reform, and the first mass demonstration was held the following month.[60] Held on a Sunday afternoon at the Los Angeles Civic Center, a location in the deserted downtown business district, the protest received no press coverage outside the already sympathetic *Advocate*. That newspaper nonetheless declared the demonstration a resounding success because of its impact on the participants themselves. "A new sense of pride" was visible, the reporter claimed, among the gathered demonstrators, who, by attending the event, "had come farther out of their 'closets' than ever before."[61] The rally was the first of a series of progressively larger demonstrations, which in December of that year also drew in the newly formed Los Angeles chapter of the GLF and its founder, Morris Kite, who collaborated with Perry to organize marches, vigils, and sit-ins. Perry's increasing political involvement at first elicited worried comments from some of the church's quietistic members.[62] "We're a church first, a community organization second, and we don't want to be politically involved," complained one member in the church newsletter.[63] Initial debates over whether to prioritize faith or politics, however, did not ultimately require an either/or choice. In the late summer of 1970, after Perry's public fast, a churchwide meeting over exactly this question widely affirmed Perry's political involvement as part of his ministry. This congregational vote established a foundational conviction: the spiritual identity of the MCC could not be separated from activism for gay rights.[64] Thus, it was also with the blessing of his congregation that Perry stepped into the national spotlight after the first commemoration of Stonewall.

Despite the outsider puzzlement over how Perry and the MCC reconciled faith and homosexuality, Perry's vocation as a minister was actually quite important to his legitimacy as a national gay rights leader. Since the 1964 founding of the Council on Religion and the Homosexual, clergy activists had served in leadership roles in the homophile movement, and many of the veteran activists in the movement saw Perry's clerical credentials as an extension of the ongoing need for the moral weight of clergy leadership. In 1970, homophile delegates to the final meeting of the North American Conference of Homophile Organizations elected Perry to moderate the meeting, a role previously held by the ministers affiliated with the CRH.[65] In a movement that already borrowed pages from the tactical playbook of the black freedom struggle, Perry's leadership was also compared to that of the slain civil rights leader Martin Luther King Jr. So often did he hear the comparison that Perry answered with a coy retort: "Martin Luther *Queen* might be more appropriate."[66] However, Perry also took up in earnest King's model of spiritual politics, a connection actively encouraged by Bob Ennis, a black gay man who moved from Arizona to join the MCC and quickly appointed himself Perry's personal assistant and founding editor of the MCC's national magazine.[67] The first issues of *In Unity*, under Ennis's editorial direction, gave homage to King and included editorials by Perry that commented on King's significance to the struggle for gay rights.[68] During the early 1970s heyday of gay liberation, Perry was undoubtedly the most widely recognized figure in the movement, with the characteristic black cassock as a memorable marker of his identity.

Perry and leaders in the growing "gay church" movement fused religion and political involvement as seamlessly as they joined faith and gay identity. Indeed, the movement seemed to grow precisely because of the way it turned seemingly unstable contradictions into a foundation for an activist ministry. The perceived conflicts—between Christianity and gay identity, faith and political involvement—cohered around a central conviction. As one MCC pastor put it in 1976, the mission of the MCC concerned a revelation from God received by Troy Perry in the wake of a bar raid. "The initial revelation was that God does love everyone, including gay men and women," this pastor explained; "the continuing revelation is that God wills a church to exist in this world to live and proclaim that message."[69] An experiential connection to divine truth—even a claim to a revelation—brought a particular power of conviction to the MCC's intertwined ministry and activism. The result, in the network of congregations that grew out of the Los Angeles church, was the formation of a Christian denomination, one of most conventional of American institutions, that took as its mission the righteous advocacy of one of the nation's most stigmatized causes.[70]

The axiom of church growth specialists in the early 1970s was that "weak churches"—liberal congregations that did not demand disciplined spiritual lifestyles and absolutist beliefs—were almost inevitably slated for decline.[71] On the face of it, the growing network of MCC congregations defied this logic: they were churches that embraced gay and lesbian lifestyles with deliberately ecumenical beliefs and practices. And they were growing, at first without any intention to branch out. The first few MCC congregations outside of Los Angeles were started by enterprising gay Christians who subsequently sought affiliation with the Los Angeles church. In response to these requests, the collective of congregations formed the United Fellowship of Metropolitan Community Churches in 1970, with five localities (Los Angeles, San Diego, San Francisco, Chicago, and Phoenix) represented at the new denomination's first General Conference. The following year, the represented localities quadrupled, and by 1976, the UFMCC had ninety church bodies in six countries.[72] The congregations adopted a governance structure modeled after Presbyterian polity, which struck a useful balance between national cohesion and local autonomy.[73] The UFMCC sustained stable, long-term growth and was, by 1977, the largest national grassroots gay organization in the United States.[74]

In many ways the UFMCC was not at all an exception to the prevailing logic of church growth. If a so-called strong church made high lifestyle demands on members and supported "absolutist" beliefs at odds with the prevailing culture, than there were few churches that fit the bill better than the growing collective of gay-welcoming congregations. As the UFMCC experienced exponential growth, 7 percent of its congregations were targets of arson or firebombing, and many local pastors also regularly experienced harassment and threats of violence. The most tragic incident occurred in New Orleans in 1973, on the day of the fourth commemoration of Stonewall. An arson attack on the Upstairs Lounge, a gay bar frequented by members of the local MCC, resulted in thirty-two lives lost, including the pastor and assistant pastor of the church.[75] As denominational leaders of the UFMCC presented it, these acts of violence were motivated by twin hatreds against the spiritual belief of the churches and their members' predominant sexual orientation.[76] The narrative told and retold in the face of these instances of violence and persecution emphasized God's solidarity with a persecuted minority and reiterated the church's commitment to stand for the truth of God's acceptance even in the face of violence. The call to "come out" as testimony to one's faith and the stance of principled critique against culturally pervasive homophobia were certainly both lifestyle demands and "absolutist" beliefs on par with what church growth specialists identified as the marks of a "strong" church.[77]

These commitments to faith and activism also made pastors and members of the UFMCC some of the most committed participants in the annual commemoration of Stonewall. In the meanings generated by gay Christians, the Stonewall narrative told a story of Christian theodicy that encouraged listeners to face homophobic violence and persecution with confidence in God's solidarity with the victimized. This narrative about triumph over suffering turned even arson into a redemption story. When the mother church in Los Angeles burned in 1973, the congregation held Sunday services in the street. "*I guess the closet has burned down!*" Perry declared to those gathered outside the fire-gutted building. "So we're hated! So what? So was the early Church! We *shall* overcome!"[78] The Upstairs Lounge fire in New Orleans, which took lives as well as a building, inspired memorial services around the country and drew in the participation of various congregations of the UFMCC, gay synagogues, and groups like Dignity and denominationally based gay caucuses.[79] For the UFMCC and for other gay and lesbian–welcoming religious organizations, gay pride was a fixture on the liturgical calendar—an opportunity for interfaith cooperation, special services, and collective participation in local events that honored the legacy of the New York riots.[80]

By the middle of the 1970s, it was clear that the UFMCC was neither an offshoot of a secular movement nor a way station to spur change in the religious establishment: it was a center and an establishment in its own right. Perry often declared, in the early years of the Los Angles MCC, that the gay-welcoming church's mission was to "preach itself out of business."[81] This axiom quickly came into question; by 1974, the UFMCC had appointed its own credentialing board with a tacit policy to encourage pastors who transferred ordination credentials from other denominations to commit wholeheartedly to the new denomination by relinquishing the other affiliations. The UFMCC was not going to put establishment churches out of business as quickly as its leaders might initially have hoped.[82] Even so, the gay-welcoming denomination did indeed provide inspiration and support to a movement for change in the Protestant establishment. Perry's unabashed stand as a gay minister and the various local outreach ministries to gay communities also motivated those in mainline churches to follow suit. For those in the mobilizing movement for establishment reform, the Stonewall narrative also resonated with intertwined spiritual and political meanings. For a generation of gay and lesbian mainline Protestants, the journey from shame to pride symbolized by Stonewall held layered meanings. It was a spiritual discipline as well as a strategy of institutional visibility; mainline Protestants made the interior journey public through coming-out confessions that made it clear that the challenge to establishment churches came from their own pulpits and pews. The most well known of these out-and-proud mainliners spent the morning of his ordination day celebrating San Francisco's first debut into gay pride.

Coming Out in the Mainline

San Francisco did not join the trend to commemorate Stonewall until 1972, the third anniversary of the riots. Except for a handful of participants in the San Francisco GLF, most of gay San Francisco sat out the first two celebrations of Christopher Street Liberation Day. The city was a latecomer not because its gay residents were politically inactive. Just the opposite: San Francisco's battles over police harassment and arrest preceded Stonewall by several years. The well-publicized response to the 1965 police raid on California Hall, which prominently involved area ministers, and protests by transgender women and drag queens in 1967 at Compton Cafeteria were both incidents in recent memory. The protests and organizing efforts galvanized by these events had helped create avenues for institutional redress against the kind of police harassment and violence that sparked the New York riots of 1969. San Franciscans were latecomers to the practice of commemoration because the struggle for identity pride symbolized by the Stonewall riots seemed to represent a battle that the proverbial "gay mecca" had already won.[83]

The San Francisco celebration showed how Stonewall could mark a collective liberation even for a community that did not see the actual event as a cause of its own political awakening—the symbol could work, in other words, even if the history did not. Organizers for San Francisco's first gay pride parade knit the Stonewall narrative into their own local history. Spearheading the plans for commemoration were two ministers, Bob Humphries and Ray Broshears, and planning meetings took place at Glide Memorial Methodist Church, which had long been a location for radical organizing.[84] Broshears and Humphries were both entrepreneurial gay ministers of a sort that seemed to flock to the Bay Area. Journalist Lester Kinsolving wrote an exposé of what he called "the paper priests," published in the San Francisco Examiner, which disparagingly cast doubt on the ministerial credentials of several self-declared priests.[85] Neither Broshears nor Humphries were named in the article, but they were certainly among the locally famous body of gay priests with credentials of an unknown provenance. An editor of Vector, newsletter of the Society of Individual Rights, gave up sorting through the priestly claims and complained that "there were so many people around S. I. R. center with clerical titles and collars that we haven't time to figure it all out."[86] Broshears and his colleagues, as part and parcel of their ministerial labor, were also skilled at creatively splicing and grafting traditions. The parade announcement that circulated in 1972 gave credit to the Compton Street riots rather than to Stonewall as the commemorative history for the parade. That earlier incident, the announcement claimed, was "the first ever recorded violence by Gays against police anywhere" and was thus the event that inspired San Francisco's celebration of "Christopher Street West." With some ritual sleight of hand, San Francisco's parade organizers replaced Stonewall with their own history, which provided local meanings for a commemorative practice imported from New York.

A similar practice of adopting and resignifying Stonewall also took place around another historic "first" that took place on that same day. The Golden Gate Association of the United Church of Christ had approved the ordination of William Johnson, a gay man, and his ordination service was scheduled for that Sunday evening. The date carried dual historic significance: it was not only the appointed anniversary celebration for Stonewall but also the fifteenth anniversary of the UCC denomination. Press coverage of the service cited both momentous anniversaries as milestones in the ordination of an openly gay minister. Fittingly, Johnson participated in two celebratory events that day: he was an honored participant in the gay pride parade, taking part in the journey to Golden Gate Park on the back of a red convertible, and that evening, at San Carlos Community Church, Johnson received ordination credentials in a ceremony that also celebrated his decision to come out as gay. The stole that marked Johnson's new religious authority was decorated with butterflies—"symbols of resurrection," the bulletin for the service explained. Just as the butterfly transformed from a "creeping, toiling caterpillar" into a "new creature, filled with new life," so Johnson's decision to come out of the closet was a personal "resurrection from fear" into "expectation and hope."[87] The symbolism took latent Christian themes in the metaphors of gay pride as a new birth and foregrounded a specifically Christian story: Johnson's decision to come out of the closet, like the caterpillar's departure from the chrysalis and Jesus's exit from the tomb, brought a spiritual transformation.[88]

The announcements that heralded Johnson's ordination also acknowledged the importance of "coming out" to the nature of this historic first. "Never before," journalist Evan Golder stated in the *Christian Century*, "has any major religious group *knowingly* ordained a homosexual."[89] The claim pointed to the novel publicity—the "*knowing*" of Johnson's sexuality. The UCC certainly had its share of gay ministers, some with identities already tacitly acknowledged. They included, most prominently, Rev. Robert Wood, the author of *Christ and the Homosexual*, which only thinly veiled the fact that the book addressed Wood's own experience. A longtime participant in the homophile movement, Wood continued to pastor a UCC congregation outside of New York City while also actively working for denominational change around homosexuality—he was the organizer, in 1971, of a Conference on Religion and Homosexuality in New York, which continued the homophile movement's ongoing efforts to educate denominational leaders. The difference: by avoiding the confessional pronoun "I" when speaking of homosexuality, Wood did not rehearse the narrative that plainly marked his own gay identity. Indeed, Wood was of the generation that coined the phrase "dropping hairpins" to refer to a different social genre, which performed gay identity without revealing it.[90] To the new generation of activists, like Johnson, the confessional declaration was more than a point of clarification; visibility was important to achieving identity pride. The elusive scripts of preceding generations were the self-loathing practices of the closet. The changing meanings of identity visibility, however, added an asterisk to the historic first. Johnson was not the first homosexual to be ordained, and he was not the first homosexual on whom church superiors knowingly conferred holy orders. But by coming out, Johnson invited a watching public into these transactions. He was the first person to be ordained with the knowledge—and democratic approval—of a broad sector of his denomination.

Johnson quite unmistakably admitted his homosexuality. He came out at a public forum that took place at the Pacific School of Religion (PSR) in November 1970, about a year and a half before the ordination. Berkeley in those days was a nest of countercultural radicalism, and the seminaries perched at the top of the colloquially dubbed holy hill were thoroughly in the mix. The Berkeley GLF was cofounded by a graduate student in theology, Nicholas Benton, who was also an editor of the radical newspaper *Gay Sunshine*.[91] From the outset, Benton connected Christianity and gay liberation—"The Homosexual Revolution Is the Jesus Revolution and It Is Total" was the title of a manifesto published in *Gay Sunshine*, which called homosexuals to follow the revolutionary example of Jesus into solidarity with all oppressed people.[92] Benton, along with seminary student Laurence de Vries, organized a gay seminarians group that began meeting at the PSR in the fall of 1970. A few weeks later, de Vries published his own manifesto in PSR's student newspaper, which proclaimed both his homosexuality and his plans to become a minister. The article sparked debate among students and faculty, with some pushing for de Vries's dismissal and others adamantly fighting for his place as both seminary student and minister. The gay seminarians group organized a chapel service and public panel to respond to the debate. In the midst of the heated question-and-answer session at the public panel, in front of some four hundred people, a soft-spoken young man with a slight southern accent stepped forward to admit that he too was gay. Johnson's disarming demeanor put a relatable face on the ordination question, and his confession also shifted the debate from the hypothetical to the specific: de Vries was someday hoping to be a minister; Johnson's ordination in the UCC was scheduled, at the time, for the following spring.[93]

Such public confession by gay ministers and seminarians surprised even progressive religious leaders, some of whom already quietly supported the ordination of homosexuals. The former president of Union Theological Seminary, who attended the session on homosexuality and ministry at PSR, told a reporter that the practice for addressing incidents of homosexuality during his tenure at Union always involved confidential "closed door meetings." The seminary did not dismiss gay students, but it did inform denominational superiors who had the ultimate say on matters of ordination.[94] A handful of progressive religious leaders had publicly stated the view that homosexuality should not be a bar from ministry, and it is likely that some of those "closed door" decisions resulted in ordination.[95] However, Protestant leaders, as well as the seminary students and ordination candidates, carefully avoided public attention on this controversial question. What surprised sympathetic religious leaders in the early 1970s was that the people who seemed most in need of confidential protection—gays and lesbians themselves—were the ones stepping forward to publicly reveal their identities.

The impetus for these confessions came in part from outrage over recently circulated sexuality studies. The United Presbyterian and the American Lutheran denominations approved sexuality education literature in the summer of 1970 that offered new guides for encouraging "healthy sexuality." The authors of this literature held to still-prevailing disease theories of homosexuality, even as they used the sickness theories to argue for moral and legal tolerance. Reviewed—and edited—by church delegates of various conservative and liberal perspectives, the study material that ultimately circulated offered a contradictory splice job that pleased almost no one. Conservatives in the denominations were not the only malcontents to accuse denominational executives of compromising their devotion to Christ with an unholy marriage to the therapeutic sciences. For some gay Christians, it was cause for revolution. "For a conscientious person to accept this pronouncement is to willingly lay himself out on a rack of ethical self flagellation," one gay Christian lamented; "in the teeth of such a quandary it is doubtless wiser to follow Luther into a rebellion against the ethical system itself."[96] Gay Christians confronted condemning religious teachings with a sense of moral outrage as they held a simultaneous crusade against disease theories: institutions of religion and science alike presented cultural legitimation for ideas that boiled down to irrational, archaic taboo. Allen Blaich, a gay Lutheran college student, lamented the focus on science found in liberal Protestant sexuality teachings. Christians should focus instead, he argued, on "the need for Christ's love and acceptance in understanding the gay person as a creation of the Father and thus a whole person."[97] For gay Christians, the newly circulating denominational literature on sexuality exposed the failure of institutional Christianity to follow a truly Christlike ethic. They confronted establishment churches with the conviction that authentic Christianity offered both a critique of antihomosexual condemnation and a model for righteous protest.

The "zaps" conducted by gay liberation groups were certainly one method in the arsenal of protest tactics, but another practice—the public avowal of gay identity—was even more destabilizing than the militant confrontations by presumed outsiders. The coming-out speeches by gay and lesbian Christians epitomized what various scholars have analyzed as a "politics of authenticity" that saturated the political Left of the 1960s and 1970s. Historian Doug Rossinow highlights the distinct Protestant influences on this political ethos. Christians on the political Left, he shows, took inspiration from avant-garde existentialist theologians like Paul Tillich and Dietrich Bonhoeffer, and they interpreted these thinkers in ways that put political teeth into ideals of spiritual wholeness and critiques of cultural alienation. In practices that resonated with this larger political sensibility, Christian gays and lesbians of the early 1970s pitted the power of genuine confession and authentic community against institutional demands for false conformity.[98]

These ideals shaped practices of self-inspection as well as public statements. Bill Silver, a Union Theological Seminary student and Presbyterian candidate for ordination, kept a journal of his coming-out process. It analyzed, in excruciating detail, his interactions with family members, friends, and other Christians with attention to the layers of shame and fear that made it difficult to authentically present his identity as a gay man. The goal of this humbling self-examination was to find the courage to "honestly relate" to himself and to others. Silver even mailed out a card to longtime friends announcing "the birth of himself as a gay person."[99] These practices of self-examination and confession also resonated through the paper that Johnson presented to the committee tasked with making a decision about his ordination. "I could not, in good conscience," Johnson stated, "take the vows of ordination without fully affirming who I am." He also acknowledged that such honesty opened up a difficult process of dialogue about his identity. This too was part of the demands of authenticity; "I do not believe the call to discipleship is a call to expediency," he wrote.[100] Coming out was a spiritual discipline as much as a political strategy: the practices of self-inspection and honest confession offered difficult paths to a new self and a genuine community. The coming-out statements of mainline Christians thus confronted the false cultural foundations of the therapeutic orthodoxy with a newly politicized gospel of authenticity.

As a strategy for institutional reform, however, the success of this practice of identity visibility rested on the foundations laid by an earlier generation of homophile organizers. The vote of approval for Johnson's ordination came out of the Golden Gate Association of Northern California, one of the few places where a broad sector of the denomination was prepared to accept a homosexual candidate for ordination. This support was not only a factor of the region's progressive demographic but also a direct result of the 1964-founded CRH, an organization formed by ministers connected to Glide Urban Center, which focused on educating ministers and local churches about homosexuality. The Golden Gate Association provided financial support to the CRH from its inception—the first denominational body to do so—and many area UCC ministers either were affiliated with the CRH or participated in the sexuality training provided through Glide Urban Center. UCC leaders' responses to Johnson's public confession drew from prior training. They chose to delay Johnson's scheduled ordination for more than a year to permit a process of education and dialogue for member churches and voting delegates in the association. When delegates finally met in May 1972 for an association-wide vote, they approved Johnson's ordination by a 2–1 majority.[101]

Coming out publicly meant that gay and lesbian ministers and ordination candidates replaced previous "closed door" processes with open, democratic deliberation by the appointed governing bodies of the denomination. Democracy was rarely kind; mainliners who "came out" in other locations and in other denominations faced decidedly mixed outcomes. A year before Johnson's ordination, another out minister— Houston Methodist Gene Leggett—was suspended from ministry by a 144–117 vote by delegates at the Southwest Texas regional Annual Conference.[102] And in March 1972, two months before Johnson's successful vote, the Northern Illinois conference of the Methodist church similarly voted to suspend out minister Charles Lamont from the ministry.[103] John Preston, an Episcopal layperson and coordinator of the Minneapolis Gay House, a ministry supported by local clergy, was denied acceptance from a course in the Lutheran Seminary of Saint Paul.[104] Presbyterian minister David Sindt, who led an outreach ministry to gays with the support of Lincoln Park Presbyterian Church in Chicago, began a long battle with the Ministerial Relations Committee of the Presbytery of Chicago, which initially denied the request to have his ordination credentials recognized.[105] In almost every case, the person in question had the support of a local congregation and sympathetic clergy, but such support was not enough to sway the majority vote of denominational delegates. It was not until 1977, when Ellen Barrett, an out lesbian, was ordained in the New York diocese of the Episcopal Church that a gay or lesbian candidate for ordination was again "knowingly" ordained to the ministry, and this was a decision made by a sympathetic (and closeted) bishop, Paul Moore. Even this victory sparked an immediate outcry from within the denomination. The subsequent meeting of the House of Bishops voted, with a dissenting minority, to forbid future ordination of homosexual candidates.[106]

In the short term, thus, the practice of openly admitting a sexual orientation was woefully ineffective as a strategy for change. The frequent result was institutional retrenchment rather than church reform. However, the various mainliners who publicly came out did achieve something else. The eye of the press and the ire of conservative church members placed a hothouse glare on individuals who became unwitting point persons for broader identity organizing within the denominations. For example, Rick Husky, a gay United Methodist, knew of the ousted Methodist Gene Leggett after reading an article about him in *Newsweek*. He recognized him at the following Methodist Annual Conference, and the collective that formed around that one publicly marked person became the organization Gay United Methodists, which in 1975 became the Methodist Gay Caucus.[107] Within a period of less than two years, between late 1973 and early 1975, gay caucuses formed within every mainline Protestant denomination, most of them mobilized around ministers and ordination candidates who publicly came out.[108] The publicity that sparked populist resistance in Protestant churches allowed gays and lesbians to find each other and organize collectively.

These efforts in collective organizing challenged church institutions but also benefited from the earlier connections forged by the CRH. When Johnson was unable to secure a church appointment, he instead became the executive director of the CRH in San Francisco. The CRH, despite the fact that it had little funding at this point, focused on supporting the efforts for change in mainline Protestant denominations. The National Council of Churches, which had also in previous years authorized study and education around homosexuality, agreed to appoint a task force on gay people in the church. However, this source of support was also tenuous: the NCC's earlier efforts encouraged dialogue and study *about* homosexuality; the task force composed *of* gays and lesbians received only an arms-length recognition as a dialogue partner.[109] None of the ordained participants on the task force, notably, had ministerial appointments in established denominations. In addition to Johnson, the group included Roy Birchard, an ordained minister in the UCC working as a secretary in the NCC; John Preston, an Episcopalian layperson and director of a CRH in Minnesota; and Roger Harrison, an American Baptist minister serving as an MCC pastor. Notably, the two women who participated—Louise Rose, an American Baptist layperson and the only African American in the group, and Susan Thornton, a Union Theological Seminary graduate and a hospital chaplain—were at that point not out publicly.[110] The task force's most significant symbolic gain was the 1975 endorsement from the NCC for gay civil rights. The vote gave formal approval to the public policy battles for nondiscrimination rights, even as it explicitly demurred on the issues of denominations' own hiring of gays and lesbians.[111] Policy statements were important ways to mark a sense of progress, but the most far-reaching gains came out of the collective networks that were built through these efforts for institutional reform.

The first histories of the new movement activism gave reflexive credit to Stonewall for sparking the church-based organizing. In 1974, Johnson, together with lesbian feminist activist Sally Gearhart, chronicled these church developments in a book published by Glide Urban Center, an organization that had been active in homosexuality politics since before Stonewall and that was still the alternative publishing center for radical Christian politics. *Loving Men/Loving Women* documented the emerging efforts for reform within the denominations and was interesting for the way that it gave homage to the Stonewall riots as an influence on the gay and lesbian activism in churches. The origin story only partly fit: the 1964-founded CRH and the momentum sparked by the 1968 formation of the MCC had as much direct influence on the denominational reform movement as the gay liberation movement that spread after 1969. Indeed, Johnson and Gearhart's narrative, after beginning with references to Stonewall, acknowledged and traced the particular influences of the CRH and the MCC on mainline Protestant reform efforts. Even activists like Gearhart and Johnson, whose histories stemmed largely from earlier influences, nonetheless credited the Stonewall riots as a symbolic beginning.[112]

What was new about the denominational activism of the 1970s was its attention to visibility through practices of "coming out." This may well be why the Stonewall narrative held such significance for those who chronicled the movement's history. Here, too, the memory of Stonewall was important for reasons other than quotidian chronology and earlier precedent. The symbolic journey from shame to pride also inhered within coming out, a practice of insider visibility that was important to the strategies for institutional reform. Johnson, in 1974, articulated this importance to a staff member of the recently formed National Gay Task Force, a nonreligious advocacy organization. Denominations, he argued, "will listen primarily to persons from *within* the respective structures, and, essentially, only when the issues have been personified, personalized via the coming out of persons whose commitment to the church is recognized."[113] Coming out thus made it clear that the challenge to institutional homophobia was not a co-optation mobilized by secular outsiders but a strategy by church members with shared Christian convictions. The mainline reformers were certainly not alone in conceiving the practice of coming out as an important way to push for institutional change from within. The National Gay Task Force was formed to mobilize a similar strategy of insider access and reform. Founded in 1973 with a focus on professional lobbying and legislative change, the task force, in one sense, represented another shift in movement activism. The manifestos and "zaps" of gay liberationists seemed a far cry from the ideals and tactics of the new political organizations, which were led by professional staff members who pressed for change in legislative offices and boardrooms. In this brave new world of insider access, the memory of the rioting queers of Christopher Street and the symbolic journey from shame to pride again shifted meaning. Reformers rehearsed what might be called "a Stonewall of the heart"—an interior journey from shame to pride confessed aloud to make visible an otherwise invisible sexual identity.

This did not mean that mainliners gave up marching in the streets. The Protestant gay caucuses, along with other gay religious organizations, were reliable participants in the annual pride commemorations. Protestant caucus leaders encouraged local chapters to march in pride parades with banners that made their presence known. Mainline church reform thus relied on a dual visibility—coming out with sexual identities in their respective churches while also publicly displaying denominational identities to a broader gay community. For countless Presbyterians, Lutherans, Episcopalians, and so on, the celebration of Stonewall held dual significance: it was a ritual that connected them to a broader lesbian and gay collective as it was also a practice of authenticity that compelled the truth-telling confessions to fellow church members.

Conclusion

Popular histories credit the riots on Christopher Street for bringing about a new moment in gay activism. Those popular accounts of the movement's "birth" exceed the evidence of history and chronology in many ways. We know that Stonewall was not the beginning of the movement or the first protest against the police or even the debut of radical activism. Stonewall did indeed serve as the inspiration for new movement activism, but even more important, those activists turned the inspirational meanings from the riots into a practice of commemoration. The collaborative efforts of veteran homophile organizers and new liberation activists put into place an annual demonstration that served as an important "first" for gay identity organizing. The nationally coordinated demonstrations that took place on the first anniversary of Stonewall brought unprecedented public participation and press attention to the lesbian and gay movement. The commemorative practice grew and expanded with each year and ultimately outlasted the gay liberation organizations that first claimed the legacy of the riots. Most of the gay liberation groups folded by 1972, and others changed their names to omit the leftist reference to a "liberation front."[114] Over time, even the annual commemoration shed its leftist and New York roots as the "Christopher Street Liberation Day"—the name adopted for the first commemoration—came to be popularly known as "gay pride."[115] But that change in name also reflected the way that the commemorative practice of Stonewall spread the movement ideology of gay liberation in ways that transcended the particular location of a street in Greenwich Village. Through the 1970s, activists in an expanding number of locales claimed the legacy of Stonewall by liberating their own streets and boulevards. The commemorative practices turned the event of the Christopher Street riots into a movement myth and a symbolic marker of a new identity. The collective displays of "out and proud" identity restructured the remembered past of Stonewall into the natal home of gay pride.[116]

This attention to the ritual and commemorative meanings of Stonewall is also important to the history of queer religious organizing, a story that has been decidedly left on the sidelines by most historical accounts of the movement in the 1970s. Most narratives about gay liberation activism, if they mention religion at all, focus on activists' critical challenge to religion, and the resulting picture is of a movement in which religion seems wholly absent. In fact, though, religious organizing intersected with every sector of an internally diverse movement. This chapter focuses on the history of lesbian and gay Protestants, but these groups were also part of organizing efforts that crossed every major faith tradition. The fact of these proliferating religious groups, I suggest, has been obscured by overly credulous approaches to the movement narrative about Stonewall. Histories focused on the rioters of Christopher Street and the radical activism they inspired convey a story of secular political origins that seems markedly at odds with religious identity. As a result, those who claimed faith during this era of movement radicalism seem like added appendages whose efforts strained to bridge the natural divide between the normatively nonreligious queer identities and the normatively antigay religious ones.

This chapter highlights the ways that the Stonewall narrative itself spanned those seemingly oppositional identities. The account of the fighting dykes and riotous drag queens of Christopher Street and the commemorative practice that their protests inspired may seem like a rejection of religion, but this narrative and its commemoration has had a peculiarly religion-like quality. For the gay Christians whose stories I tell in this chapter, the Stonewall narrative and its commemoration conformed to the plotlines of a familiar Christian story. This scripted performance of identity did not uproot religion and replace it with gay pride; it performed gay pride as a religious identity. In the Christian terms, that is, the protesting dykes and drag queens were figures of ritual identification in a narrative about the triumphant overcoming of the despised and the rejected. They were more than historical agents; they were Christ-figures whose suffering and triumph could be claimed by those who retraced their steps to be reborn into a new identity. We see these echoes in the MCC's celebration of a "freedom revival in lavender"; in a gay Christian's circulated announcement of his new birth into gay identity; and in the ordination candidates' allusions to "coming out" as a Christian resurrection. This Christian hagiography seems like a wild appropriation only for those who credulously hold to the Stonewall narrative and the attached claims about rupture and rebirth as a simple fact of chronology. The Christian interpretations overlapped with the broader ritual meanings of a movement myth.

This overlap between Christian and secular narrations of Stonewall were especially visible in the gay pride protests of June 1977. The date was significant: gay pride that year took place just three weeks after an overtly religious antigay campaign succeeded in South Florida. With Southern Baptist gospel singer Anita Bryant at the helm, the campaign riled up lesbian and gay communities across the country with condemning moral rhetoric and comparisons of homosexuals to child molesters. The timing of the antigay defeat—on June 7—gave communities a running start to prepare for gay pride. When thousands gathered in the nation's largest cities and hundreds showed up for debut protests in other locations, *Time* called it "the biggest nation-wide protest demonstration since the days of the anti-war movement."[117] Mainstream newspapers put particular emphasis on activists' anger against religion—a Boston gay man's attempted Bible burning circulated widely, as did New Yorkers' protest in front of St. Patrick's Cathedral.[118] However, the gay newspaper the *Advocate* presented a different story about religion. The cover of the magazine's "Pride issue" presented "A Movement 'Born Again.'"[119] The language was in part a tongue-and-cheek response to Bryant's own born-again faith, but journalists and editors discussed how the antigay campaign did indeed bring a kind of renewal to the movement. What some authors presented as metaphor, however, was for one minister a testament of faith. A featured quotation from a Houston-based lesbian minister of the MCC suggested that the surge in activism was indeed a kind of born-again renewal. The antigay campaign was an "instrument of the Lord," she claimed; "it took Anita Bryant to bring this many of our brothers and sisters out of their closets. And after tonight, they'll never return."[120] Religious metaphors held multivalent meanings in this article. "Coming out," to various spokespersons, both *was* and was *like* a religious conversion. The fact that both meanings could coexist showed the ways that narratives of sexual identity already overlapped at a porous border between the secular and the religious.

Those overlapping meanings, however, would come to seem only more fraught and more oppositional over time. The antigay campaign of 1977, as the epilogue will show, brought the beginnings of a new religious politics and with it a newly consolidated antigay tradition.

EPILOGUE
Afterlives of an Invented Past

Truth is undoubtedly the sort of error that cannot be
refuted because it was hardened into an unalterable form
in the long baking process of history.

—Michel Foucault, "Nietzsche, Genealogy, History"

In June 30, 1986, the Supreme Court ruled on the constitutionality of sodomy laws in *Bowers v. Hardwick*. The case concerned a gay man in Atlanta,
Georgia, whom police arrested for an act of consensual oral sex that took
place in his own bedroom. At the time, Georgia was one of twenty-five
states that continued to outlaw sodomy, holdouts against a national trend
toward repeal that began in the mid-1960s and gained momentum through
the 1970s. Advocates for lesbian and gay rights watched hopefully as this
case wended its way through the legal system. Sponsored by the American
Civil Liberties Union, it seemed to offer a textbook example of how the law
violated citizens' right to privacy, a right with considerable precedent in
recent rulings. Gay rights advocates responded with dismay when the ruling, closely split 5–4, upheld the particular enforcement of these sodomy
laws to target same-sex behavior. The majority ruling held that the American
Constitution did not confer the "right to engage in homosexual sodomy."[1]

A concurring opinion by Justice Warren Burger controversially invoked
religion as a rationale for legal sanctions against homosexual behavior.
Burger's opinion provided a hasty genealogy of sodomy laws and cited biblical texts and Christian teachings as historical anchors for a prohibition
that was "firmly rooted in Judeo-Christian moral and ethical standards."
To repeal the law, Burger insisted, was to "cast aside millennia of moral
teaching." In Burger's own terms, the law's religious underpinnings were
justified because they were rooted in a broad moral consensus. The reference to a "Judeo-Christian" tradition invoked a shared inheritance of
Protestant, Catholic, and Jewish condemnation against homosexuality to
make the point that this law did not enshrine a particular creed but a shared

moral ideal. However, Burger cited an odd source for this religiously capacious condemnation. Information about the "millennia of moral teaching" supporting the law came from a single footnoted source— Derrick Sherwin Bailey's *Homosexuality and the Western Christian Tradition*.[2]

Those who disagreed with the ruling pointed to Burger's opinion as something of a slip-up—an unwitting revelation of the unconstitutional establishment of religion that propped up what was already an unconstitutional violation of privacy rights. Justice Harry Blackmun, in a blistering dissent, singled out Burger's opinion as a view that actually undermined the majority ruling. Just because "religious groups condemn the behavior at issue," Blackmun argued, "gives the State no license to impose their judgments on the entire citizenry."[3] According to Blackmun, what his fellow justice's opinion confirmed was that the animating rationale for sodomy laws was religious intolerance. Later commentators added to Blackmun's critique by exploring the odd reference to Bailey's book on Western Christianity as a supposedly definitive source of the law's Judeo-Christian foundations. Janet Jakobsen and Ann Pellegrini, in their analysis of this case, point to the footnote as smoking-gun evidence of Burger's overreach—the reference and the history outlined in the opinion offered not a moral consensus nor religion in general nor even a broad Christian heritage. Rather, Jakobsen and Pellegrini argue, this religious rationale for American sodomy laws rested on a distinctly Protestant genealogy. Burger's origin story told of laws bequeathed to the early American colonies through the codes of Protestant-governed Great Britain. "*Hardwick* is an example," they argue, of the "maintenance of religious—Protestant—authority in the guise of sexual law."[4] Burger's opinion raised the curtain, so to speak, on the otherwise invisible Protestant scaffolding that propped up the legal regulation of sex.

This book suggests that Protestantism did much more than prop up the legal regulation of sodomy. It played an important role on all sides of the twentieth-century politics of homosexuality. Jakobsen and Pellegrini allude to the influences of a "stealth Protestantism" in the politics on both sides of gay rights battles, and this book traces out the history supporting this claim.[5] Indeed, Bailey's *Homosexuality and the Western Christian Tradition* could be taken as a linchpin in the broader history of Protestant influence on homosexuality politics. Tracing out Bailey's ideas and their expansive connections illuminates more than the vestigial Protestant influences in American law or the reanimated Protestant force in antigay politics. It also shows how Protestant ideals and practices were important to pro-gay politics in general and to the history of sodomy law repeal in particular. What that telltale footnote highlights is the way that a particular liberal Protestant tradition helped to establish the ground rules for a late twentieth-century debate over sexuality, which appeared to take place across a religious-versus-secular divide.

Bailey's book was an odd choice as a reference to support sodomy laws. It was odd not only because the title made specific reference to Christianity but also because the book plainly supported the other side of the case. Bailey, an Anglican clergyman, published *Homosexuality and the Western Christian Tradition* in 1955 as a supporting treatise for the movement to repeal sodomy law in Great Britain. Bailey had served on the Wolfenden Committee, which influentially advocated for sodomy law repeal. The book supported two sides of an axiomatic legal argument, which proceeded on the logic of religious disestablishment. Matters of private morality—and particularly sexual behavior committed in private by consenting adults—should be the business of the church, but they should not be the concern of civil magistrates. On the first point, Bailey's book made the case that homosexual behavior was indeed immoral according to Christian teaching. Bailey's thorough survey of biblical texts confirmed that a handful of "definite cases" condemned what Bailey carefully termed "homosexual behavior." On the second point, however, Bailey also roundly challenged the idea that the Bible was a law book. "Accurate exegesis" of the Bible, he argued, did not support the punitive reach of the law in matters of homosexuality any more than in other issues of sexual morality.[6] The book and Bailey's influential involvement also provided an influential model for liberal clergy, effectively establishing a third mandate for sodomy law repeal: clergy, as public arbiters of morality, should offer their principled opposition to legal practices that singled out homosexuals for unfair harassment and punishment. By the time the British Parliament voted to repeal English sodomy laws in 1967, this cause also gained acknowledged support from leading Protestants and other religious figures in the United States. In both Britain and the United States, established liberal Protestants advocated for sex law repeal. For these voices of the religious establishment, separating private morality from public law was not simply a procedure for secularization; it was also a religious principle.

Previous chapters of this book trace the changing nature of progressive American clergy support for gay rights. The postwar argument for separating morality from law evolved over time to become a robust moral imperative for the social and legal inclusion of an unjustly stigmatized sexual minority. When *Homosexuality and the Western Christian Tradition* was first published, it was widely discussed in the pages of homophile journals, and the British model of clergy support for homosexual law reform encouraged American organizers in the emerging identity movement to cultivate alliances with liberal clergy. Through the 1960s, the cause of sodomy law reform gained increasing support from liberal and moderate clergy. By the late 1960s, even the conservative evangelical periodical *Christianity Today* included reviews of Bailey's book that agreed with his legal recommendations. Even more important, the homophile movement, working hand in hand with progressive clergy, began to stretch the mandate for legal reform from disestablishment to identity pride. Activists working with the Council on Religion and the Homosexual in various cities authored and circulated a robust moral imperative for ending punitive laws and for challenging stigma and harassment. Clergy allies gave both symbolic cover and instrumental support for a coalescing identity movement for gay rights. Liberal Protestant ideas and practices, as I show in the previous chapter, continued to shape the liberationist politics of the 1970s. What looked like a secular movement predicated on challenging religious condemnation had from the very beginning drawn on liberal Protestant involvement and support.

What was not visible in either the politics of disestablishment or the politics of liberation was that the condemning tradition of antihomosexual regulation was in fact a recent invention. Liberal Protestants, including Bailey, had played an important, if unwitting, part in producing a new Christian tradition. The "definite cases" that Bailey found in his exegesis of the Bible and homosexuality offered a new set of biblical texts that were detached from an earlier interpretive tradition centered on Sodom and reinterpreted to focus specifically on same-sex behavior. These interpretive choices ratified views of sexual disease and health coming out of the fields of psychology and psychiatry, which divided sex in two: they presented heterosexuality as right and natural and homosexuality as a lurking illness. The opposition between healthy heterosexuality and unhealthy homosexuality took up the patina of longstanding tradition as Christians implanted these assumptions into their texts and teachings and thus into a retroactive sense of the past. American liberal Protestants were particularly eager purveyors of this medical approach. Their burgeoning postwar genre of therapeutic advice popularized a new therapeutic approach to sexuality. These texts labored to instill a wholesome view of sex (as heterosexual desire and attraction) by dispelling lingering taboos and old dogmas that might inhibit natural development. This therapeutic approach was also central to leading liberal Protestants' advice on homosexuality: it could be prevented and possibly cured through a nonjudgmental approach, which would emancipate (and straighten) the natural attractions. What these leading thinkers did was to circulate and ratify what I call a "therapeutic orthodoxy," a Christian understanding of sexuality that effectively reconfigured received prohibitions against unnatural and disordered sex to increasingly point toward same-sex sexuality. At the same time, they also insisted that the mechanism for preventing and curing homosexuality was to lift—through therapy—the condemnatory weight of precisely these dogmas. The judgments from which liberal Protestants sought to emancipate unhealthy homosexuals were in large part a tradition of their own making, a modern mutation of a religious past that newly specified same-sex behavior as a singular category of deviance.

This invented past also influenced Protestant conservatives. Here, too, previous chapters of this book show the way that evangelical and conservative Protestants worked to adopt and adapt the therapeutic views of sexuality first circulated by their liberal counterparts. It was Protestant liberals like Bailey and the American translators of the Revised Standard Version of the Bible who first began to systematically appraise—and thus to reshape—a set of biblical texts "about" homosexuality. It was liberals, in step with broader establishment Protestant engagement with the therapeutic sciences, who first used the medical neologism "homosexuals," as an apt English translation for a particular passage in 1 Corinthians. It was liberals who first interpreted a particular passage in Romans through the disease theories of developmental psychiatry. Those verses, in earlier decades, had communicated other commonsense meanings. Conservative Protestant leaders, even into the mid-1960s, continued to interpret these texts as references to masturbation or as warnings against deviant lust between unmarried women and men. Through the 1960s, however, evangelicals followed the precedent of liberals and began to sift through the insights of psychology and psychiatry on their own terms. Conservatives, too, began to implant into their texts and traditions the doubled assumption that heterosexuality was innate to the created order and homosexuality was a sinful perversion. They began to reorient previous prohibitions against unnatural and deviant sex to point specifically toward same-sex behavior. Those shifting teachings helped clear the way for a distinct evangelical version of the sexual revolution—by the 1970s, conservative Christian advice books circulated to married couples a born-again and biblically-bounded pro-sex gospel. The rising injunctions to heterosexual married pleasure proceeded with the logic of binary opposition to an unnatural and unhealthy homosexuality. The tradition that animated antigay politics was formed as conservatives adopted and adapted their liberal counterparts' therapeutic orthodoxy.

This book shows that Protestant ideas and practices played a formative role across all sides of twentieth-century sexuality politics. Tracing out the prior influence of liberal Protestant authors, reformers, and activists thus highlights a dynamic process of cultural innovation that was decidedly eclipsed, even obscured, by a political and religious shift of the late 1970s that was widely—and inaccurately—portrayed as a "religious backlash." The language of backlash presented religion as a retrogressive force that preserved an older social order of gender and sexual regulation. Thus, it was not only the developments of the late 1970s but also the interpretive narratives about those developments that obscured the more expansive influence of religious liberals on the politics of sexuality. Turning to the history of those developments answers a final perplexity about the 1986 Hardwick case: how a liberal Protestant treatise for sodomy law repeal could so easily be repurposed as uncontested support for precisely the opposite cause.

By the time of the Bowers v. Hardwick ruling, the earlier history of liberal Protestant support had been thoroughly eclipsed by a very different public voice in the politics of homosexuality. The pivotal year was 1977, when an antigay campaign in South Florida brought the first of a longer line of antigay voter initiatives. With Southern Baptist gospel singer Anita Bryant as a figurehead, the Save Our Children campaign canvassed for grassroots support from the diverse religious population of the Miami area, which overwhelmingly voted to roll back the slim gains of Florida gay rights activists.[7] Although Save Our Children soon folded, it proved to be only one part of a growing network of conservative Protestant lobbying and activist organizations founded around the same time, including the Moral Majority, Focus on the Family, Christian Voice, and Washington for Jesus. Over the next few years, this network, collectively known as the Christian Right, gained grassroots support and political influence for a socially conservative politics of "moral values." These activists presented religion as a sui generis source for a politics led by the convictions of true believers, and they cast the gains of gay rights, feminism, and abortion (among other issues) as the antireligious encroachment of secular move- ments. Partisan narrative and outsider commentary alike presented a consolidating Christian Right as a "religious backlash" against secular gains.[8]

The broad narratives about a religious backlash elided the cultural and demographic shifts at work in these developments: this was not a generic return of religion but rather the mobilization of a particular sectarian alliance. Nor did the new voting bloc represent a "return" of religion to politics. Religious leaders and practitioners had been prominently involved in political movements of the previous decades—they were a visible part of the African American civil rights movement and the feminist movement and, as previous chapters show, were involved in supportive activism for gay rights.[9] Nor did the new conservative politics represent the political debut of conservative white Protestants, who had been politically active in various campaigns and issues of the previous decades. Rather, the shift toward conservative religious political influence was not a return but a consolidation. The rhetoric of moral values skirted important dynamics of race, class, and geography, which were important to the formation of a particular alliance between socially conservative white voters and the Republican Party. Over the course of the 1980s, this alliance of white conservative Protestants and Republican operatives succeeded, as historian Daniel Williams quips, "in turning the GOP into 'God's Own Party.'"[10] Although this collective of Christian Right organizations was never able to completely achieve the groups' legislative goals, the partisan inroads gave them broad influence over public discourses of religion and politics. Their intervention in public policy discussions of gender and sexuality worked to effectively define religion as social conservatism.

To be sure, such public influence was possible in part because of the absence of an equally visible religious counternarrative. Conservative Protestants' longtime liberal contenders were rapidly losing ground. The once-influential "mainline" was now a "sideline" or "oldline."[11] Adding to the woes of declining numbers and finances was the fact of these denominations' own internal battles over homosexuality. In the 1960s and through the early 1970s, progressive-leaning wings of mainline denominations actively supported radical activism on a number of political issues, including gay rights. The support cultivated by that early activism was critical to the 1970s formation of denomination-based gay and lesbian identity groups, even as the "coming-out" practices by the new activists made it seem as if gay and lesbian organizing was taking place for the first time. Within a few years, these organizing efforts began to run up against bureaucratic processes, as the appeals for lesbian and gay inclusion were taken up as policy issues to be addressed by task forces, committees, and denominational legislative bodies. Mainline institutions were already navigating recurring conflicts among internally divided memberships, which spanned evangelical-leaning traditionalists to adamant liberals. The debates over homosexuality, in most denominations, fell into the familiar conflict cycle over scriptural authority and modern interpretation that animated recent disagreements over women's ordination and sexuality education. The mobilization and countermobilization across these fissures brought the beginnings of policy battles over ordination and same-sex unions that would continue well into the twenty-first century. Churches' official statements and policies visibly reflected the internal dissent. By the 1980s, most mainline denominations had adopted formal bans against ordaining open lesbians and gays to ministry even as they also endorsed public policy support for gay rights. Mainline churches continued to have dedicated supporters of lesbian and gay rights, but the internal dissent made it difficult if not impossible for these supporters to stake out a direct moral imperative in the public policy debates over gay rights.[12]

The very terms of the debate, moreover, obscured the history of liberal Protestants' prior involvement in gay rights history. The debates figured gay and lesbian "inclusion" as a question of Christians' openness to challenges and changes that originated from outside of their traditions. The rhetoric made it seem, as theologian Mark Jordan has stated, as if lesbian and gay appeals for inclusion were "an alien menace that attacks churches from the stratosphere."[13] The spatial metaphors of the debate figured the ethics of homosexuality as a question prompted by secular developments. With a picture of the tradition as normatively antihomosexual, those who pressed for welcome seemed to be advocating that Christians should make the tradition less religious—to leave behind some of the strictures of piety in order to accommodate new secular interlopers. The anxious questions over Christian teaching concerned the ends to this process of liberalization—what would be left of the faith once its boundaries were dissolved by the practice of increasing openness and inclusion? These terms set practitioners before a forked path; the options were either orthodoxy or inclusion.

The dynamics of religious insides and secular outsides were especially visible in the debates over biblical interpretation. The particular terms, however, were a legacy of earlier liberal Protestants' inquiries. Indeed, Derrick Sherwin Bailey was one important influence on the pathways of this rhetorical battle. *Homosexuality and the Western Christian Tradition* effectively circulated a particular interpretive approach to the biblical record on homosexuality. It distinguished between "act" and "condition" as a way to mark an epistemological gap between biblical and modern views of sex. This distinction, to be sure, had precedent in the earlier writing of psychiatrists and psychologists. Sexologist Havelock Ellis in 1897 parsed through the ways that his approach to a "psychic sexual condition" addressed an interior clockwork of same-sex desire that could not be equated with the older category of sodomy (which Ellis defined as a "sexual act of intercourse *per anum*, even when carried out heterosexually").[14] But it was Bailey and other midcentury liberal Protestant writers who made a version of this conceptual distinction into a hermeneutical principle for biblical exegesis. In doing so, these interpreters also retroactively redefined the older sodomy discourse. "Strictly speaking," Bailey wrote in 1955, "the Bible and Christian tradition know nothing about *homosexuality*; both are concerned with the commission of homosexual *acts*."[15] It was this distinction that not only interpreted but rather actively generated a category called "homosexual acts" as an idea with ancient and biblical meaning. The modern foil, of course, was the interiorized "condition," a category that users recognized as a modern innovation, a discovery of the medical sciences. Later authors exchanged the disease reference of "condition" for the more neutral term "sexual orientation," but the hermeneutical distinction remained the same. What stood in for tradition was the Bible's act-based condemnation. The dominant terms of the debate reinforced a sense of the Christian past as normatively homophobic. Those who advocated for lesbian and gay inclusion seemed to be drawing from resources for critique and reform that came not from Christianity itself but from a secular ethos of inclusion and tolerance.

This perception—that churches staged derivative sectarian versions of a broader secular battle—overlooked the ways that defining terms of public policy battles overlapped with a long-standing Protestant theological divide. James Davidson Hunter's now classic *Culture Wars* offers what is still a reigning account of the political divisions of the 1980s. Hunter's argument was that 1980s debates over social issues like gay rights, abortion, and gun rights fractured the American public across a new divide that crossed faith communities as well as public politics. Competing factions were driven by either "the impulse toward orthodoxy" or "the impulse toward progressivism."[16] Hunter argued that this division split Protestant, Catholic, and Jewish communities as well as American public politics more broadly. However, his analysis also suggests that the language of public square debates over tradition and progress were fought in a Protestant idiom that reanimated the terms of a residual Protestant fundamentalist/modernist divide.[17] The seemingly descriptive terms for tradition and modernity and the seemingly neutral categories of the religious and the secular in fact followed a Protestant map. Even the part of the secularists—who argued that religion should be disestablished from public politics and that sexuality should be emancipated from religious restrictions—took up a cause that proceeded from the Protestant logic of religious disestablishment. It was not that liberals in churches adopted a version of secularism but that the entire terms of public policy battles proceeded on Protestant terms.

But the analysis of what counted as religion and tradition also missed the way that the entire map and its compass point had already been reconfigured to fit within modern categories. The spokespersons of the Christian Right presented the plain testimonies of their Bibles as evidence for a traditional worldview. The narratives both by and about these religious activists presumed a long antigay religious tradition. Newly galvanized believers sought to defend that tradition and to reinstate its authority in civic law. They saw their challengers as secular activists who wished to sever the nation from its rightful religious anchors. Evangelicals— and many conservative religionists—spoke of the prohibitions against homosexuality as an important part of this biblical worldview, and they found support for that world in the plain words of their Bibles. However, the new antihomosexual tradition appeared plainly in the Word of God because those words themselves had been recently revised. For conservative Protestants, those revisions were also recent history. It was not until the mid-1970s that conservative Protestants began to write and reflect at length on the biblical teaching about homosexuality. The direct impetus to stake out this orthodoxy was not a secular movement for gay rights but the heterodox interpretations within conservative Protestants' own ranks. Leading conservatives were concerned about liberal Christian pro-gay interpretations, and they were also worried about a small but vocal movement for gay and lesbian acceptance emerging within evangelical institutions.[18] This group included Ralph Blair, who led the organizing efforts for Evangelicals Concerned, an affinity group for gay evangelicals that formed in 1975; and Letha Scanzoni and Virginia Ramey Mollenkott. Both respected Christian authors, Scanzoni and Mollenkott's best-selling, pro-gay treatise, *Is the Homosexual My Neighbor?*, made an argument that even critics acknowledged took biblical authority seriously.[19] When those critics responded to pro-gay Christian arguments, they adopted the pre-existing map of relevant passages even as they upturned the arguments for toleration and acceptance. The first systematic writing by conservative Protestants to defend a biblical condemnation of homosexuality, in other words, was a defensive response to previous liberal and pro-gay Christian arguments.

These debates were important because they showed the covert ways that the interpreted meanings of the Bible changed over time, even for conservatives who strongly insisted upon biblical authority. What conservatives defended as tradition was in many ways a reanimated version of what Bailey, in *Homosexuality and the Western Christian Tradition*, presented as evidence of the Bible's condemnation against "homosexual acts." Antihomosexual conservatives hewed closely to what they saw as the plain evidence of biblical authority—that scripture did indeed prohibit "homosexual acts." Their opponents argued that Christians needed to carefully interpret these prohibitions in historical context and with attention to recent evidence that homosexuality was an unchangeable condition or orientation. The debates fell into preexisting disagreements between Protestant liberals and conservatives about how to interpret the Bible. Liberals emphasized historical critical methods that cultivated a critical distance between the reader and the perceived meanings of scripture. Through this deliberate attention to interpretation, liberals challenged and reinterpreted seemingly plain Bible prohibitions on the grounds that they should not be seen as timeless rules but as contextual practices. In contrast, those who professed an attachment to the plain or literal meanings of the Bible accused their opponents of arguing away those clear meanings that conveyed the Bible's unchanging authority.

In practice, however, conservatives' attachment to biblical authority was key to a process of authorizing change in the supposedly bedrock text. Critical to the process of consolidating a new orthodoxy was the 1978 publication of the New International Version (NIV). This Bible translation was the evangelical answer to the "liberal" Revised Standard Version, and it quickly surpassed the King James as America's best-selling Bible. The RSV was the first Bible to use the term "homosexuals" in the plain text—in a New Testament passage in 1 Corinthians. The RSV also excised some "sodomites" from the plain text as well. The KJV has several Old Testament passages that reference "sodomites" as ancient pagan idolaters; the RSV and most subsequent translations changed these figures to "cult prostitutes." These changes tracked along a therapeutic logic, which narrowed the meanings of sodomy to homosexual behavior and thus sloughed off the previously attached meanings of idolatry. This set of translation changes were also carried forward by the evangelical translators of the NIV, whose choices challenged a number of the other RSV precedents. In the translation choices for passages referencing sodomites and other ancient sexual sinners, evangelicals belatedly followed liberals' modern therapeutic paradigm. They, too, reconfigured an older sodomy tradition into an emergent homosexuality tradition.[20] Thus, the NIV translation worked to ratify and authorize a new antihomosexual tradition. Translators not only changed the Bible's meanings but changed the wording to make plain newly understood meanings. The debate over whether a modern notion of a sexual orientation should moderate the Bible's plain prohibitions against "homosexual acts" obscured the more fundamental changes in modern Bibles. The seemingly plain tradition of homosexual prohibition was itself a product of earlier interpretive changes that through the process of translation became embedded into the words of the text.

Conservative Christians encountered a newly manufactured anti-gay tradition in the pages of their Bibles, and the late twentieth-century explosion of new Bible products also further expanded and cultivated readers' connections to those newly plain meanings. Conservative Protestant publishing companies offered an expanding array of what religion scholar Paul Gutjahr calls the "culturally relevant Bible."[21] Glossy covers, attractive images, and magazine-like styles were important to the consumer packaging of new translations, paraphrase editions, and Bible study tools. They offered the Bible as a lifestyle product with to-the-minute wisdom for everyday choices. These Bible products illustrate a second important aspect of conservative Christian practices of literalism. In addition to avowed fidelity to biblical authority, the practice of literalism also conveyed a personal and affective relationship to the text and its divine author—the Bible not only speaks authoritatively but speaks *to me*.[22] Indeed, the format of late twentieth-century Bible products actively cultivated this sense of closeness. Formats that elicited readers' personal engagement with the text also gave material meaning to the repeated injunction to "hide God's word in your heart." The Bible's meanings were not an external authority but an interiorized truth. The personal attachment to the Bible's meanings served as a mechanism for the production of a distinctive sexual self. When evangelicals spoke of the ways that biblical authority marked out a distinct practice of sexual behavior—sexual abstinence, heterosexuality, and marital fidelity—they were not speaking of a rote performance of external rules but were referring, rather, to living out a deeply embedded sense of self. The political rhetoric of "defending moral values" might communicate to outsiders an adherence to external rules and authorities; for the born again, however, the affective personal life of faith was about being authentic to an interior truth.

Indeed, we should notice at this juncture how religious claims to sexual authenticity worked to form identities in ways similar to those of gays and lesbians. An example from the late 1970s illustrates the comparable patterns in sex and lifestyle advice represented in two subcultural iterations of sex manuals. The standard in this genre was Alex Comfort's *The Joy of Sex* (1972), a runaway best-seller that translated recent sex research into practical how-to techniques. Evangelicals followed suit with Tim and Beverly Lahaye's *The Act of Marriage: The Beauty of Sexual Love* (1976). Published the next year were Charles Silverstein and Edmund White's *The Joy of Gay Sex: An Intimate Guide for Gay Men to the Pleasures of a Gay Lifestyle* and Emily L. Sisley and Bertha Harris's *The Joy of Lesbian Sex: A Tender and Liberated Guide to the Pleasures and Problems of a Lesbian Lifestyle*. There were certainly important differences in these texts—the books for gays and lesbians addressed lovers rather than spouses and offered advice for navigating non-monogamous and multiple-partner encounters. But evangelicals also fostered ideals of sexual authenticity and pleasure for a distinctive subcultural identity, one marked by a unique sexual essence that was created by God and set apart by principled avowal to moral boundaries. Christian sex advice texts, not unlike the gay and lesbian version of this genre, coached couples who identified with an outside-the-mainstream sexual lifestyle in the techniques that helped them realize the intrinsic pleasures of that outsider status. Taken together, these texts added a maxim to the Sermon on the Mount: blessed are the marginalized, for they shall have the greatest sex.

In many ways, it makes sense to speak of the moral politics of Christian Right supporters as a kind of identity politics—even a particular *sexual* identity politics. A number of religion scholars have emphasized that evangelical commitments of biblical authority and born-again identity were important in staking out a distinct subcultural identity. And rightly ordered practices of gender and sexuality were also an important part of that identity. In the late 1970s and early 1980s, a list of new books by conservative Christian authors outlined this new orthodoxy in respect to homosexuality. That emergent tradition insisted on the Bible's plain condemnation of homosexual acts and acknowledged the psychiatric research on sexual orientation. Conservatives' embrace of the therapeutic sciences, however, took up recently discredited theories of disease and cure, and both conservative church members and leaders in Christian Right organizations insisted that homosexuals could be cured of their same-sex desires. What seemed to provide evidence for these claims was a crop of Christian therapeutic ministries that promised help for homosexuals who wished to change their attractions. Christian Right spokespersons touted these ex-gay ministries as evidence that lesbians and gays were not "born that way" but could "choose" a righteous lifestyle. In practice, as the ethnographic work of scholars Tanya Erzen and Lynne Gerber shows, that lifestyle looked much like an evangelical variant of a gay subculture. Ex-gay communities, Gerber argues, marked out a "queer-ish" sexual identity that was symbolically bounded by biblical orthodoxy and born-again conversion.[23] Along similar lines, the Christian abstinence campaigns of the 1990s also presented sexuality in identity terms. Evangelical spokespersons urged chaste young people to express identity pride by "coming out of the closet."[24] These campaigns relied on visibility tactics that mirrored what had been a long-standing strategy in movements for sexual and gender rights. As lesbians and gays publicly professed their identities by coming out, evangelicals similarly presented Christian sexuality as the public expression of an interior truth.

What most chroniclers of the culture wars have taken for granted, however, is that sexual identity and biblical orthodoxy point to wholly separate sources of truth. And in many ways, this assumption has stood as patently true precisely because of the ways that Americans of various faith traditions—and of none at all—perceive the Bible as an accurate map of a religious past. The Bible's antihomosexual meanings guided the practice of faith communities and informed the political agendas of social conservatives. Denominations and public politics alike have proceeded on questions of biblical meaning but with the central question focused on whether the Bible should have any standing in civil legislation.

For many Americans—religious and not—the Bible has served as a neutral measure of a regulatory past. To repeat Mark Noll's observation of the nineteenth-century debates over biblical teachings about slavery: not only did both sides "read the same Bible," he notes, but "they also read the Bible *in the same way*."[25] The primacy of conservatives' claims to religion stand, in part, because their ways of representing religion and homosexuality seem to represent what Americans of the late twentieth century took to be an established fact: religion had always condemned homosexual acts.

This notion—that religion's primary relationship to sexuality is one of regulation and suppression—may well be the most important assumption that foreclosed the complex and capacious history of a particular footnote published in June 1986. Derrick Sherwin Bailey's *Homosexuality and the Western Christian Tradition* stood as the uncontested authorization for sodomy laws because few people could imagine a book on this topic being otherwise. However, the set of influences and practices that I trace in this book show what else we might discover by looking beyond narratives of religious regulation to consider the way that religion—and a particular Protestant tradition—has been a productive source for the twentieth-century politics of sexual emancipation. Teasing out the history of this other relationship between religion and sexuality, however, requires looking for religion within a site defined by its absence. Secularism is so often positioned alongside sexuality that one scholar coined the neologism "sexularism" to illustrate the "assumed synonymity" of the secular and the sexually liberated.[26] But this perceived congruity should also suggest sexuality as a paradigmatic site for the kind of rethinking taking place in the recent critical studies of secularism. This scholarship urges inquiry into the ways in which a Protestant ideology remains most pervasively in force in the seemingly religiously uninhabited domain of the secular. The point that religion scholar Tracy Fessenden makes of secularism should also hold true of sexuality, where it is likewise important "to consider the consolidation of a Protestant ideology that has grown more entrenched and controlling even as its manifestations have often become less visibly religious."[27] If this is so, then nowhere is Protestantism more pervasive or more invisible than in what seems to be the quintessentially secular quest of finding and expressing a liberated sexual self, a practice critical to the politics on all sides of the late twentieth-century culture wars. What may well give continued animus to the political debates over religion and sexuality is not their difference but their similarity. Both sides claim a proprietary relationship to a small but inviolable plot of interior real estate that promises nothing less than the freeing key to the authentic self. Where a reigning Protestant ideology continues to govern most securely, it seems, is in this domain of the innermost heart.

Notes

ABBREVIATIONS

CL   Congregational Library and Archives, Boston, Mass.

CRH   Council on Religion and the Homosexual

FLHL   Flora Lamson Hewlett Library, Graduate Theological Union,
              Berkeley, Calif.

GA Records   General Assembly Records of the Presbyterian Church (USA)

GEC   Gender Equity Collections, Elihu Burritt Library, Central
              Connecticut State University, New Britain, Conn.

GLBTHS   Gay, Lesbian, Bisexual, Transgender Historical Society, San
              Francisco, Calif.

IGIC   International Gay Information Center Collections, Rare Books and
              Manuscripts Division, New York Public Library, New York, N.Y.

JHGLC   James C. Hormel Gay and Lesbian Center, San Francisco Public
              Library, San Francisco, Calif.

KJV   King James Version

LGBTRAN   Lesbian Gay Bisexual Transgender Religious Archives Network

MCC   Metropolitan Community Church

ONGLA   ONE National Gay and Lesbian Archives, Los Angeles, Calif.

PHS   Presbyterian Historical Society, Philadelphia, Pa.

RSV   Revised Standard Version

SBC   Archives of the Southern Baptist Church

UPCUSA   United Presbyterian Church in the United States of America

INTRODUCTION

1. 1 Corinthians 6:9–10, RSV: "Do you not know that the unrighteous will not inherit the kingdom of God? Do not be deceived; neither the immoral, nor idolaters, nor adulterers, nor homosexuals, nor thieves, nor the greedy, nor drunkards, nor

revilers, nor robbers will inherit the kingdom of God." In the 1971 revision of the RSV, "homosexuals" was changed to "sexual perverts."

2. 1 Corinthians 6:9–10, KJV: "Know ye not that the unrighteous shall not inherit the kingdom of God? Be not deceived: neither fornicators, nor idolaters, nor adulterers, nor effeminate, nor abusers of themselves with mankind, nor thieves, nor covetous, nor drunkards, nor revilers, nor extortioners, shall inherit the kingdom of God."

3. Buttrick, *Interpreter's Bible*, 10:72.

4. Jones, *Principles and Practice of Preaching*, 77.

5. Eiselen, Lewis, and Downey, *Abingdon Bible Commentary*, 1178, 232, 724.

6. Balmer and Winner, *Protestants in America*, 149.

7. Eiselen, Lewis, and Downey, *Abingdon Bible Commentary*, 1178, 232, 724, 1140. The commentary on Romans 1 mentions "sexual enormities," but the cross-linked texts are Mark 7:20 and Galatians 5:19–21, and the commentary underscores that the lists of sins in all of these passages highlight the ways in which the apostle condemns "dispositions or conduct which non-Christian codes treat with indifference" (1140).

8. R. Davis, "'My Homosexuality Is Getting Worse Every Day,'" 355.

9. Kinsey Pomeroy, and Martin, *Sexual Behavior in the Human Male*, 483.

10. The most commonly debated Bible texts since the 1970s are Genesis 1:27 (creation of Adam and Eve); Genesis 19:1–38 (the Sodom story); Leviticus 18:22 and 20:13; Romans 1:26–28; 1 Corinthians 6:9–11; and, less frequently, 1 Timothy 1:10. Not discussed are a handful of texts that reference "sodomite(s)" in the King James Version. These verses are now taken as references to pagan cultic practices: Deuteronomy 23:17; 1 Kings 14:24; 1 Kings 15:12; 1 Kings 22:46; 2 Kings 23:7. Also rarely discussed in contemporary debates is Jude 1:7, a reference to the Sodom account that specifies the perversion involved—in the King James, they went "after strange flesh" (in context, the reference is to the angels). The New International Version now renders the phrase "they gave themselves up to sexual immorality and perversion." The original Greek terms ἕτερος (literally "hetero," translated "strange" in KJV) and σάρξ (flesh) makes a same-sex reading problematic. There is need for further scholarship on the history of textual translations; a review of the translation changes that produced homosexual-focused interpretations may be found in the appendices to Boswell, *Christianity, Social Tolerance, and Homosexuality*.

11. This literature is immense. Two examples: Stone, *Practicing Safer Texts*; and Martin, *Sex and the Single Savior*.

12. This literature is also immense. Key texts include Halperin, *How to Do the History of Homosexuality*; M. Canaday, *Straight State*; Jordan, *Invention of Sodomy*; and Goldberg, *Sodometries*.

13. Keane, *Christian Moderns*, 6.

14. Ibid., 4–7.

15. Klassen, *Spirits of Protestantism*, xviii.

16. Ibid., xviii.

17. Holifield, *History of Pastoral Care*.

18. Muravchik, *American Protestantism*, 2.

19. Rose, "Assembling the Modern Self," 224.

20. See R. Davis, *More Perfect Unions*.

21. See DeRogatis, *Saving Sex*.

22. Foucault, *History of Sexuality*, 43.

23. See Katz, *The Invention of Heterosexuality*.

24. See, for example, Chauncey, "'What Gay Studies Taught the Court.'"

25. Boswell, *Christianity, Social Tolerance, and Homosexuality*, 147.

26. See, for example, Trexler, *Sex and Conquest*; Goldberg, *Sodometries*; Puff, *Sodomy in Reformation Germany and Switzerland*; Boone, *The Homoerotics of Orientalism*; Hutchison, "The Sodomitic Moor"; and Tortorici, "Against Nature."

27. Rubin, "Thinking Sex."

28. Scholarship on homosocial spaces in American Christianity includes Chauncey, "Christian Brotherhood or Sexual Perversion?"; Gustav-Wrathall, *Take the Young Stranger by the Hand*; Smith-Rosenberg, *Disorderly Conduct*; Lofton, "Queering Fundamentalism"; and Best, *Passionately Human, No Less Divine*.

CHAPTER I

1. Miller, *Harry Emerson Fosdick*, 149.

2. Hedstrom, *Rise of Liberal Religion*, 175–76, 207.

3. Fosdick, *On Being a Real Person*, viii.

4. Fosdick, *Living of These Days*, 218.

5. Holifield, *History of Pastoral Care*, 274.

6. Ibid., 271–72. See also Myers-Shirk, *Helping the Good Shepherd*.

7. Hedstrom, *Rise of Liberal Religion*, 175.

8. D'Emilio, *Sexual Politics*, 13.

9. Chauncey, *Gay New York*, 353; D'Emilio, *Sexual Politics*, 13, 147.

10. On these debates, see Marsden, *Fundamentalism and American Culture*; and Hutchison, *Modernist Impulse*.

11. See also Hutchison, *Modernist Impulse*; and Lofton, "Methodology of the Modernists."

12. Bayer, *Homosexuality and American Psychiatry*, 15.

13. Holifield, *History of Pastoral Care*. See also Rieff, *Triumph of the Therapeutic*; and Lasch, *Culture of Narcissism*.

14. On the history of early theological reference to "sodomy," see Jordan, *Invention of Sodomy*.

15. Genesis 19:1–24.

16. Eiselen, Lewis, and Downey, *Abingdon Bible Commentary*, 724.

17. Smith, *Historical Geography*, 504–5.

18. George Frederick Wright, "Sodom," in Orr, *International Standard Bible Encyclopaedia*, 2821. See also George Barton, "Sodomy," in Hastings, *Encyclopaedia of Religion and Ethics*, 672; and Davis, *Dictionary of the Bible*.

19. Barton, "Sodomy," 672–74; Brooks, "Fertility Cult Functionaries."

20. Eiselen, Lewis, and Downey, *Abingdon Bible Commentary*, 1178, 232, 724.

21. Quoted in Oosterhuis, *Stepchildren of Nature*, 42.

22. The book was cowritten with British homosexual John Addington Symonds, but the American edition lists only Ellis as the author. See Terry, *American Obsession*, 50–53.

23. Ellis, *Studies in the Psychology of Sex*, 3. In many cases, these laws prohibited sodomy and buggery together, which also lumped in interspecies sex with anal penetration. On the evolution of sodomy laws, see Eskridge, *Dishonorable Passions*.

24. Ellis, *Studies in the Psychology of Sex*, 3–4, v–vi.

25. The earliest American edition of Freud's theories of sexuality was the translation by A. A. Brill. See Sigmund Freud and A. A. Brill, *Three Contributions to the Sexual Theory* (New York: The Journal of Nervous and Mental disease Publishing Company, 1910). On Freud's views of homosexuality and their reception in the United States, see Terry, *American Obsession*, 55–68.

26. For discussion of pastoral counselors' responses to Freud, see Roberts, "Psychoanalysis and American Christianity."

27. Walter M. Horton, "The Psychological Approach to Theology," *Journal of Religion* 9.3 (July 1929): 338–39.

28. Boisen, *Exploration of the Inner World*, 275; Holifield, *History of Pastoral Care*, 244–49.

29. Council of Christian Associations, *Sex Life of Youth*, 51.

30. Gray, *Men, Women, and God*; Council of Christian Associations, *Sex Life of Youth*; Piper, *Christian Interpretation of Sex*. For historical treatment of early twentieth-century sex education, see Terry, *American Obsession*, 120–58; and Gustav-Wrathall, *Take the Young Stranger by the Hand*, 63–69.

31. For more on postwar Christian discussions of homosexuality, see Jordan, *Recruiting Young Love*, 50–66; Waller, "'A Man in a Cassock Is Wearing a Skirt'"; and R. Davis, "'My Homosexuality Is Getting Worse Every Day.'"

32. Holifield, *History of Pastoral Care*, 259–306.

33. Gregory, "The Chaplain and Mental Hygiene," 422.

34. Bérubé, D'Emilio, and Freedman, *Coming Out under Fire*, 165 n. 59. Bérubé also suggests two other interesting aspects of World War II chaplaincy. First, the procedures of referral may have unknowingly conscripted chaplains into military policies of penalizing and discharging suspected homosexuals. Second, many of his informants also reported that chaplains' offices were an informal gathering place for gay men.

35. On wartime cooperation and its influence in postwar pastoral counseling, see Holifield, *History of Pastoral Care*, 260–61.

36. Bertram Crocker, "Pastoral Aid for the Abnormal," *Crozer Quarterly* 22 (1945): 242–45.

37. Ibid., 242–44.

38. Other pastoral counseling discussions of homosexuality and men in the armed services include Walter Cowen, "The Consultation Clinic," *Pastoral Psychology* 1.4 (May 1950): 51–54; and Bonnell, *Psychology for Pastor and People*, 67.

39. On Rado's influence in American psychiatry, see Bayer, *Homosexuality and American Psychiatry*, 28–29. For a pastoral theologian's views on Rado, see Cole, *Sex in Christianity and Psychoanalysis*.

40. Margaretta K. Bowers, "The Psychotherapy of Homosexual Clergymen," in Episcopal Church Bishop's Committee on Pastoral Counseling, *Papers on Homosexuality: Presented at the House of Bishops of the Protestant Episcopal Church* (Committee on Pastoral Counseling of the Protestant Episcopal Church, 1962), 28, mimeographed copy, University of Rochester Library, http://catalog.lib.rochester.edu/vwebv/holdingsInfo?bibId=4816779; Charles D. Brand, "Margaretta K. Bowers, M.D.," *Pastoral Psychology* 16.8 (November 1965): 4, 65–66. For more on Bowers, see Waller, "'A Man in a Cassock Is Wearing a Skirt.'"

41. Kinsey, Pomeroy, and Martin, *Sexual Behavior in the Human Male.*

42. Religious News Service, "Indiana Religious Leaders Attack Kinsey Report," August 24, 1953, 1, Papers of the National Council of Churches, PHS. For further discussion of religious responses to Kinsey, see Griffith, "Religious Encounters."

43. Rollin J. Fairbanks, "A Christian View of Homosexuality," *Journal of Pastoral Care* 3.2 (June 1949): 14–16.

44. George W. Henry, "Pastoral Counseling for Homosexuals," *Pastoral Psychology* 2.8 (November 1951): 33 (ghostwritten by Alfred Gross)

45. Luther E. Woodward, "The Bearing of Sexual Behavior on Mental Health and Family Stability," in Doniger, *Sex and Religion Today*, 203–4.

46. Hiltner, *Sex Ethics and the Kinsey Reports*, 125.

47. See also Alfred A. Gross, "The Homosexual in Society: The Minister Has a Primary Obligation to Relieve Guilt Feelings and Restore the Homosexual's Self-Respect," *Pastoral Psychology* 1.3 (April 1950): 38–45; Judge Morris Ploscowe, "Homosexuality, Sodomy, and Crimes against Nature," *Pastoral Psychology* 2.8 (November 1951): 40–48; Gotthard Booth, "The Meaning of Sex," *Pastoral Psychology* 3.6 (September 1952): 44–56; Carroll A. Wise, "Pastoral Problems of Sex," *Pastoral Psychology* 3.6 (September 1952): 57–64; John A. P. Millet, "A Psychoanalyst's Viewpoint on Sexual Problems," *Pastoral Psychology* 4.1 (February 1953): 38–46.

48. Joe McCarthy to the editors of the *Saturday Evening Post*, August 8, 1950, cited in Johnson, *Lavender Scare*, 225 n. 42.

49. Johnson, *Lavender Scare*.

50. Howard Whitman, "The Biggest Taboo," *Collier's*, February 15, 1947, 24, 38–40.

51. R. Davis, "'My Homosexuality Is Getting Worse Every Day,'" 357–60.

52. Reuel L. Howe, "A Pastoral Theology of Sex and Marriage," in Doniger, *Sex and Religion Today*, 101, 102, 113.

53. Northridge, *Psychology and Pastoral Practice*, 54, 57. Northridge was British, and the book was published in the United States in the Pastoral Psychology book series.

54. Ibid., 54, 57.

55. Carroll A. Wise, "Pastoral Problems of Sex," *Pastoral Psychology* 3.6 (September 1952): 165.

56. John Millet, Phillip Q. Roche, Walter Stokes, Camilla Anderson, and Seward Hiltner, "The Consultation Clinic: The Church and the Homosexual," *Pastoral Psychology* 2.18 (November 1951): 49–57.

57. Both quotations are from ibid.

58. Seward Hiltner, "Sex—Sin or Salvation," *Pastoral Psychology* 3.6 (September 1952): 33.

59. Roberts, *Psychotherapy and a Christian View of Man*, 129.

60. Henry, *All the Sexes*, 583.

61. Northridge, *Psychology and Pastoral Practice*, 54, 57.

62. Carroll A. Wise, "Pastoral Problems of Sex," *Pastoral Psychology* 3.6 (September 1952): 165, 161–62. On the therapeutic process, see also Myers-Shirk, *Helping the Good Shepherd*, 92.

63. I. Gerber, *Man on a Pendulum*.

64. Ibid., 14, 317–20.

65. John A. P. Millet, Philip Q. Roche, Walter R. Stokes, Sandor Rado, Camilla M. Anderson, and Seward Hiltner, "The Consultation Clinic: The Church and the Homosexual," *Pastoral Psychology* 2.8 (November 1951): 49–57.

66. Ibid., 57.

67. Ibid., 57, 54.

68. Ibid., 57.

69. See Holifield, *History of Pastoral Care*; and Rieff, *Triumph of the Therapeutic*.

70. Robert Wright and Carroll Wise, "Theology Questions Counseling," *Pastoral Psychology* 6.2 (March 1955): 52.

71. Seward Hiltner, "Sex—Sin or Salvation," *Pastoral Psychology* 3.6 (September 1952): 33.

72. Seward Hiltner, "The Consultation Clinic on Homosexuality," *Pastoral Psychology* 6.56 (September 1955): 49.

73. Advertisement, *Life*, October 6, 1952. For a history of the RSV translation, see Thuesen, *In Discordance with the Scriptures*.

74. A 1971 revision to the RSV changed the term "homosexuals" to "sexual perverts." The translation committee records offer no explanation for the earlier choice of the word "homosexuals" in 1 Corinthians 6:9. There apparently was some debate over the Genesis 19 Sodom account. Early drafts for the RSV suggested the phrase "to know carnally" for a Hebrew verb that the KJV rendered simply "to know." The final revisions deleted the overtly sexual meaning for the more ambiguous earlier phrasing. The working drafts and revisions for the RSV are collected in the Papers of the Standard Bible Committee, Yale Divinity School Archives.

75. See, for example, Fletcher, *Morals and Medicine*, 118; and Northcote, *Christianity and Sex Problems*, 34.

76. Buttrick, *Interpreter's Bible*, Romans, 9:401–3.

77. Ibid., Deuteronomy, 1:471.

78. Thomas Fleming, "Sex and the Bible," *American Weekly*, April 24, 1960, 7; "Notes and Footnotes," *Berkshire Eagle* (Pittsfield, Mass.), October 5, 1959, 16.

79. Cole, *Sex and Love in the Bible*, 433.

80. Ibid., 435–36.

81. Ibid., 343, 363, 362.

82. Ibid., 365.

83. D. Bailey, *Homosexuality and the Western Christian Tradition*, 52–53.

84. Leviticus 18:22 and 20:13, Romans 1:28, 1 Corinthians 6:9, and 1 Timothy 1:9–10.

85. D. Bailey, *Homosexuality and the Western Christian Tradition*, 1–28.

86. Ibid., x.

87. Ibid., xi.

88. Bailey, "Homosexual and Christian Morals," 56.

89. O. J. Baab, "Homosexuality," in Buttrick, *Interpreter's Dictionary of the Bible*, 639.

90. "The Bible: The Sins of Sodom," *Time*, September 6, 1963, 54.

91. Martin, *Sex and the Single Savior*, 64.

92. Harry Emerson Fosdick, "The Ministry and Psychotherapy," *Pastoral Psychology* 11.101 (February 1960): 12.

93. Ibid., 13.

94. Narramore, *Life and Love*, 166–68.

95. Chauncey, *Gay New York*, 358. On this theme, also see M. Canaday, *Straight State*, 169.

CHAPTER 2

1. Quoted in R. Davis, "'My Homosexuality Is Getting Worse Every Day,'" 357.

2. George W. Henry, "Pastoral Counseling for Homosexuals," *Pastoral Psychology* 2.8 (November 1951): 33 (ghostwritten by Alfred Gross).

3. Advertisement for *The Homosexual in America: A Subjective Approach*, *Pastoral Psychology* 2.8 (November 1951): 39.

4. Sagarin, *Structure and Ideology*. For biographical information on Sagarin, see Duberman, "Dr. Edward Sagarin."

5. Cory, *Homosexual in America*, 10.

6. Ibid., 178.

7. Ibid., 15–25, 209.

8. See Cutler, *Homosexuals Today*; and Streitmatter, *Unspeakable*, 17–50.

9. Jones, "Stained Glass Closet."

10. Wood, *Christ and the Homosexual*.

11. Miss J. (pseudonym of Lorraine Hansberry) "As for Me," ONE 5.5 (May 1957): 18–19. On Lorraine Hansberry's relationship to the homophile movement, see Anderson, "'Education of Another Kind.'"

12. Henry and Committee for the Study of Sex Variants, *Sex Variants*.

13. Minton, *Departing from Deviance*. Before the Henry Foundation, from 1946 to 1948, Gross and Henry also worked with the Readjustment Committee of the Quaker Emergency Service in a short-lived counseling program very similar in aim to the subsequent Henry Foundation.

14. Alfred A. Gross to Paul Moore, October 12, 1983, file 137-30, Paul Moore Papers, Archives of the Episcopal Diocese of New York,.

15. Gross admitted this anachronism in his final annual report, "The Twenty-fourth Annual Report of the George W. Henry Foundation," April 1, 1972, 1, Wells Collection, GEC.

16. On Moore's decision to ordain Ellen Barret, see P. Moore, *Take a Bishop Like Me*; on his hidden homosexuality, see H. Moore, *Bishop's Daughter*.

17. Chauncey, *Gay New York*, 6.

18. "Second Annual Report of the George W. Henry Foundation," April 1, 1950, 1, Wells Collection, GEC.

19. Henry, *All the Sexes*, 575.

20. "Seventh Annual Report of the Psychiatrist in Chief," April 1, 1955, 9, Wells Collection, GEC.

21. "Seventeenth Annual Report of the George W. Henry Foundation," April 1, 1965, 4, Wells Collection, GEC.

22. George W. Henry, "Pastoral Counseling for Homosexuals," *Pastoral Psychology* 2.8 (November 1951): 40, 43, 45, 39 (ghostwritten by Alfred Gross).

23. "The Eighth Annual Report of the George W. Henry Foundation," April 1, 1956, 47, Wells Collection, GEC; "Fourth Annual Report of the Psychiatrist in Chief," April 1, 1952, 17, 19, Wells Collection, GEC.

24. "Fourth Annual Report of the Psychiatrist in Chief," April 1, 1952, 19, Wells Collection, GEC.

25. Alfred Gross, "An American Experiment," *Man and Society* 10 (Winter 1966): 13–14.

26. Wells's case, under the pseudonym "Tom," is discussed in "Third Annual Report of the Psychiatrist in Chief," April 1, 1951, 5, Wells Collection, GEC; Robert Wells, "The Henry Foundation," e-mail to archivist Frank Gagliardi, June 9, 2005, Wells Collection, GEC. See also Robert Wells, interview with the author, February 25, 2009.

27. "Third Annual Report of the Psychiatrist in Chief," April 1, 1951, 5, Wells Collection, GEC; Alfred Gross to William T. Wells, October 23, 1950, 1, Wells Collection, GEC.

28. Robert Wells to Thurman Wells, September 23, 1950, 4, Wells Collection, GEC.

29. Ibid., 4.

30. Alfred Gross to Robert Well, November 15, 1954, 1–2, Wells Collection, GEC. Despite the caution against public behavior, Gross was tolerant of Well's sexual behavior. Another letter offers advice ("get a blood test immediately") in response to Wells's concern that he contracted syphilis from anal sex. "Papa" to Robert Wells, April 21, 1955, 1, Wells Collection, GEC.

31. Gross to Wells, June 2, 1952, Wells Collection, GEC.

32. Ibid., January 8, 1953.

33. "The Eighth Annual Report of the George W. Henry Foundation," April 1, 1956, 39, Wells Collection, GEC; "Sixth Annual Report of the Psychiatrist in Chief," April 1, 1954, 4, Wells Collection, GEC; "Third Annual Report of the Psychiatrist in Chief," April 1, 1951, 3, Wells Collection, GEC.

34. Gross to Wells, November 12, 1953, 1, Wells Collection, GEC.

35. ONE did list the Henry Foundation in its 1956 handbook of "homosexual organizations" with the caveat that the foundation itself objected to the listing. The author insisted that the listing in itself "made no determination as to the personal lives of its memberships." See Cutler, *Homosexuals Today*, 91.

36. Loftin, *Masked Voices*, 20.

37. "Fifth Annual Report of the George W. Henry Foundation," April 1, 1953, Wells Collection, GEC, excerpt quoted in Sagarin, *Structure and Ideology*, 60.

38. W. L., "The Case of the Well-Meaning Lyncher," *ONE*, November 1953, 10–11.

39. Loftin, *Masked Voices*, 23.

40. See Streitmatter, *Unspeakable*, 17–50.

41. On homophile commentary about gender presentation, see Loftin, "Unacceptable Mannerisms."

42. My thinking in reading publics here is informed by Warner, *Publics and Counterpublics*.

43. Cory, *Homosexual in America*, 28.

44. Donald Webster Cory, "Address to the International Committee for Sex Equality," *ONE*, February 1953, 2. See also Elwin Volk, "The Common Law Notions of Decency in California," *ONE*, March 1953, 14–15.

45. James Barr [Fugaté], "James Barr on Organized Religion," *ONE*, June 1954, 19–20.

46. Frank Golovitz, "The Lonely Season," *ONE*, December 1957, 10.

47. Robert Gregory, "Editorial," *ONE*, December 1955, 22.

48. Kenneth McIntosh, "St. Paul on Sodomy," *ONE*, April 1958, 23–24.

49. R. H. Crowther, "Sodom: A Homosexual Viewpoint," *ONE*, January 1955, 24.

50. Wallace David, "A Minister and His Conscience," *ONE*, June 1954, 14–16.

51. Ibid.

52. Rev. Davis Stephens, "No Need to Despair," *Mattachine Review* 3.2 (February 1957): 16–17.

53. For other articles on Christian theology and biblical interpretation, see Luther Allen, "Homosexuality, Morality and Religion," *Mattachine Review* 2.3 (June 1956): 26; and "Letters," *ONE*, April 1955, n.p.

54. "Letters," *ONE*, April 1955, n.p.

55. "Letters," *ONE*, March 1960, n.p.

56. "Letters," *ONE*, November 1958, 29–30.

57. Committee on Homosexual Offences and Prostitution, *Wolfenden Report*, 24.

58. This exchange, which took place in 1954, is archived in box: Religion, ONE Records, ONGLA.

59. D. Bailey, "Homosexual and Christian Morals."

60. Lyn Pedersen [Jim Kepner], "Church of England Recommendations on Homosexuality," *ONE*, July 1956, 10–11.

61. "Religious Viewpoint Defined," *Mattachine Review* 2.2 (April 1956): 43–44.

62. Jim Kepner, "World Religion," *ONE Institute Quarterly: Homophile Studies*, Fall 1959, 131.

63. Ibid., 128.

64. Ibid., 130.

65. Ibid., 132. See also Lyn Pedersen [Jim Kepner], "Editorial," *ONE*, December 1960; and Lyn Pedersen [Jim Kepner], "Thorn in the Spirit." *ONE*, June 1955, 21.

66. Pedersen [Kepner], "Editorial," 4–5.

67. Advertisement for *Christ and the Homosexual*, *Pastoral Psychology* 11.5 (June 1960): 23.

68. Thomas J. Bigham, "Pastoral and Ethical Notes on Problems of Masturbation," *Pastoral Psychology* 11.5 (June 1960): 19–23. The first mention of Wood's

work in a pastoral counseling journal was in 1967 in a largely unflattering review. See Robert E. Buxbaum, "Homosexuality and Love," *Journal of Religion and Health* 6.1 (January 1967): 17–32.

69. Advertisement for *Christ and the Homosexual*, 23.

70. William E. Jacob, review of *Christ and the Homosexual*, by Robert Watson Wood, in *United Church Herald* 4.1 (January 1961): 22–23.

71. Albert Ellis, "Introduction," in Wood, *Christ and the Homosexual*, 18.

72. Noel I. Garde, "Review, *Christ and the Homosexual*," *Mattachine Review* 6.4 (April 1960): 20–21.

73. Jordan, *Recruiting Young Love*, 74.

74. Garde, "Review," 20–21; Robert Wood, interview with the author, August 17, 2006, transcript in the author's possession. See also Jordan, *Recruiting Young Love*, 74–79.

75. Wood, *Christ and the Homosexual*, 127.

76. Ibid., 193.

77. Ibid.

78. Ibid., 21.

79. Cutler, *Homosexuals Today*, 105–7; Kepner, *Rough News*, 10–11.

80. Rev. Edward Egan to Rev. Robert Wood, December 7, 1957, p. 1, Robert Wood Papers, CL.

81. George Hyde, interview with James Anderson and Gordon Melton, January 2005. Oral History Collection, LGBTRAN, http://www.lgbtran.org/Exhibits/Hyde/GHyde.pdf (January 30, 2007).

82. For a history of Independent Catholics, see Anson, *Bishops at Large*.

83. Hyde takes credit for the advertisement in ONE magazine, which invited readers to correspond to "Father John-Martin" to find our more about "a liberal church offering freedom to the inquiring mind, we do not attempt to judge, but only to serve." Advertisement, *ONE* 2.10 (December 1954): 32; letter to the editor, *Advocate*, September 30–October 13, 1970, 19.

84. Rt. Reverend John Augustine to D. Cone, September 30, 1961, 3; and George Hyde (Bishop John Augustine) to ONE editors, September 30; both in box: Religion, ONE Records, ONGLA.

85. A. G. to Robert Wood, January 24, 1961, pp. 1–2, Robert Wood Papers, CL.

86. A. B. and J. W. to Robert Wood, July 18, 1960, p. 1, Robert Wood Papers, CL.

87. Gross, *Strangers in Our Midst*, 96.

CHAPTER 3

1. "Chronology of Events Occurring in Connection with Arrest of Above Individuals on Jan 1, 1965," n.d., handwritten depositions from Ted McIlvenna, Mrs. Winnie McIlvenna, Cecil Willians, Mrs. Evelyn Williams, Fred Bird, Lewis Durham, and Mrs. Patricia Durham, file: Donaldson, Smith, Leighton and May vs. city and county of San Francisco, Smith and Donaldson Papers, JHGLC; Del Martin, "The Conspiracy Revealed," n.d., box 18, file: New Year's Ball Documents, CRH 1965, Lyon/Martin Papers, GLBTHS.

2. "Chronology of Events Occurring in Connection with Arrest of Above Individuals on Jan 1, 1965," n.d., pp. 1–9, handwritten depositions from Ted McIlvenna, Mrs. Winnie McIlvenna, Cecil Willians, Mrs. Evelyn Williams, Fred Bird, Lewis Durham, and Mrs. Patricia Durham, file: Donaldson, Smith, Leighton and May vs. city and county of San Francisco, Smith and Donaldson Papers, JHGLC.

3. Ibid.; John Moore, "Glide Memorial Church 1962–1966," p. 8, John Moore Manuscript, in the Farmworker Movement Documentation Project, http://www.farmworkermovement.org/essays/essays.shtml (April 11, 2006); "Here's What Really Happened" (January 2, 1965), Council on Religion and the Homosexual Exhibition, LGBTRAN, http://www.lgbtran.org/Exhibits/CRH/Image.aspx?AID=49 (May 3, 2014).

4. Charles Lewis, interview with Paul Gabriel, video recording, Shedding a Straight Jacket Collection, GLBTHS; Larry Littlejohn, interview with Scott Bishop, tape recording, San Francisco, April 27, 1990, Scott Bishop Papers, JHGLC.

5. Boyd, *Wide-Open Town*, 232.

6. Hal Call, "New Years Ball Planned as Church Council Benefit," *Town Talk* 1.6 (December 1964): 2.

7. Report on Council on Religion and the Homosexual, November 6, 1964, box 17, file: Minutes 1964–1974 CRH, Lyon/Martin Papers, GLBTHS.

8. "Chronology of Events Occurring in Connection with Arrest of Above Individuals on Jan 1, 1965," n.d., p. 2, handwritten depositions from Ted McIlvenna, Mrs. Winnie McIlvenna, Cecil Willians, Mrs. Evelyn Williams, Fred Bird, Lewis Durham, and Mrs. Patricia Durham, file: Donaldson, Smith, Leighton and May vs. city and county of San Francisco, Smith and Donaldson Papers, JHGLC.

9. Ibid., 3–4.

10. Donovan Bess, "Incidents at a Homosexual Benefit," *San Francisco Sunday Chronicle*, January 3, 1965, 1A; "Uproar over Dance," *San Francisco Examiner*, Sunday, January 3, 1965.

11. Paul Gabriel uses this phrase in his oral history interviews with CRH ministers. See Council on Religion and the Homosexual Exhibition, LGBTRAN, http://www.lgbtran.org/Exhibits/CRH/Exhibit.aspx?P=I (May 4, 2014).

12. Boyd, *Wide-Open Town*, 231.

13. Ibid., 203.

14. Ibid.; D'Emilio, *Sexual Politics*, 194–95.

15. Martin and Lyon, *Lesbian/Woman*, 240.

16. King, "The Current Crisis in Race Relations," 88.

17. "Treading Lightly in a Delicate Subject," *Christian Century* 74.38 (September 18, 1957): 1092–93.

18. See, for example, Carleton Simon, "Homosexualists and Sex Crimes" (paper presented before the International Association of Chiefs of Police at Duluth, Minnesota, September 21–25, 1947), 1.

19. Report of the Florida Legislative Investigation Committee, *Homosexuality and Citizenship in Florida* (Tallahassee, 1964), 9, http://ufdc.ufl.edu/UF00004805/00001?m=hmh (November 14, 2014).

20. Howard, "Library, the Park, and the Pervert," 182.

21. Eskridge, *Dishonorable Passions*, 75.

22. On changes in sodomy laws, see Eskridge, *Dishonorable Passions*; and Chauncey, "'What Gay Studies Taught the Court.'"

23. Eskridge, *Dishonorable Passions*, 118–24; Committee on Homosexual Offences and Prostitution, *Wolfenden Report*; Heron, *Towards a Quaker View of Sex*. For liberal Christian support, see Fletcher, "Sex Offenses"; Winfred Overholser, "Homosexuality: Sin or Disease?," *Christian Century* 80.37 (September 11, 1963): 1099–1101; John C. Bennett, "Questions on the Jenkins Case," *Christianity and Crisis* 24.19 (November 16, 1964): 223; and "Reappraising Laws on Homosexuality," *Christian Century* 82.21 (May 26, 1965): 669–70.

24. Thomas F. Driver, "On Taking Sex Seriously," *Christianity and Crisis* 23.17 (October 1963): 175–79.

25. "Bishop Pike Asks Reforms in Sex Law," *Chicago Tribune*, October 11, 1966, B11.

26. See, for example, Humphreys, *Tearoom Trade*, 23.

27. Joe Allison, "Treat Homosexuals as Human Beings," *San Francisco News Call Bulletin*, September 13, 1963.

28. Sweet, "Political and Social Action," 78–93. Sweet's informants (who were white) also suggested that "Negroes" had their own gay bars in San Francisco. See also Stryker, *Transgender History*, 66–67; and Boyd, *Wide-Open Town*, 113–14.

29. "Homosexuality in America," *Life*, June 26, 1964, 66; Boyd, *Wide-Open Town*, 202.

30. Cromey, *Essays Irreverent*, 25–28.

31. James G. Manz, "Pastoral Counseling in the Inner City," *Springfielder* 27.1 (March 1963): 30.

32. Cox, *Secular City*, 278–79.

33. Alinsky, *Reveille for Radicals*.

34. For histories of Christian urban ministries, see Green, *Churches, Cities, and Human Community*; and Luecke, "Protestant Clergy."

35. Durham, *Glide Foundation*.

36. Lewis Durham, interview with Paul Gabriel, July 18, 1998, transcript, pp. 6–8, Shedding a Straight Jacket Collection, GLBTHS.

37. Interviews with Ted McIlvenna and Hal Call in Sears, *Behind the Mask*, 285–86; Ted McIlvenna, interview with Paul Gabriel, September 26, 1996, video recording, Shedding a Straight Jacket Collection, GLBTHS.

38. Boyd, *Wide-Open Town*, 221–31.

39. Hal Call, "Planning Meeting for the Upcoming 'Consultation on the Church and the Homosexual,'" May 12, 1964, p. 1, box 17, file: Founding and History, CRH, Homophile Organizations, Lyon/Martin Papers, GLBTHS.

40. Kuhn, *Church and the Homosexual*, 32.

41. The interpersonal dynamics may have been influenced by the encounter sessions held at the neighboring Esalen Institute. Other urban training centers also hosted similar confrontation sessions. See Luecke, "Protestant Clergy"; and Kripal, *Esalen*, 183.

42. Clergy participating in the consultation were William Black, a Lutheran urban specialist in San Francisco; Orville Luster, the director of the Youth for

Service, a project of the American Friends Service Committee, and the only African American at the consultation; Jan Marinessen, penal affairs secretary with the American Friends Service Committee in San Francisco; Walter Press, a United Church of Christ minister from San Francisco; Robert Cromey, special assistant to the Episcopal bishop of California; Keith Wright, UCC minister working with the National Council of Churches; C. Kilmer Myers, Episcopal clergy from the Chicago Urban Training Center; Dennis Nyberg, Methodist minister from Minneapolis; Roger Burgess and Dale White, staff at the Methodist Board of Christian Social Concerns in Washington, D.C.; Charles Mowry and B. J. Stiles, staff at the Methodist Board of Education in Nashville; and Ted McIlvenna, Donald Kuhn, Lewis Durham, and John Moore, ministers at Glide Urban Center. Kuhn, *Church and the Homosexual*; Peter Crysdale, "Dealing with What's Wrong in Our Society: A Visit with Jan Marinessen," *FCL Newsletter*, January 2000, http://www.fclca.org/jannews/jan2000.html (April 11, 2006); Demian Bulwa, "Orville B. Luster—Social Worker, Friend to S.F.'s Youth," *SFGate*, July 7, 2005, http://www.sfgate.com/bayarea/article/Orville-B-Luster-social-worker-friend-to-2657195.php#src=fb (May 3, 2014); C. Dale White, phone interview with the author, April 30, 2006. Referring to Jan Marinessen and Orville Luster as "clergy" is not entirely accurate (the Religious Society of Friends does not have a professional clergy), but this was the designation used by the consultation.

43. Durham interview; Kuhn, *Church and the Homosexual*, 2.

44. Kuhn, *Church and the Homosexual*, 3, 31.

45. Del Martin, "The Church and the Homosexual: A New Rapport," *Ladder* 8.12 (September 1964): 9–13.

46. Ibid., 9.

47. Kuhn, *Church and the Homosexual*, 32.

48. Richard Hallgren, "S. F. Clergyman's View of the Homosexuals," *San Francisco Chronicle*, December 7, 1964, 1, 22; "Clergy Shatter Another Taboo," *Christian Century* 81.52 (December 23, 1964): 1581.

49. See interviews with McIlvenna and Hal Call in Sears, *Behind the Mask*, 289; Ted McIlvenna, interview with the author, August 24, 2005.

50. "The Defenders: Herb Donaldson and Evander Smith," in Marcus, *Making Gay History*, 158.

51. Ibid., 158.

52. John V. Moore, interview with Chris Waldrep, January 7, 2010, Oral History Collection, LGBTRAN, http://www.lgbtran.org/Exhibits/OralHistory/Moore/JMoore.pdf (June 21, 2013).

53. John Moore, "Church, Community, and Homosexuality," January 17, 1965, p. 6, Special Collections, Shields Library, University of California Davis, http://www.worldcat.org/title/church-community-and-homosexuality/oclc/537720007.

54. "A Brief of Injustices," *ONE*, October 1965, 17; various, "Letters to the Editor" responding to the "Brief of Injustices," *ONE*, December 1965, 31–32.

55. Durham, *Glide Foundation*.

56. R. Sweet, "Political and Social Action," 120, 158–59, 171–72, 212–14.

57. See Stryker, *Transgender History*, 69–72.

58. See Johnson, *Lavender Scare*, 192–208.

59. "Frank Kameny," in Marcus, *Making Gay History*, 93–99; D'Emilio, *Sexual Politics*, 150–52.

60. D'Emilio, *Sexual Politics*, 154–62.

61. Stein, *City of Sisterly and Brotherly Loves*, photographic image, 249.

62. Ibid., 248.

63. "Cross-Currents," *Ladder* 9.12 (September 1965): 13–14.

64. Report by Neale Secor to San Francisco Council of Religion and the Homosexual, "Washington D.C. CRH" (October 31, 1965), p. 1, box 17, file 16, Lyon/Martin Papers, GLBTHS. See also H. Jones, *Toward a Christian Understanding*, 126–28.

65. "Scanning the Conference," *Ladder* 10.4 (January 1966): 8–10.

66. Existing historiography on gay organizing in Los Angeles gives only brief reference to the SCCRH. This account draws from a file on the SSCRC included in box: religion, ONE Records and a collection description for the Southern California Council on Religion and the Homophile Collection, ONGLA. See also Faderman and Timmons, *Gay L.A.*, 154–65.

67. "General Report on the First Year Activities of the CRH," n.d., p. 2, box 9, file 10, Donald Stewart Lucas Papers, GLBTHS.

68. Foster Gunnison, "The Homophile Movement in America," in Weltge, *Same Sex*, 119. Gunnison counts seventeen organizations in 1965 and almost forty by the end of 1968.

69. Paul Jones, interview with the author, June 20, 2013; W. Paul Jones, "Homosexuality and Marriage: Exploring on the Theological Edge," *Pastoral Psychology* 21.10 (December 1970): 29–37. On the history of the Phoenix Society, see John D'Emilio, *Sexual Politics*, 200; and Jackson, *Changing Times*. Records for the Phoenix Society are also located at "Phoenix Society for Individual Freedom," http://www.mickeyray .com/phoenix-society.asp (June 6, 2013). Louis Crompton, "North American Conference of Homophile Organizations Report of the Religious Committee," December 1969, box: Religion, file: Southern California Council on Religion and the Homophile, ONE Records, ONGLA.

70. Moye, "Cathedral of Hope," 21–34.

71. Atkins, *Gay Seattle*, 97–98, 119.

72. Kohl, *Curious and Peculiar People*, 41–45.

73. C. Jones, "Pastoral Counselor and the Male Homosexual," 166–68.

74. Annual President's Report of the CRH, presented by Phyllis Lyon, January 25, 1967, p. 1, box: Homophile Orgs, file: CRH, Meeting Minutes and other documents, Donald Stewart Lucas Papers, GLBTHS.

75. "Board of Directors Meeting: CRH," February 7, 1967, box: Religion, file: CRH Meetings, ONE Records, ONGLA.

76. Ibid.

77. Quoted in Marotta, *Politics of Homosexuality*, 62–63.

78. Warren D. Adkins (pseudonym for Jack Nichols), "Homosexuals Confer with Clergy," *Eastern Mattachine Magazine* 10.5 (June 1965), http://www.rainbowhistory .org/EMMX5.pdf (June 4, 2007); "Gay Is Good: Resolution Adopted Unanimously by the North American Conference of Homophile Organizations," August 1968, http://

www.rainbowhistory.org/nachogayisgood.pdf (June 4, 2007). For biographical work on Frank Kameny, see DeLeon, *Leaders from the 1960s*, 253–59.

79. Robert Cromey, "Gay Is Good—So What?," n.d., box 17, file: Mailings and Publicity, Lyon/Martin Papers, GLBTHS.

80. Elizabeth Johns to Robert Wood, July 8, 1964, p. 1, box 2: Correspondence UCC leaders, Robert Wood Papers, CL. Wood also had other letters in a correspondence file with UCC leaders dating back to 1959.

81. Zan Harper to Robert Wood, January 23, 1967, ibid.

82. Robert Wood to Council for Christian Social Action, January 27, 1967, p. 1, box 2: Correspondence UCC leaders, ibid.

83. Keith Wright to Edward Egan, August 26, 1965, p. 1, box 1, folder: Seminar, Special Needs Planning 1965–1967, ibid.

84. Ibid.; "Department of Ministry, Vocation and Pastoral Services Consultation on the Church's Ministry to the Sexually Variant," March 11, 1966, p. 1, ibid.

85. Barbara Gittings presentation, untitled, October 1966, p. 1, ibid.

86. Sources on this committee and the agenda for this meeting are held in the Robert Wood Collection, CL, and in the Canon Clinton Jones Papers, GEC.

87. "Motive is Sought in Cleric Slaying," *New York Times*, October 19, 1966, 92.

88. Spike, *Photographs of My Father*, 225.

89. Paul Spike's comments on the aftermath: "Few people had known my father might actually be bisexual. Very few people. But thanks to the Columbus police, now few people thought of him as anything but some kind of sexual deviate. And the panicked reaction of the National Council of Churches was obvious." The crime was never solved, but Spike's memoir counters the police suspicions of its sexual connection and uncovers some evidence that it may have been a politically motivated assassination. Ibid., 224, 230, 236–44. On Spike's career and the impact of his death on the Protestant left, see also Hulsether, *Building a Protestant Left*, 121–22; and Findlay, *Church People in the Struggle*, 175–77.

90. Robert Cromey, "Ministry to the Homosexual," *Living Church*, January 8, 1967, 18–19.

91. Council for Christian Social Action, United Church of Christ, "Resolution on Homosexuals and the Law" (adopted April 12, 1969), http://www.ucc.org/lgbt_statements (January 24, 2015).

92. Lewis I. Maddocks, "The Homosexual and the Law," *Social Action* 34.4 (December 1967): 18–20.

93. C. A. Tripp, "Who Is a Homosexual?," *Social Progress* 58.2 (November/December 1967): 21.

94. Carlyle Marney, "The Christian Community and the Homosexual," *Social Progress* 58.2 (November/December 1967): 36, 38.

95. Marcus Paine, "Views of a Hidden Homosexual," *Social Progress* 58.2 (November/December 1967): 24–25.

96. Neale A. Secor, "A Brief for a New Homosexual Ethic," in Weltge, *Same Sex*, 75.

97. Bayer, *Homosexuality and American Psychiatry*, 41–66.

98. Secor, "Brief for a New Homosexual Ethic," 78.

99. Treese, *Homosexuality*; "Robert Treese—Obituary—Bostonia Fall 2008," www .bu.edu/bostonia/fa1108/obituaries (July 15, 2013).

100. Treese, *Homosexuality*, 25.

101. Paul W. Jones, "Homosexuality and Marriage: Exploring on the Theological Edge," *Pastoral Psychology* 21.10 (December 1970): 35–37.

102. C. Jones, "Pastoral Counselor and the Male Homosexual"; Treese, *Homosexuality*; Pittenger, *Time for Consent*.

103. Lloyd Wake, interview with the author, August 25, 2005; Ron Moskowitz, "Two Men Take Vows: A Covenant of Friendship," *San Francisco Chronicle*, March 22, 1971. Wake remembers that there were same-sex ceremonies in the late 1960s.

104. Cecil Williams, "A New Word and World for the Homosexual," October 27, 1968, "Gay Scrapbook," William Billings Papers, JHGLC.

105. P. Jones, "Homosexuality and Marriage," 37.

106. Sears, "Bob Basker," 198.

107. Hadden, *Gathering Storm*, 99.

108. Louis Crompton, "North American Conference of Homophile Organizations Report of the Religious Committee," December 1969, box: Religion; file: Southern California Council on Religion and the Homophile, ONE Records, ONGLA.

CHAPTER 4

1. Will Oursler, "Religious Storm Center: New Sex Code," *Parade Magazine*, May 17, 1970, 1.

2. Janet M. Brunger to Presbyterian General Assembly, n.d., box 8, file 26-12-1, Office of the Stated Clerk Records, 1967–73, GA Records, PHS.

3. UPCUSA, *Minutes of the General Assembly*. Includes the study guide "Sexuality and the Human Community" and appended material, 888–926.

4. Ibid.

5. Irvine, *Talk about Sex*, 35.

6. DeRogatis, *Saving Sex*, 3.

7. Presbyterian Office of Formation, "A Special Communication to Presbyterian Pastors," May 13, 1970, p. 1, box 8, file 26-12-1, GA Records, PHS.

8. On Presbyterian polity and democratic process, see Little, "Calvinism and American National Identity."

9. UPCUSA, *Minutes of the General Assembly*, 889.

10. Louis Cassels, "Church Statements Have Built-in 'Cop Out,'" *Middlesboro (Ky.) Daily News*, June 13, 1970, 4.

11. Mark O'Connell, "Presbyterians Give Green Light to Sexual Freedom," *National Informer*, July 19, 1970, 11.

12. Billy James Hargis, "Presbyterian Church Approves Sex Code That Repudiates Biblical View of Sin," *Christian Crusade Weekly* (Tulsa, Okla.), July 5, 1970, 1.

13. On media reports of the sexual revolution, see Bailey, *Sex in the Heartland*.

14. Williams, *God's Own Party*, 80–83; Lassiter, *Silent Majority*, 232–37.

15. See Roof and McKinney, *American Mainline Religion*.

16. Ervin Drake, "The Second Sexual Revolution," *Time*, January 24, 1964, http://www.time.com/time/magazine/article/0,9171,875692,00.html (October 30, 2009).

17. Oursler, "Religious Storm Center."

18. On sexual liberalism, see D'Emilio and Freedman, *Intimate Matters*.

19. UPCUSA, *Minutes of the General Assembly*, 924, 925.

20. On these debates, see Irvine, *Talk about Sex*.

21. A list of these Protestant sexuality studies is found in William H. Genné, "A Synoptic of Recent Denominational Statements on Sexuality, Second Edition," National Council of the Churches, December 31, 1975, box 23: Sexuality, 1950s–1960s, Christian Life Commission Resources Files, SBC. Also see Genné et al., *Foundations for Christian Family Policy*; Genné, *Christians and the Crisis in Sex Morality*; and Wynn. *Sex, Family, and Society*.

22. Roy W. Fairchild, "John Charles Wynn," *Pastoral Psychology* 11.6 (September 1960): 6.

23. Ray Ranner to Dr. William P. Thompson, May 19, 1970, p. 1, box 8, file 26-12-1, GA Records, PHS.

24. Fairchild, "John Charles Wynn," 6; John Charles Wynn, "What Churches Say Today," in Duvall and Duvall, *Sex Ways*, 41.

25. Evelyn Millis Duvall, "Facing Facts and Issues," in Duvall and Duvall, *Sex Ways*, 15–25; Wynn, "What Churches Say Today," 64.

26. Lester A. Kirkendall and Peter B. Anderson, "Authentic Selfhood: Basis for Tomorrow's Sexual Morality," *Pastoral Psychology* 21.9 (November 1970): 19–32.

27. J. Robinson, *Honest to God*; Fletcher, *Situation Ethics*.

28. J. Robinson, *Honest to God*, 115.

29. William H. Genné, "The Churches and Sexuality," Fall 1966, box 23: Sexuality, 1950s–1960s, Christian Life Commission Resources Files, SBC.

30. See my discussion of these terms in White, "'Love Is the Only Norm,'" 227–31, 239.

31. UPCUSA, *Minutes of the General Assembly*, 892. An almost identical approach can be seen in Cedric W. Tilberg, ed., *Sex, Marriage and Family: A Contemporary Christian Perspective* (New York: Commission on Marriage, Board of Social Ministry, Lutheran Church in America, 1970), 52.

32. UPCUSA, *Minutes of the General Assembly*, 892.

33. Ibid., 899.

34. Ibid., 914.

35. Ibid., 915–17.

36. Ibid., 917–19.

37. Ibid., 907.

38. On Bergler and disease theories, see Terry, *American Obsession*, 309–10.

39. Edmund Bergler, "Homosexuality: Disease or Way of Life?," *Pastoral Psychology* 8.5 (June 1957): 49–52; Edmund Bergler and Paul B. Maves, "Homosexuality: Disease or Way of Life?," *Pastoral Psychology* 8.9 (December 1957): 51–55; Thomas Franklyn Hudson, "Homosexuality," *Pastoral Psychology* 8.6 (September 1957): 7; Robert E. Buxbaum, "Homosexuality and Love," *Journal of Religion and Health* 6.1 (January 1967): 17–32.

40. Valente, "Evelyn Gentry Hooker."

41. Evelyn Hooker, "Homosexuality—Summary of Studies," in Duvall and Duvall, *Sex Ways*, 166–83.

42. UPCUSA, *Minutes of the General Assembly*, 905.

43. Ibid., 905.

44. D. Bailey, *Homosexuality and the Western Christian Tradition*; Macquarrie, *Dictionary of Christian Ethics*.

45. Thielicke, *Ethics of Sex*, 282.

46. UPCUSA, *Minutes of the General Assembly*, 905.

47. L. Nelson Bell, "A Layman and His Church: Yes, There Are 'Rules,'" *Presbyterian Journal*, July 22, 1970, 13.

48. Broyles, "Fractured Body of Christ"; Worthen, *Apostles of Reason*, 26–27.

49. Virginia Culver, "Graham's Targets Include Radical Clergy," *Denver Post*, June 1, 1970, 1.

50. R. Norman Herbert, "Something Sacred Was Missing at General Assembly," *Presbyterian Layman*, September 1970, 3.

51. The session of the Waverly U.P. Church to Board of Christian Education (December 15, 1970), p. 1; personal statement of William McCreery to the High Plains Presbytery on the Report, Sexuality and the Human Community (May 11, 1971), p. 3, both in box 1: Responses to Sex Report 1971, GA Records, PHS.

52. Rev. J. Mark Irwin to Elis Butler, May 14, 1970, box 8, file 26-12-1, ibid.

53. Edward C. Thedens to Office of the General Assembly, October 31, 1970, box 1: Responses to Sex Report 1970, ibid.

54. On the history of fundamentalist/modernist debates, see, for example, Hutchison, *Modernist Impulse*; and Ammerman, *Baptist Battles*.

55. On fundamentalism and modernity, see, for example, Lofton, "Preacher Paradigm."

56. Williams, *God's Own Party*, 4, 93.

57. R. J. Rushdooney, "Do-It-Yourself Religion," *Christianity Today* 2.3 (November 11, 1957): 35.

58. Walter Vail Watson, "Review, Leslie Weatherhead, *Prescription for Anxiety*," *Christianity Today* 2.14 (April 14, 1958): 36.

59. See, for example, Bernard Ramm, "Christian Experience and Psychiatry," *Christianity Today* 2.17 (May 26, 1958): 13–14, 22.

60. See also May, *Homeward Bound*.

61. Charles Woodbridge, introduction to Wyrtzen, *Sex and the Bible*, i.

62. On evangelical sexual culture in the 1960s and 1970s, see R. Davis, *More Perfect Unions*, 176–213; DeRogatis, "What Would Jesus Do?"; and Williams, "Sex and the Evangelicals."

63. See also Myers-Shirk, *Helping the Good Shepherd*, 206–33.

64. Billy Graham, "Questions Teens Are Asking," *Moody Monthly*, June 1967, 70.

65. See, for example, Geldenhuys, *Intimate Life*, 85.

66. Ibid.; Mow, *Secret of Married Love*; Williams, "Sex and the Evangelicals," 9.

67. See also Myers-Shirk, *Helping the Good Shepherd*, 206–33.

68. See, for example, Billy Graham, "The Unpardonable Sin," October 8, 1958, http://www.wheaton.edu/bgc/archives/docs/bg-charlotte/1008.html (October 3, 2014), which references texts and terms later seen to be "about" homosexuality to speak of lust between women and men.

69. See, for example, "Sodom in America," *Christianity Today* 8.9 (October 25, 1963): 14.

70. Narramore, *Life and Love*, 167.

71. Wilkerson, *Hope for Homosexuals*. See also Wyrtzen, *Sex and the Bible*; and Babbage, *Christianity and Sex*, 56–57.

72. Brian R. Munday, Stanley H. Mullen, Paul E. Adolph, Lucy Jane King, and William Standish Reed, "The Homosexual: Does He Belong in the Church?," *Christian Life*, October 1967, 38, 63–68.

73. Reader's letters, "Pro and Con Homosexual," *Christian Life*, January 1968, 16.

74. J. R. Dolby, "The Minister's Workshop—Helping the Homosexual," *Christianity Today* 12 (February 16, 1968): 29–30.

75. Janet M. Brunger to Presbyterian General Assembly, n.d., box 8, file 26-12-1, Office of the Stated Clerk Records, 1967–73, GA Records, PHS, 1.

76. "Evaluation Study of the Committees of the Pioneer and Pleasant Grove United Presbyterian Churches, Ligonier, Penn.," December 19, 1970, pp. 1, 4, box 8, file 26-12-1, GA Records, PHS.

77. Mrs. T. D. (Lucille) Moehl to William Thompson, stated clerk, September 25, 1970, p. 1, ibid.

78. Notably, the first extensive discussion of biblical views of homosexuality in *Christianity Today* was written by an Anglican, who was responding to D. S. Bailey's work and concurs with his support for sodomy law repeal. Bruce L. Smith, "Homosexuality in the Bible and the Law," *Christianity Today* 13.21 (July 18, 1969): 7–10. A much shorter discussion of biblical texts also responded to liberal views. See "The Bible and the Homosexual," *Christianity Today* 12.8 (January 19, 1968): 24–26.

79. L. Sweet, "1960s," 44.

80. See Foucault, *History of Sexuality*, 101.

81. Clergy connected to the Council on Religion and the Homosexual were already publishing challenges to homosexual disease theories in the late 1960s: Morton T. Kelsey, "The Church and the Homosexual," *Journal of Religion and Health* 7.1 (January 1968): 61–78; W. Paul Jones, "Homosexuality and Marriage: Exploring on the Theological Edge," *Pastoral Psychology* 21.10 (December 1970): 29–37; Neale A. Secor, "A Brief for a New Homosexual Ethic," in Weltge, *Same Sex*, 67–82.

82. Patricia Maxwell, "A Radical Perspective," *New/World Outlook* 31.1 (September 1970): 28–29.

CHAPTER 5

1. Dick Leitsch, "The Hairpin Drop Heard Round the World," supplemental leaflet to *New York Mattachine Newsletter*, July 1969.

2. Craig Rodwell, "Get the Mafia and the Cops Out of Gay Bars," Homophile Youth Movement flyer, June 29, 1969; Dick Leitsch, "The Stonewall Riots: The Police Story,"

New York Mattachine Newsletter, August 1969, 5–6; Lige Clark and Jack Nichols, "The Stonewall Riots: The Gay View," *New York Mattachine Newsletter*, August 1969, 13–14; Dick Leitsch, "NY Gays: Will the Spark Die?" *Los Angeles Advocate*, September 1969, 3; "Police Raid on NY Club Sets Off First Gay Riot," *Los Angeles Advocate*, September 1969, 3; "Gay Power in New York City," *Ladder* 14.1/2 (October–November 1969): 40.

3. Howard Smith, "Full Moon over the Stonewall," *Village Voice*, July 3, 1969, 1; Lucian Truscott IV, "Gay Power Comes to Sheridan Square," *Village Voice*, July 3, 1969, 1; "No Place for Gaiety, " *New York Post*, June 28, 1969; "Village Raid Stirs Melee," *New York Post*, June 28, 1969; Dennis Eskow, "3 Cops Hurt as Bar Raid Riles Crowd," *New York Daily News* (Sunday ed.), June 29, 1969, 30.

4. "Four Policemen Hurt in 'Village' Raid: Melee Near Sheridan Square Follows Action at Bar," *New York Times*, June 29, 1969, 33; "Hostile Crow Dispersed near Sheridan Square," *New York Times*, July 3, 1969, 19.

5. Lacy Fosburgh, "Thousands of Homosexuals Hold a Protest Rally in Central Park," *New York Times*, June 29, 1970, 1, 26; "The 'Gay' People Demand Their Rights," *New York Times*, July 5, 1970; Associated Press, "Gays Celebrate Their Own Week," *San Antonio Express*, June 26, 1972; "Gay Pride," *Time*, July 13, 1970, 12; "Hope for the Homosexual," *Time*, July 13, 1970, 60.

6. Duberman, *Stonewall*, xv; for a critical commentary on Duberman's historical telling of Stonewall, see Bravmann, *Queer Fictions of the Past*, 68–96.

7. Kissack, "Freaking Fag Revolutionaries," 105.

8. The riots actually took place early Saturday morning, but the popular history almost universally places the event on Friday night. See Carter, *Stonewall*.

9. For reflection on this point, see Jordan, *Recruiting Young Love*, 105–7.

10. Angelo d'Arcangelo, "To Seek Beauty and Pleasure," *Gay*, February 1, 1970, 4.

11. Birchard, "Metropolitan Community Church."

12. Marotta, *Politics of Homosexuality*, 65–66.

13. These anecdotes appear in several histories of the Stonewall riots. See Sears, *Rebels*, 27; and Carter, *Stonewall*, 147.

14. Craig Rodwell, memo to All East Coast Homophile Organizations, April 10, 1970, box 4, file: Christopher Street Liberation Day Committee, 1970, Rodwell Papers, IGIC.

15. Teal, *Gay Militants*, 30–31.

16. Kissack, "Freaking Fag Revolutionaries," 110–11.

17. Most of these groups were on or near university or college campuses. See Eisenbach, *Gay Power*, 140–41.

18. This history has been widely chronicled. See, for example, ibid. and Kissack, "Freaking Fag Revolutionaries."

19. "Gay Holiday," *New York HYMNAL*, January 1970, 8.

20. Ibid.

21. Foster Gunnison, "Bulletin No. Two," April 10, 1970, 1, box 4, file: Christopher Street Liberation Day Committee, 1970, Rodwell Papers, IGIC.

22. Gay Pride Week announcement and invitation, June 22–28, 1969, ibid.

23. Christopher Street Liberation Day announcement in *Come Out!*, quoted in Teal, *Gay Militants*, 323.

24. Christopher Street Liberation Day Committee, flier, n.d., box 4, file: Christopher Street Liberation Day Committee, 1970, Rodwell Papers, IGIC.

25. Activists in Chicago chose a similarly symbolic route held on Saturday, June 27. It began at Bughouse Square, representing "fear, shame, and repression," and proceeded to the Water Tower, a famous landmark, via Michigan Avenue or the Magnificent Mile. Demonstrators had also initially planned to burn closets at Bughouse Square. "Gay Pride Week in Chicago" (planned demonstration by Chicago Gay Liberation), n.d., and "Gay Pride Week, June 21–28," *Mattachine Midwest Newsletter*, June 1970, 1. Both archived in box 4, file: Christopher Street Liberation Day Committee, 1970, Rodwell Papers, IGIC.

26. Perry Brass, "We Did It!," *Come Out!* 1.5 (October 1970): 11. Teal's account of the march in *Gay Militants*, 322–33, quotes these phrases from contemporaneous accounts.

27. Martha Shelley, "Power . . . and the People!," *Come Out!* 2.7b (Spring/Summer 1971): 18.

28. Jordan, *Recruiting Young Love*, 105–9.

29. Hollinger, "After Cloven Tongues of Fire," 46.

30. Ibid., 21–48.

31. "To Accept Homosexuals," *Christian Century* 88.9 (March 3, 1971): 275; Elliot Wright, "The Church and Gay Liberation," *Christian Century* 88.9 (March 3, 1971): 281–85. Other reporting on these events included "Gays Go Radical" and "Militant Homosexuals," *Christianity Today* 15.5 (December 4, 1970): 40–41. A similar instance of militant confrontation alongside dialogue also occurred in a Detroit meeting of the Episcopal diocese of Michigan.

32. Paul Breton, interview with the author, September 3, 2005, transcript in the author's possession.

33. Ibid.; "Metropolitan Community Church of Washington," February 1973, 1–3, file: NE District UFMCC, Birchard Papers, FLHL.

34. See Kuhn, *Church and the Homosexual*.

35. Ernest Reagh, "Can a Person Be Different and Accepted—in Love?," *Engage*, April 15, 1971, 6–7.

36. Teal, *Gay Militants*, 281, note.

37. Humphreys, *Out of the Closets*, 143.

38. John P. Rash, "Reforming Pastoral Attitudes toward Homosexuality," *Union Seminary Quarterly Review* 25.4 (June 1, 1970): 439–55.

39. John Preston, "Beyond Rhetoric," *motive: Gay Men's Liberation Edition* 12.2 (1972): 11–14, http://www.rainbowhistory.org/html/gmotive.htm (August 10, 2013).

40. "Texas Methodists Sack Admitted Gay Minister," *Advocate*, July 23, 1971, 4.

41. Roy Birchard to Lawrence L. Durgin, May 17, 1971, 3, box 1, file 13, Birchard Papers, FLHL. Donn Teal also reports that the GAA's "first bitter floor fight" was touched off by members' request for authorization for a committee to educate clergymen. Teal, *Gay Militants*, 172.

42. Robert Clement, interview with the author, August 30, 2005, transcript in the author's possession. "A New Church for Gay People," n.d., file: American Church, Ephemera—Subject Files—Religion, IGIC.

43. Flier, "Christopher Street West: A Freedom Revival in Lavender," box 4, file: Christopher Street Liberation Day Committee, 1970, Rodwell Papers, IGIC. Also printed in *MCC News*, June 28, 1970, 1.

44. God's presence, many participants claimed, was made visible in a miracle—a rainbow ring around the sun—that occurred during the protest in Sacramento. "Rally's Organizer's See God's Hand in Rainbow," *Advocate*, July 21, 1971, 12.

45. Swicegood, *Our God Too*, 195–96.

46. Press release, June 28, 1970, box 1, file 59: Troy Perry, MCC Historical Collection, ONGLA.

47. Jim Kepner, "A Homosexual Minister Fasts for Justice," *Gay News*, August 3, 1970, 4, 12. See also "Perry Busted as He, 7 Others Start Fast," *Advocate*, July 22–August 4, 1970, 2, 7; Angela Douglas, "Gays Federal Fast," *Los Angeles Free Press*, July 10, 1970, 5; "Troy Perry Breaks 10 Day Fast," *Gay News*, August 3, 1970, 3.

48. For analysis of press coverage of the MCC and gay activism in Los Angeles, see D. Robinson, "Rhetoric of Troy Perry," 87–90.

49. Swicegood, *Our God Too*, 204.

50. Edward Fiske, "Color Some of the Churches Lavender," *New York Times*, March 28, 1971, E7. The first mainstream press attention to the MCC was John Dart, "A Church for Homosexuals," *Los Angeles Times*, December 3, 1969, C1.

51. Enroth and Jamison, *Gay Church*, 113; Robert L. Cleath, "Homosexual Church," *Christianity Today* 14.24 (September 11, 1970): 48–50; "Metropolitan Community Church: Deception Discovered," *Christianity Today* 18.15 (April 26, 1974): 13–14.

52. John Francis Hunter, "The Lord Is My Shepherd and He Knows I'm Gay!," *Gay*, March 29, 1970.

53. On Perry's life, see Perry, *Lord Is My Shepherd*; on the conservative Christian realignment of the Sunbelt, see Dochuk, *From Bible Belt to Sunbelt*.

54. D. Robinson, "Rhetoric of Troy Perry"; Perry, *Lord Is My Shepherd*.

55. A. B. T., "'God Loves All': Bold New Church Welcomes Gays," *Los Angeles Advocate*, February 1969, 3; Lee Spangenberg, "Are You Ready?," *MCC News*, June 28, 1970, 2; "Members Celebrate MCC's First Anniversary," *MCC News*, October 6, 1969, n.p.

56. D. Robinson, "Rhetoric of Troy Perry," 59–83; Swicegood, *Our God Too*, 114–21, 135–37.

57. "MCC Church for Everyone," *MCC News*, October 26, 1969, 1–2; D. Robinson, "Rhetoric of Troy Perry," 151.

58. Jim Kepner, "Angles on the News," *Los Angeles Advocate*, October 1969, 23.

59. These statistics come from a study of the church conducted by sociologist Barry Dank, who reported that the MCC-LA was 96 percent white while also noting that the congregation appeared to include more racial/ethnic diversity than the survey participation indicated. He hypothesized that whites participated in the survey at higher levels. See Dank, "Development of a Homosexual Identity," 35–37, 48–50; and Warner, "Metropolitan Community Churches," 88.

60. "Not Afraid Anymore," *Los Angeles Advocate*, January 1970, 1; "More Demonstrations," *Los Angeles Advocate*, January 1970, 1.

61. "Not Afraid Any More," 2. A description and transcript of the rally is available in D. Robinson, "Rhetoric of Troy Perry."

62. An earlier protest, called by homophile activists in San Francisco, picketed the State Steamship lines for firing a gay employee. Perry and eight others participated. Swicegood, *Our God Too*, 147–49.

63. "MCC Goes to SF," *MCC News*, December 25, 1969, 1–2.

64. Jim Kepner, "Angles on the News," *Advocate*, August 19–September 1, 1970, 2, 7; Rob Cole, "Just Call It Metropolitan Community Church U.S.A.," *Advocate*, August 19– September 1, 1970, 2, 5; Swicegood, *Our God Too*, 180–210.

65. For an account of the final meeting, which was "zapped" by gay liberation radicals, see Humphreys, *Out of the Closets*. Louis Crompton, who summarized developments in religion for a report written before the meeting, called the founding of the MCC "the most remarkable development in the field of homosexuality and religion during the last two years." Report of the Religious Committee, North American Conference of Homophile Organizations, December 1969, p. 3, box: Religion, file: Southern California Council on Religion and the Homophile, ONE Records, ONGLA.

66. Humphreys, *Out of the Closets*, 151.

67. For more on Robert (Bob) Ennis, see Swicegood, *Our God Too*, 180–210.

68. Troy Perry, "Dr. King and the Homosexual Community," *In Unity* 1.2 (May 1970): 1. A drawing of King was also the cover illustration for this issue of *In Unity*.

69. Birchard, "Metropolitan Community Church," 127–32.

70. My analysis here is indebted to Warner, "Metropolitan Community Churches." My argument challenges Warner's contention that MCC was "first of all" a religious community with the point that Perry and MCC congregations folded politics into their religious mission in such a way as to make the question of priorities a moot issue. See also Wilcox, "Of Markets and Missions."

71. See, for example, Kelley, *Why Conservative Churches Are Growing*.

72. Birchard, "Metropolitan Community Church," 127; Donna J. Wade, "We Are Family," *In Unity* (August/September 1979): 11, 14, 31.

73. "Bylaws of the Universal Fellowship of Metropolitan Community Churches," *In Unity* 1.3 (August 1970): 1–10.

74. Fejes, *Gay Rights and Moral Panic*, 72.

75. The Upstairs Lounge Fire Exhibition, LGBTRAN, http://exhibits.lgbtran.org/exhibits/show/upstairs-lounge-fire (April 4, 2014).

76. Rev. Elder Troy D. Perry and Rev. Elder Nancy Wilson, Report to the President for the White Conference on Hate Crimes, November 1, 1997, LGBTRAN; The Upstairs Lounge Fire Exhibition, LGBTRAN, http://exhibits.lgbtran.org/exhibits/show/upstairs-lounge-fire/gallery?those-who-died# (April 4, 2014).

77. R. Canaday, "Church Growth," 10–11.

78. Swicegood, *Our God Too*, 256.

79. Martin St. John, "A Part of Our Souls Was Ignited," *Advocate*, August 1, 1973, 1, 16–17.

80. Events calendars and reporting in the *Advocate* coverage of gay pride during the 1970s give substantial attention to religious events.

81. Wade, "We Are Family," 11, 14, 31.

82. Ibid.

83. See Boyd, *Wide-Open Town*.

84. "History of Christopher Street West–S.F.," *Gay Pride*, June 25, 1972, 8.

85. Lester Kinsolving, "The Paper Priests," *San Francisco Examiner*, October 11, 1971, 33.

86. Editorial response in *Vector*, November 1970, file: Evangelical Catholic Communion, Community of the Love of Christ, Broshears Papers, GLBTHS.

87. "Worship Program," June 25, 1972, The Ordination of William R. Johnson Exhibition, LGBTRAN, http://www.lgbtran.org/Exhibits/Johnson/ (January 24, 2015)

88. *A Position of Faith*, 1973,The Ordination of William R. Johnson Exhibition, LGBTRAN, http://www.lgbtran.org/Exhibits/Johnson/ (April 4, 2014).

89. W. Evan Golder, "Ordaining a Homosexual Minister," *Christian Century* 89.25 (June 28, 1972): 713.

90. There is evidence that some progressive church leaders had no issue with homosexual ministers who kept their sexuality under wraps. A 1962 brief on this issue for Episcopal bishops included an opinion paper that discouraged removing pastors from their positions solely for reasons of homosexuality. The brief was marked "CONFIDENTIAL." See Margaretta K. Bowers, "The Psychotherapy of Homosexual Clergymen," and Thomas J. Bigham, "Pastoral Care in Problems of Homosexuality among the Clergy," included in Episcopal Church Bishop's Committee on Pastoral Counseling, *Papers on Homosexuality: Presented at the House of Bishops of the Protestant Episcopal Church* (Committee on Pastoral Counseling of the Protestant Episcopal Church, 1962), 24–46, mimeographed copy, University of Rochester Library, http://catalog.lib.rochester.edu/vwebv/holdingsInfo?bibId=4816779.

91. Benton, *Extraordinary Hearts*, 142; Teal, *Gay Militants*, 81.

92. Nicholas Benton, "The Homosexual Revolution Is the Jesus Revolution and It Is Total," reprinted in Nicholas Benton, "God and My Gay Soul" (n.d.), file: Articles on Homosexuality, 1969–1971, Birchard Papers, FLHL.

93. John Coleman, "The Churches and the Homosexual," *America*, February 6, 1971, 112–17; Benton, "God and My Gay Soul," 5–6.

94. Coleman, "Churches and the Homosexual," 112–17.

95. Bigham, "Pastoral Care in Problems of Homosexuality among the Clergy."

96. Roy Birchard, memo to Dr. Lewis I. Maddocks and the United Church ad hoc committee on homosexuality, p. 3, file: Gay Liberation, 1970, Birchard Papers, FLHL.

97. Allen Blaich, "Editorial," *The Gay Considered: A Factsheet on the Homosexuality Resolution of the Lutheran Student Movement*, issue no. 1 (n.d.), p. 1, box 1, file 1, Lutherans Concerned San Francisco Records, GLBTHS.

98. Rossinow, "'The Break-Through to New Life,'" 309–40.

99. Bill Silver, coming-out journal, Silver Papers, Yale University Library Special Collections.

100. Quoted in W. Evan Golder, "Ordaining a Homosexual Minister," *Christian Century* 89.25 (June 28, 1972): 714.

101. John Dart, "Believed First in Major Denomination," *Los Angeles Times*, May 2, 1972, C1; "Homosexual's Ordination Voted in the United Church of Christ," *New York Times*, May 2, 1972, 28; "Ordaining of Homosexual OKd," *Chicago Tribune*, May 2, 1972, 3.

102. "Texas Methodists Dismiss Task Force Report," *Northwest Arkansas Times*, June 1, 1972; "Self-Described Homosexual Clergyman Suspended from Ministry," *Spartanburg Herald*, June 3, 1971, A2; "Gene Leggett" Profiles Gallery, LGBTRAN, http://www.lgbtran.org/Profile.aspx?ID=236 (August 26, 2013).

103. "Chicago Minister Faces Suspension," *Advocate*, March 29, 1972, 13; "Minister 'Comes Out,' Asks for Assignment," *Advocate*, December 8, 1971, 24.

104. "Lutheran Seminary Bars 'Gay House' Coordinator," *Advocate*, April 28, 1971, 4.

105. David B. Sindt, "Proposal to the Presbytery of Chicago," April 7, 1972, pp. 1–5, box 1, file 22, Birchard Papers, FLHL; "Chicago Affirms Twin Cities Action," *Presbyterian Gay Caucus Newsletter*, September 15, 1975, 1. The Chicago presbytery reversed its decision in 1975 and approved Sindt's ministerial standing.

106. P. Moore, *Take a Bishop Like Me*; on Moore's sexual history, see H. Moore, *Bishop's Daughter*.

107. Rick Husky, phone interview with the author, July 30, 2013.

108. In mainline Protestant denominations: the UCC gay caucus (1973); the Gay Presbyterian Caucus (1974); Lutherans Concerned for Gay People (1974); Integrity Gay Episcopal Caucus (1974); the Methodist Gay Caucus (1975); and the American Baptist Gay Caucus (founding date unknown; contact person listed in 1974). In seminaries and divinity schools, a 1974 listing cited contact persons for gay seminarian groups at the Graduate Theological Union, Yale Divinity School, New Brunswick Theological Seminary, Atlanta Theological Association, Chicago Theological Seminary, and Union Theological Seminary; see "Contact Persons in Seminaries," 1974, box 3, file 2, Birchard Papers, FLHL. Outside the mainline, gay caucuses formed in the Unitarian-Universalist Church in 1970 and in the Society of Friends in 1971. Dignity began in 1969.

109. "Gay Task Force Recognized," *Advocate*, November 21, 1973, 10; "National Gay Task Force Meets in New York," June 8, 1973, 1–2, box 2, file 16, Birchard Papers, FLHL.

110. The task force later also involved David Sindt, the Presbyterian minister from Chicago, and Ernest Reaugh, the Methodist layperson from Albany. See also Sally Gearhart and Bill Johnson, "The Gay Movement in the Church," in Gearhart and Johnson, *Loving Men/Loving Women*, 61–118.

111. "Gay Task Force Recognized," 10; "National Gay Task Force Meets in New York," 1–2.

112. Gearhart and Johnson, "Gay Movement in the Church," 61–118.

113. Bill Johnson to Joseph L. Norton of the National Gay Task Force, July 9, 1974, pp. 1–2, box 3, file 2, Roy Birchard Papers, FLHL.

114. See Stein, *Rethinking the Gay and Lesbian Movement*.

115. In New York, the formal name change of the organizing committee took place in 1984, when the Christopher Street Liberation Day Committee reorganized

as Heritage of Pride. Records for all of these organizations are held at the archives of the LGBT Community Center in New York.

116. On history and commemorative narrative, see Zerubavel, *Recovered Roots*, 3–12 On ritual interpretations of gay pride, see Armstrong, *Forging Gay Identities*.

117. "The Band Gets Bigger," *Time*, July 11, 1977, 30.

118. "Homosexuals March for Equal Rights," *New York Times*, June 27, 1977, 1, 20.

119. Cover of the *Advocate*, July 27, 1977.

120. Randy Shilts and Robert McQueen, "The Movement's 'Born Again' from Apathy to Action," *Advocate*, July 27, 1977, 7–9.

EPILOGUE

1. *Bowers v. Hardwick*, 478 U.S. 186 (1986); see also Eskridge, *Gaylaw*, 149–73.

2. Burger, concurring opinion, *Bowers v. Hardwick*. Discussions of this opinion include McGarry, "Crimes of Moral Turpitude"; Jakobsen and Pellegrini, *Love the Sin*, 22–24; and Taves, "Sexuality and American Religious History," 54–55.

3. Blackmun, dissenting opinion, *Bowers v. Hardwick*.

4. Jakobsen and Pellegrini, *Love the Sin*, 31–34.

5. Ibid., 114.

6. D. Bailey, *Homosexuality and the Western Christian Tradition*, ix.

7. On Bryant and conservative politics, see Frank, "'Civil Rights of Parents'"; and Fejes, *Gay Rights and Moral Panic*.

8. For discussion of "backlash," see Schäfer, *Counterculture Conservatives*, 3–14; and Butler, "Jack-in-the-Box Faith."

9. Marsh, *God's Long Summer*; Braude, "Faith, Feminism, and History."

10. Williams, *God's Own Party*, 9; on evangelicals and the Christian right, also see Dochuk, *From Bible Belt to Sunbelt*.

11. On mainline decline and influence, see Smith and Snell, *Souls in Transition*, 287–89.

12. For an overview of mainline homosexuality debates, see Cadge, "Vital Conflicts"; and Moon, *God, Sex, and Politics*.

13. Jordan, *Blessing Same-Sex Unions*, 5.

14. Ellis, *Studies in the Psychology of Sex*, 3–4.

15. D. Bailey, *Homosexuality and the Western Christian Tradition*, x.

16. Hunter, *Culture Wars*, 43.

17. See ibid., 85–86.

18. See, for example, Harold Lindsell, "Homosexuals and the Church," *Christianity Today* 17.25 (September 28, 1973): 8–12; Klaus Bockmühl, "Homosexuality in Biblical Perspective," *Christianity Today* 17.10 (February 16, 1973): 12–18; Dennis Kinlaw, "A Biblical View of Homosexuality," in Collins, *Secrets of Our Sexuality*, 104–16; Lovelace, *Homosexuality and the Church*; and Kirk, *Homosexual Crisis*.

19. Blair, *Evangelical Look at Homosexuality*; Letha Scanzoni, "On Friendship and Homosexuality," *Christianity Today* 18.25 (September 27, 1974): 11–14; Scanzoni and Mollenkott, *Is the Homosexual My Neighbor?*; Lewis B. Smedes, "Homosexuality: Sorting Out the Issues," *Reformed Journal* 28 (1978): 9–12.

20. On American Bible translations, see Beal, *Rise and Fall of the Bible*.

21. Gutjahr, "The Bible-zine *Revolve*," 326.

22. On practices of evangelical Bible reading, see Malley, *How the Bible Works*; and Harding, *Book of Jerry Falwell*.

23. L. Gerber, "Opposite of Gay," 8; Erzen, *Straight to Jesus*.

24. White, "Virgin Pride."

25. Noll, "Bible and Slavery," 43.

26. Scott, *Sexularism*, 1–2.

27. Fessenden, *Culture and Redemption*, 5.

Selected Bibliography

ARCHIVAL COLLECTIONS

Archives of the Episcopal Diocese of New York, N.Y.
 Bishop Donagan Files
 Paul Moore Papers
Archives of the Southern Baptist Church, Nashville, Tenn.
 Christian Life Commission Resources Files
Congregational Library and Archives, Boston, Mass.
 Robert Wood Papers
Flora Lamson Hewlett Library, Graduate Theological Union, Berkeley, Calif.
 Universal Fellowship of Metropolitan Community Churches Collection
  Roy Birchard Papers
Gay, Lesbian, Bisexual, Transgender Historical Society, San Francisco, Calif.
 Ray Broshears Papers
 Charles Lewis Papers
 Donald Stewart Lucas Papers
 Lutherans Concerned San Francisco Records
 Lyon/Martin Papers
Gender Equity Collections, Elihu Burritt Library, Central Connecticut State
  University, New Britain, Conn.
 George W. Henry Foundation / Canon Clinton Jones Papers
 Robert P. Wells Collection
International Gay Information Center Collections, Rare Books and Manuscripts
  Division, New York Public Library, New York, N.Y.
 Robert Clement Papers
 Craig Rodwell Papers
 Ephemera—Subject Files—Religion
James C. Hormel Gay and Lesbian Center, San Francisco Public Library,
  San Francisco, Calif.
 William Billings Papers
 Scott Bishop Papers
 Evander Smith and Herbert Donaldson Papers
Lesbian, Gay, Bisexual, Transgender Religious Archives Network (lgbtran.org)
 Council on Religion and the Homosexual
 Oral History Collection
 The Ordination of William R. Johnson
 Profiles Gallery

The Upstairs Lounge Fire

ONE National Gay and Lesbian Archives, Los Angeles, Calif.

    MCC Historical Collection

    ONE Records (unprocessed)

    Southern California Council on Religion and the Homophile Collection

Presbyterian Historical Society, Philadelphia, Pa.

    General Assembly Records of the Presbyterian Church (USA)

    Papers of the National Council of Churches

Yale Divinity School Archives, Yale Divinity School Library, New Haven, Conn.

    Papers of the Standard Bible Committee

Yale University Library Special Collections, New Haven, Conn.

    William Silver Papers

PERIODICALS

America

American Weekly

Berkshire Eagle

Chicago Tribune

Christian Century

Christian Crusade Weekly

Christianity and Crisis

Christianity Today

Christian Life

Collier's

Come Out!

Crozer Quarterly

Denver Post

Eastern Mattachine Magazine

Engage

FCL Newsletter

Gay

Gay News

Gay Pride

In Unity

Journal of Pastoral Care

Journal of Religion and Health

The Ladder

Law and Contemporary Problems

Life

Living Church

Los Angeles Advocate / The Advocate

Los Angeles Free Press

Los Angeles Times

Man and Society

Mattachine Review

MCC News

Middlesboro (Ky.) Daily News

Moody Monthly

motive

National Informer

New/World Outlook

New York Daily News

New York HYMNAL

New York Mattachine Newsletter

New York Post

New York Times

Northwest Arkansas Times

ONE

ONE Institute Quarterly: Homophile Studies

Parade Magazine

Pastoral Psychology

Presbyterian Gay Caucus Newsletter

Presbyterian Journal

Presbyterian Layman

Reformed Journal

San Antonio Express

San Francisco Examiner

San Francisco News Call Bulletin

San Francisco Sunday Chronicle

Social Action

Social Progress

Springfielder

Time

Town Talk

Union Seminary Quarterly Review

United Church Herald

Village Voice

BOOKS, ARTICLES, AND DISSERTATIONS

Alinsky, Saul David. *Reveille for Radicals*. Chicago: University of Chicago Press, 1946.

Ammerman, Nancy Tatom. *Baptist Battles: Social Change and Religious Conflict in the Southern Baptist Convention*. New Brunswick, N.J.: Rutgers University Press, 1990.

Anderson, Michael. "'Education of Another Kind'—Loraine Hansberry in the Fifties." In *Gender Nonconformity, Race, and Sexuality: Charting the Connections*, edited by Toni Lester, 210–16. Madison: University of Wisconsin Press, 2002.

Anson, Peter F. *Bishops at Large*. London: Faber and Faber, 1964.

Armstrong, Elizabeth A. *Forging Gay Identities: Organizing Sexuality in San Francisco, 1950–1994*. Chicago: University of Chicago Press, 2002.

Atkins, Gary. *Gay Seattle: Stories of Exile and Belonging*. Seattle: University of Washington Press, 2003.

Babbage, Stuart Barton. *Christianity and Sex*. Chicago: Inter-Varsity Press, 1963.

Bailey, Beth L. "Sexual Revolution(s)." In *The Sixties: From Memory to History*, edited by David Farber, 235–62. Chapel Hill: University of North Carolina Press, 1994.

Bailey, Derrick Sherwin. "The Homosexual and Christian Morals." In *They Stand Apart: A Critical Survey of the Problem of Homosexuality*, edited by J. Tudor Rees and Harley V. Usil, 36–66. New York: Macmillan, 1955.

———. *Homosexuality and the Western Christian Tradition*. London: Longmans, Green, 1955.

Balmer, Randall, and Lauren F. Winner. *Protestants in America*. New York: Columbia University Press, 2002.

Bayer, Ronald, *Homosexuality and American Psychiatry: The Politics of Diagnosis*. Princeton, N.J.: Princeton University Press, 1981.

Beal, Timothy Kandler. *The Rise and Fall of the Bible: The Unexpected History of an Accidental Book*. New York: Houghton Mifflin Harcourt, 2011.

Benton, Nick. *Extraordinary Hearts: Reclaiming Gay Sensibility's Central Role in the Progress of Civilization*. Maple Shade, N.J.: Lethe Press, 2013.

Bérubé, Allan, John D'Emilio, and Estelle B. Freedman. *Coming Out under Fire: The History of Gay Men and Women in World War II*. Chapel Hill: University of North Carolina Press, 2010.

Best, Wallace. *Passionately Human, No Less Divine: Religion and Culture in Black Chicago, 1915–1952*. Princeton: Princeton University Press, 2007.

Birchard, Roy. "Metropolitan Community Church: Its Development and Significance." *Foundations: A Baptist Journal of History and Theology* 20.2 (June 1997): 127–32.

Blair, Ralph. *An Evangelical Look at Homosexuality.* New York: Homosexual Community Counseling Center, 1972.

Boisen, Anton T. *The Exploration of the Inner World: A Study of Mental Disorder and Religious Experience.* Philadelphia: Willett, Clark, 1936.

Bonnell, John Sutherland. *Psychology for Pastor and People: A Book on Spiritual Counseling.* New York: Harper, 1948.

Boone, Joseph Allen. *The Homoerotics of Orientalism.* New York: Columbia University Press, 2014.

Boswell, John E. *Christianity, Social Tolerance, and Homosexuality.* Chicago: University of Chicago Press, 1980.

Boyd, Nan Alamilla. *Wide-Open Town: A History of Queer San Francisco to 1965.* Berkeley: University of California Press, 2003.

Braude, Ann. "Faith, Feminism and History." In *American Christianities: A History of Dominance and Diversity,* edited by Catherine A. Brekus and W. Clark Gilpin, 232–52. Chapel Hill: University of North Carolina Press, 2011.

Bravmann, Scott. *Queer Fictions of the Past: History, Culture, and Difference.* New York: Cambridge University Press, 1997.

Brooks, Beatrice A. "Fertility Cult Functionaries in the Old Testament." *Journal of Biblical Literature* 60.3 (1941): 227–53.

Broyles, Vernon S. "The Fractured Body of Christ: Recollections, Reflections and Observations on the Presbyterian Church in America (PCA) Schism by an Alabama Pastor." *Journal of Presbyterian History* 86.1 (Spring/Summer 2008): 5–16.

Bullough, Vern L., ed. *Before Stonewall: Activists for Gay and Lesbian Rights in Historical Context.* New York: Harrington Park Press, 2002.

Bullough, Vern L., and Martha Voght. "Homosexuality and Its Confusion with the 'Secret Sin' in Pre-Freudian America." *Journal of the History of Medicine and Allied Sciences* 28.2 (1973): 143–55.

Butler, Jon. "Jack-in-the-Box Faith: The Religion Problem in Modern American History." *Journal of American History* 90.4 (March 2004): 1357–78.

Buttrick, George Arthur, ed. *The Interpreter's Bible: The Holy Scriptures in the King James and Revised Standard Versions.* 12 vols. New York: Abington Press, 1951–57.

———. *The Interpreter's Dictionary of the Bible: An Illustrated Encyclopedia.* New York: Abingdon Press, 1962.

Cadge, Wendy. "Vital Conflicts: The Mainline Denominations Debate Homosexuality." In *The Quiet Hand of God: Faith-Based Activism and the Public Role of Mainline Protestantism,* edited by Robert Wuthnow and John Evans, 265–86. Berkeley: University of California Press, 2002.

Canaday, Margot. *The Straight State: Sexuality and Citizenship in Twentieth-Century America.* Princeton, N.J.: Princeton University Press, 2009.

Canaday, Rudd Hoover. "Church Growth in the Universal Fellowship of Metropolitan Community Churches." M.Div. thesis, Union Theological Seminary, 1990.

Carey, J. S. "DS Bailey and 'The Name Forbidden Among Christians.'" *Anglican Theological Review* 70.2 (1988): 152–73.

Carpenter, Joel A. *Revive Us Again: The Reawakening of American Fundamentalism.* Oxford: Oxford University Press, 1999.

Carter, David. *Stonewall: The Riots That Sparked the Gay Revolution.* New York: Macmillan, 2010.

Chauncey, George. "Christian Brotherhood or Sexual Perversion? Homosexual Identities and the Construction of Sexual Boundaries in the World War One Era." *Journal of Social History* 19.2 (December 1985): 189–211.

———. *Gay New York : Gender, Urban Culture, and the Makings of the Gay Male World, 1890–1940.* New York: Basic Books, 1994.

———. "'What Gay Studies Taught the Court': The Historians' Amicus Brief in *Lawrence v. Texas*." *GLQ: A Journal of Lesbian and Gay Studies* 10.3 (2004): 509–38.

Cole, William Graham. *Sex and Love in the Bible.* New York: Association Press, 1959.

———. *Sex in Christianity and Psychoanalysis.* New York: Oxford University Press, 1955.

Collins, Gary, ed. *The Secrets of Our Sexuality* Waco: Word Books, 1976.

Committee on Homosexual Offences and Prostitution. *The Wolfenden Report: Report of the Committee on Homosexual Offences and Prostitution.* Authorized American ed. New York: Stein and Day, 1963.

Cory, Donald Webster [Edward Sagarin]. *The Homosexual in America: A Subjective Approach.* New York: Greenberg, 1951.

Council of Christian Associations. *The Sex Life of Youth.* New York: Association Press, 1929.

Cox, Harvey. *The Secular City: Secularization and Urbanization in Theological Perspective.* New York: MacMillan, 1965.

Cromey, Robert Warren. *Essays Irreverent.* iUniverse, 2012.

Cutler, Marvin [pseud.], ed. *Homosexuals Today: A Handbook of Organizations and Publications.* Los Angeles: Publication Division of ONE, Inc., 1956.

Dank, Barry. "The Development of a Homosexual Identity: Antecedents and Consequents." Ph.D. diss., University of Wisconsin, 1973.

Davis, John D. *A Dictionary of the Bible.* Philadelphia: Westminster Press, 1917.

Davis, Rebecca. *More Perfect Unions: The American Search for Marital Bliss.* Cambridge, Mass.: Harvard University Press, 2010.

———. "'My Homosexuality Is Getting Worse Every Day': Norman Vincent Peale, Psychiatry and the Liberal Protestant Response to Same-Sex Desires in Mid-Twentieth Century America." In *American Christianities: A History of Dominance and Diversity,* edited by Catherine A. Brekus and W. Clark Gilpin, 347–65. Chapel Hill: University of North Carolina Press, 2011.

DeLeon, David. *Leaders from the 1960s: A Historical Sourcebook.* Westport, Conn.: Greenwood Press, 1994.

D'Emilio, John. *Sexual Politics, Sexual Communities: The Making of a Homosexual Minority in the United States, 1940–1970.* Chicago: University of Chicago Press, 1983.

D'Emilio, John, and Estelle B. Freedman. *Intimate Matters: A History of Sexuality in America.* 2nd ed. Chicago: University of Chicago Press, 1998.

DeRogatis, Amy. *Saving Sex: Sexuality and Salvation in American Evangelicalism.* New York: Oxford University Press, 2014.

————. "What Would Jesus Do? Sexuality and Salvation in Protestant Evangelical Sex Manuals, 1950s to the Present." *Church History: Studies in Christianity and Culture* 74.1 (2005): 97–137.

Dicks, Russell Leslie. *Pastoral Work and Personal Counseling.* New York: Macmillan, 1944.

Dochuk, Darren. *From Bible Belt to Sunbelt: Plain-Folk Religion, Grassroots Politics, and the Rise of Evangelical Conservatism.* New York: W. W. Norton, 2012.

Doniger, Simon, ed. *Sex and Religion Today.* New York: Association Press, 1953.

Duberman, Martin. *Stonewall.* New York: Dutton, 1993.

Duberman, Martin B. "Dr. Edward Sagarin and Mr. Cory: The 'Father' of the Homophile Movement." *Harvard Gay and Lesbian Review* 4.4 (Fall 1997): 7–17.

Durham, Lewis. *Glide Foundation from 1962 through 1967.* San Francisco: Glide Foundation, 1968.

Duvall, Evelyn M., and Sylvanus M. Duvall, eds. *Sex Ways—In Fact and Faith: Bases for Christian Family Policy.* New York: Association Press, 1961.

Eiselen, Frederick Carl, Edwin Lewis, and David G. Downey, eds. *The Abingdon Bible Commentary.* New York: Abingdon Press, 1929.

Eisenbach, David. *Gay Power: An American Revolution.* New York: Carroll and Graf, 2006.

Ellis, Havelock. *Studies in the Psychology of Sex: Sexual Inversion.* Philadelphia: F. A. Davis, 1915.

Enroth, Ronald M., and Gerald E. Jamison. *The Gay Church.* Grand Rapids, Mich.: Eerdmans, 1974.

Erzen, Tanya. *Straight to Jesus: Sexual and Christian Conversions in the Ex-Gay Movement.* Berkeley: University of California Press, 2006.

Eskridge, William. *Dishonorable Passions: Sodomy Laws in America, 1861–2003.* New York: Viking, 2008.

————. *Gaylaw: Challenging the Apartheid of the Closet.* Cambridge, Mass.: Harvard University Press, 2009.

Faderman, Lillian, and Stuart Timmons. *Gay L.A.* New York: Perseus Books, 2006.

Fejes, Fred. *Gay Rights and Moral Panic: The Origins of America's Debate on Homosexuality.* New York: Palgrave Macmillan, 2008.

Fessenden, Tracy. *Culture and Redemption: Religion, the Secular, and American Literature.* Princeton, N.J.: Princeton University Press, 2011.

Fetner, Tina. *How the Religious Right Shaped Lesbian and Gay Activism.* Minneapolis: University of Minnesota Press, 2008.

Findlay, James F. *Church People in the Struggle: The National Council of Churches and the Black Freedom Movement, 1950–1970.* New York: Oxford University Press, 1997.

Fletcher, Joseph F. *Morals and Medicine: The Moral Problems of: The Patient's Right to Know the Truth, Contraception, Artificial Insemination, Sterilization, Euthanasia.* Beacon Press, 1960.

————. "Sex Offenses: An Ethical View." *Law and Contemporary Problems* 25.2 (Spring 1960): 244–57.

———. *Situation Ethics: The New Morality*. Philadelphia: Westminster John Knox Press, 1966.

Fosdick, Harry Emerson. *The Living of These Days: An Autobiography*. New York: Harper, 1956.

———. *On Being a Real Person*. New York: Harper and Brothers, 1943.

Foucault, Michel. *The History of Sexuality: Volume 1, An Introduction*. Translated by Robert Hurley. New York: Random House, 1978.

———. "Nietzsche, Genealogy, History." In *Language, Counter-Memory, Practice: Selected Essays and Interviews*, edited by Michel Foucault and Donald F. Bouchard, 139–64. Ithaca: Cornell University Press, 1980.

Frank, Gillian. "'The Civil Rights of Parents': Race and Conservative Politics in Anita Bryant's Campaign against Gay Rights in 1970s Florida." *Journal of the History of Sexuality* 22.1 (January 2013): 126–60.

Freud, Sigmund. "Letter to an American Mother (1935)." *American Journal of Psychiatry* 107 (1951): 786–87.

Freud, Sigmund, A. A Brill, and James Jackson Putnam. *Three Contributions to the Sexual Theory*. New York: Journal of Nervous and Mental Disease, 1910.

Gearhart, Sally, and Bill Johnson, *Loving Men/Loving Women*. San Francisco: Glide Publications, 1974.

Geldenhuys, Norval. *The Intimate Life*. Grand Rapids, Mich.: Eerdmans, 1957.

Genné, Elizabeth. *Christians and the Crisis in Sex Morality: The Church Looks at the Facts about Sex and Marriage Today*. New York: Association Press, 1962.

Genné, Elizabeth, William H. Genné, North American Conference on Church and Family, National Council of the Churches of Christ in the United States of America, and Department of Family Life. *Foundations for Christian Family Policy: The Proceedings of the North American Conference on Church and Family, April 30–May 5, 1961*. New York: Published for the Canadian and National Councils of Churches by the Dept. of Family Life, National Council of Churches of Christ in the USA, 1961.

Gerber, Israel J. *Man on a Pendulum: A Case History of an Invert*. New York: American Press, 1955.

Gerber, Lynne. "The Opposite of Gay: Nature, Creation, and Queer-ish Ex-Gay Experiments." *Nova Religio* 11.4 (May 2008): 8–30.

Goldberg, Jonathan. *Sodometries: Renaissance Texts, Modern Sexualities*. Stanford, Calif.: Stanford University Press, 1992.

Gray, A. Herbert. *Men, Women, and God: A Discussion of Sex Questions from the Christian Point of View*. New York: Association Press, 1938.

Green, Clifford J., ed. *Churches, Cities, and Human Community: Urban Ministry in the United States, 1945–1985*. Grand Rapids, Mich.: Eerdmans, 1996.

Gregory, W. Edgar. "The Chaplain and Mental Hygiene." *American Journal of Sociology* 52.5 (March 1, 1947): 420–23.

Griffith, R. Marie. "The Religious Encounters of Alfred C. Kinsey." *Journal of American History* 95.2 (2008): 349–77.

Gross, Alfred A. *Strangers in Our Midst: Problems of the Homosexual in American Society*. Washington, D.C.: Public Affairs Press, 1962.

Gustav-Wrathall, John Donald. *Take the Young Stranger by the Hand: Same-Sex Relations and the YMCA*. Chicago: University of Chicago Press, 1998.

Gutjahr, Paul C. "The Bible-zine *Revolve* and the Evolution of the Culturally Relevant Bible in America." In *Religion and the Culture of Print in Modern America*, edited by Charles L. Cohen and Paul S. Boyer, 326–48. Madison: University of Wisconsin Press, 2008.

Hadden, Jeffrey K. *The Gathering Storm in the Churches*. New York: Doubleday, 1969.

Halperin, David M. *How to Do the History of Homosexuality*. Chicago: University of Chicago Press, 2004.

Harding, Susan Friend. *The Book of Jerry Falwell: Fundamentalist Language and Politics*. Princeton, N.J.: Princeton University Press, 2001.

Hastings, James, ed. *Encyclopaedia of Religion and Ethics*. New York: C. Scribner's Sons, 1921.

Hedstrom, Matthew. *The Rise of Liberal Religion: Book Culture and American Spirituality in the Twentieth Century*. New York: Oxford University Press, 2012.

Henry, George William. *All the Sexes: A Study of Masculinity and Femininity*. New York: Rinehart, 1955.

Henry, George William, and Committee for the Study of Sex Variants. *Sex Variants: A Study of Homosexual Patterns*. New York: P. B. Hoeber, 1941.

Herman, Didi. *The Antigay Agenda: Orthodox Vision and the Christian Right*. Chicago: University of Chicago Press, 1997.

Heron, Alastair. *Towards a Quaker View of Sex: An Essay by a Group of Friends*. 2nd ed. London: Friends Home Service Committee, 1963.

Hewitt, Thomas Furman. "The American Church's Reaction to the Homophile Movement, 1948–1978." Ph.D. diss., Duke University, 1983.

Hiltner, Seward. *Sex Ethics and the Kinsey Reports*. New York: Association Press, 1953.

Holifield, E. Brooks. *A History of Pastoral Care in America: From Salvation to Self-Realization*. Nashville: Abingdon Press, 1983.

Hollinger, David A. "After Cloven Tongues of Fire: Ecumenical Protestantism and the Modern American Encounter with Diversity." *Journal of American History* 98.1 (June 2011): 21–48.

Howard, John. "The Library, the Park, and the Pervert: Public Space and Homosexual Encounter in Post–World War II Atlanta." *Radical History Review* 62 (1995): 166–87.

Huffer, Lynne. *Mad for Foucault: Rethinking the Foundations of Queer Theory*. New York: Columbia University Press, 2010.

Hulsether, Mark. *Building a Protestant Left: Christianity and Crisis Magazine, 1941–1993*. Knoxville: University of Tennessee Press, 1999.

Humphreys, Laud. *Out of the Closets: The Sociology of Homosexual Liberation*. New York: Prentice-Hall, 1972.

———. *Tearoom Trade*. Chicago: Aldine, 1975.

Hunter, James Davidson. *Culture Wars: The Struggle to Define America*. New York: Basic Books, 1991.

Hutcheson, Gregory S. "The Sodomitic Moor: Queerness in the Narrative of Reconquista." In *Queering the Middle Ages*, edited by Glenn Burger and Steven F. Kruger, 99–122. Minneapolis: University of Minnesota Press, 2001.

Hutcheson, William R. *The Modernist Impulse in American Protestantism*. Durham, N.C.: Duke University Press, 1992.

Irvine, Janice. *Talk about Sex: The Battles over Sex Education in the United States*. Berkeley: University of California Press, 2004.

Jackson, David W. *Changing Times: Almanac and Digest of Kansas City's Gay and Lesbian History*. Kansas City: Orderly Pack Rat, 2011.

Jakobsen, Janet R., and Ann Pellegrini. *Love the Sin: Sexual Regulation and the Limits of Religious Tolerance*. New York: New York University Press, 2003.

———, eds. *Secularisms*. Durham, N.C.: Duke University Press, 2008.

Johnson, David K. *The Lavender Scare: The Cold War Persecution of Gays and Lesbians in the Federal Government*. Chicago: University of Chicago Press, 2004.

Jones, Clinton R. "The Pastoral Counselor and the Male Homosexual." Master's thesis, New York Theological Seminary, 1969.

Jones, H. Kimball. *Toward a Christian Understanding of the Homosexual*. New York: Association Press, 1966.

Jones, Ilion Tingnal. *Principles and Practice of Preaching*. Nashville: Abingdon Press, 1956.

Jones, Timothy. "The Stained Glass Closet: Celibacy and Homosexuality in the Church of England to 1955." *Journal of the History of Sexuality* 20.1 (December 2010): 132–52.

Jordan, Mark D. *Blessing Same-Sex Unions: The Perils of Queer Romance and the Confusions of Christian Marriage*. Chicago: University of Chicago Press, 2005.

———. *The Invention of Sodomy in Christian Theology*. Chicago: University of Chicago Press, 1997.

———. *Recruiting Young Love: How Christians Talk About Homosexuality*. Chicago: University of Chicago Press, 2011.

———. "Sodomites and Churchmen: The Theological Invention of Homosexuality." In *Michel Foucault and Theology: The Politics of Religious Experience*, edited by James William Bernauer and Jeremy R. Carrette, 233–44. Burlington, Vt.: Ashgate, 2004.

Katz, Jonathan. *The Invention of Heterosexuality*. New York: Dutton, 1995.

Keane, Webb. *Christian Moderns: Freedom and Fetish in the Mission Encounter*. Berkeley: University of California Press, 2007.

Kelley, Dean M. *Why Conservative Churches Are Growing: A Study in Sociology of Religion*. New York: Harper and Row, 1972.

Kepner, Jim. *Rough News, Daring Views: 1950s' Pioneer Gay Press Journalism*. New York: Harrington Park Press, 1997.

King, Martin Luther, Jr. "The Current Crisis in Race Relations" (1958). In *A Testament of Hope: The Essential Writings and Speeches of Martin Luther King, Jr.*, edited by James W. Washington, 88. San Francisco: HarperCollins, 1986.

Kinsey, Alfred C., and the Institute for Sex Research. *Sexual Behavior in the Human Female*. Philadelphia: W. B. Saunders, 1953.

Kinsey, Alfred C., Wardell Baxter Pomeroy, and Clyde Eugene Martin. *Sexual Behavior in the Human Male*. Philadelphia: W. B. Saunders, 1948.

Kirk, Jerry R. *The Homosexual Crisis in the Mainline Church: A Presbyterian Minister Speaks Out*. Nashville: T. Nelson Incorporated, 1978.

Kissack, Terence. "Freaking Fag Revolutionaries: New York's Gay Liberation Front, 1969–1971." *Radical History Review* 62 (1995): 104–34.

Klassen, Pamela. *Spirits of Protestantism: Medicine, Healing, and Liberal Christianity.* Berkeley: University of California Press, 2001.

Kohl, David Grant. *A Curious and Peculiar People: A History of the Metropolitan Community Church of Portland, Oregon, and the Sexual Minority Communities of the Pacific Northwest.* Portland: Spirit Press, 2006.

Kripal, Jeffrey J. *Esalen: America and the Religion of No Religion.* Chicago: University of Chicago Press, 2007.

Kuhn, Donald. *The Church and the Homosexual: A Report on a Consultation.* San Francisco: Glide Urban Center, 1965.

Lasch, Christopher. *The Culture of Narcissism: American Life in the Age of Diminishing Expectations.* New York: W. W. Norton, 1979.

Lassiter, Matthew D. *The Silent Majority: Suburban Politics in the Sunbelt South.* Princeton, N.J.: Princeton University Press, 2006.

Little, David. "Calvinism and American National Identity." In *John Calvin's American Legacy*, edited by Thomas Davis, 43–64. New York: Oxford University Press, 1981.

Loftin, Craig M. *Masked Voices: Gay Men and Lesbians in Cold War America.* Albany: State University of New York Press, 2012.

———. "Unacceptable Mannerisms: Gender Anxieties, Homosexual Activism, and Swish in the United States, 1945–1965." *Journal of Social History* 40.3 (2007): 577–96.

Lofton, Kathryn. "The Methodology of the Modernists: Process in American Protestantism." *Church History: Studies in Christianity and Culture* 75.2 (2006): 374–402.

———. "The Preacher Paradigm: Promotional Biographies and the Modern-Made Evangelist." *Religion and American Culture* 16.1 (2006): 95–123.

———. "Queering Fundamentalism: John Balcom Shaw and the Sexuality of a Protestant Orthodoxy." *Journal of the History of Sexuality* 17.3 (2008): 439–68.

Lovelace, Richard F. *Homosexuality and the Church.* Old Tapan, N.J.: F. H. Revell, 1978.

Luecke, Richard Henry. "Protestant Clergy: New Forms of Ministry, New Forms of Training." *The Annals of the American Academy of Political and Social Science* 387.1 (January 1970): 86–95.

Macquarrie, John. *Dictionary of Christian Ethics.* Philadelphia: Westminster Press, 1967.

Malley, Brian. *How the Bible Works: An Anthropological Study of Evangelical Biblicism.* Walnut Creek, Calif.: Altamira Press, 2004.

Marcus, Eric. *Making Gay History.* New York: HarperCollins, 2009.

Marotta, Toby. *The Politics of Homosexuality.* Boston: Houghton Mifflin Harcourt, 1981.

Marsden, George M. *Fundamentalism and American Culture.* New York: Oxford University Press, 2006.

Marsh, Charles. *God's Long Summer: Stories of Faith and Civil Rights.* Princeton, N.J.: Princeton University Press, 1999.

Martin, Dale. *Sex and the Single Savior: Gender and Sexuality in Biblical Interpretation.* Louisville, Ky.: Westminster John Knox Press, 2006.

Martin, Del, and Phyllis Lyon. *Lesbian/Woman*. Volcano, Calif.: Volcano Press, 1991.

May, Elaine Tyler. *Homeward Bound: American Families in the Cold War Era*. New York: Basic Books, 2008.

McGarry, Molly. "Crimes of Moral Turpitude: Questions at the Borders of Religion, the Secular and the U.S. Nation State." In *Religion, the Secular, and the Politics of Sexual Difference*, edited by Tracy Fessenden and Linell E. Cady. New York: Columbia University Press, 2013. E-book.

Miller, Robert Moats. *Harry Emerson Fosdick: Preacher, Pastor, Prophet*. New York: Oxford University Press, 1985.

Miller, Steven P. *The Age of Evangelicalism: America's Born Again Years*. New York: Oxford University Press, 2014.

Minton, Henry. *Departing from Deviance : A History of Homosexual Rights and Emancipatory Science in America*. Chicago: University of Chicago Press, 2002.

Moon, Dawne. *God, Sex, and Politics: Homosexuality and Everyday Theologies*. Chicago: University of Chicago Press, 2004.

Moore, Honor. *The Bishop's Daughter: A Memoir*. New York: W. W. Norton, 2009.

Moore, Paul, Jr. *Take a Bishop Like Me*. New York: Harper and Row, 1979.

Mow, Anna. *The Secret of Married Love*. New York: A. J. Holman, 1970.

Moye, J. Todd. "Cathedral of Hope: A History of Progressive Christianity, Civil Rights, and Gay Social Activism in Dallas, Texas, 1965–1992." Master's thesis, University of North Texas, 2009.

Muravchik, Stephanie. *American Protestantism in the Age of Psychology*. New York: Cambridge University Press, 2011.

Myers-Shirk, Susan E. *Helping the Good Shepherd: Pastoral Counselors in a Psychotherapeutic Culture, 1925–1975*. Baltimore: Johns Hopkins University Press, 2009.

Narramore, Clyde M. *Life and Love: A Christian View of Sex*. Grand Rapids, Mich.: Zondervan House, 1956.

Niebuhr, H. Richard. *Christ and Culture*. San Francisco: HarperCollins, 1951.

Noll, Mark A. "The Bible and Slavery." In *Religion and the American Civil War*, edited by Randal M. Miller, 43–73. New York: Oxford University Press, 1998.

Northcote, Hugh. *Christianity and Sex Problems*. Philadelphia: F. A. Davis, 1906.

Northridge, W. L. *Psychology and Pastoral Practice*. Great Neck, N.Y.: Pastoral Psychology Book Club, 1953.

Oosterhuis, Harry. *Stepchildren of Nature: Krafft-Ebing, Psychiatry, and the Making of Sexual Identity*. Chicago: University of Chicago Press, 2000.

Orr, James, ed. *The International Standard Bible Encyclopaedia, Volume 5*. Chicago: Howard-Severance Company, 1915.

Perry, Troy. *The Lord Is My Shepherd and He Knows I'm Gay*. Los Angeles: Nash, 1972.

Piper, Otto A. *The Christian Interpretation of Sex*. New York: Scribner, 1941.

Pittenger, W. *Time for Consent*. 2nd ed., rev. and enlarged. London: S. C. M. Press, 1970.

Puff, Helmut. *Sodomy in Reformation Germany and Switzerland, 1400–1600*. Chicago: University of Chicago Press, 2003.

Rieff, Philip. *The Triumph of the Therapeutic: Uses of Faith after Freud*. Chicago: University of Chicago Press, 1966.

Roberts, David. *Psychotherapy and a Christian View of Man*. New York: Charles Scribner's Sons, 1950.

Roberts, Jon H. "Psychoanalysis and American Christianity." In *When Science and Christianity Meet*, edited by David C. Lindberg and Ronald L. Numbers, 239–45. Chicago: University of Chicago Press, 2008.

Robinson, David Joe. "The Rhetoric of Troy Perry: A Case Study of the Los Angeles Gay Rights Rally, November 16, 1969." Ph.D. diss., University of Southern California, 1972.

Robinson, John Arthur Thomas. *Honest to God*. Philadelphia: Westminster John Knox Press, 1963.

Roof, Wade Clark, and William McKinney. *American Mainline Religion: Its Changing Shape and Future*. New Brunswick, N.J.: Rutgers University Press, 1987.

Rose, Nikolas. "Assembling the Modern Self." In *Rewriting the Self: Histories from the Renaissance to the Present*, edited by Roy Porter, 224–48. New York: Routledge, 1997.

Rossinow, Doug. "'The Break-Through to New Life': Christianity and the Emergence of the New Left in Austin, Texas, 1965–1964." *American Quarterly* 46.3 (September 1994): 309–40.

————. *The Politics of Authenticity: Liberalism, Christianity, and the New Left in America*. New York: Columbia University Press, 1998.

Rubin, Gayle. "Thinking Sex: Notes for a Radical Theory of the Politics of Sexuality" (1984). Republished in *Deviations: A Gayle Rubin Reader*, 137–81. Durham, N.C.: Duke University Press, 2011.

Sagarin, Edward. *Structure and Ideology in an Association of Deviants*. New York: Arno Press, 1975.

Scanzoni, Letha, and Virginia Ramey Mollenkott. *Is the Homosexual My Neighbor? Another Christian View*. New York: Harper and Row, 1978.

Schäfer, Axel R., ed. *Countercultural Conservatives: American Evangelism from the Postwar Revival to the New Christian Right*. Madison: University of Wisconsin Press, 2011.

Scott, Joan Wallach. *Sexularism*. Florence, Italy: European University Institute, 2009.

Sears, James Thomas. *Behind the Mask of the Mattachine: The Hal Call Chronicles and the Early Movement for Homosexual Emancipation*. New York: Harrington Park Press, 2006.

————. "Bob Basker (1918–2001): Selling the Movement." In *Before Stonewall: Activists for Gay and Lesbian Rights in Historical Context*, edited by Vern L. Bullough, 193–203. New York: Harrington Park Press, 2002.

————. *Rebels, Rubyfruit, and Rhinestones: Queering Space in the Stonewall South*. New Brunswick, N.J.: Rutgers University Press, 2001.

Smedes, Lewis B. *Sex for Christians: The Limits and Liberties of Sexual Living*. Grand Rapids, Mich.: Eerdmans, 1976.

Smith, Christian, and Patricia Snell. *Souls in Transition: The Religious and Spiritual Lives of Emerging Adults*. New York: Oxford University Press, 2009.

Smith, George Adam. *The Historical Geography of the Holy Land: Especially in Relation to the History of Israel and of the Early Church*. London: Hodder and Stoughton, 1894.

Smith-Rosenberg, Carroll. *Disorderly Conduct: Visions of Gender in Victorian America*. New York: Oxford University Press, 1986.

Spike, Paul. *Photographs of My Father*. New York: Alfred A. Knopf, 1973.

Stein, Marc. *City of Sisterly and Brotherly Loves: Lesbian and Gay Philadelphia, 1945–1972*. Chicago: University of Chicago Press, 2000.

———. *Rethinking the Gay and Lesbian Movement*. New York: Routledge, 2012.

Stone, Ken. *Practicing Safer Texts: Food, Sex and Bible in Queer Perspective*. London: T and T Clark, 2005.

Streitmatter, Rodger. *Unspeakable: The Rise of the Gay and Lesbian Press in America*. Boston: Faber and Faber, 1995.

Stryker, Susan. *Transgender History*. Berkeley: Seal Press, 2008.

Swartz, David R. *Moral Minority: The Evangelical Left in an Age of Conservatism*. Philadelphia: University of Pennsylvania Press, 2012.

Sweet, Leonard. "The 1960s: The Crisis of Liberal Christianity." In *Evangelicalism and Modern America*, edited by George Marsden, 29–45. Grand Rapids, Mich.: Eerdmans, 1984.

Sweet, Roxanna Beryl Thayer. "Political and Social Action in Homophile Organizations." Ph.D. diss., University of California, 1968.

Swicegood, Tom. *Our God Too: Biography of a Church and a Temple*. 1974; repr., iUniverse, 2003.

Taves, Ann. "Sexuality and American Religious History." In *Retelling U.S. Religious History*, edited by Thomas Tweed, 27–56. Berkeley: University of California Press, 1997.

Teal, Donn. *The Gay Militants*. New York: Stein and Day, 1971.

Terry, Jennifer. *An American Obsession: Science, Medicine, and Homosexuality in Modern Society*. Chicago: University of Chicago Press, 1999.

Thielicke, Helmut. *The Ethics of Sex*. New York: Harper and Row, 1964.

Thuesen, Peter Johannes. *In Discordance with the Scriptures: American Protestant Battles over Translating the Bible*. New York: Oxford University Press, 2002.

Tortorici, Zeb. "Against Nature: Sodomy and Homosexuality in Colonial Latin America." *History Compass* 10.2 (2011): 161–78.

Treese, Robert L. *Homosexuality: A Contemporary View of the Biblical Perspective*. San Francisco: Glide Urban Center, 1966.

Trexler, Richard C. *Sex and Conquest: Gendered Violence, Political Order, and the European Conquest of the Americas*. Ithaca, N.Y.: Cornell University Press, 1997.

United Presbyterian Church in the United States of America. *Minutes of the General Assembly of the United Presbyterian Church in the United States of America, Part I*. Philadelphia: Office of the General Assembly, 1970.

Valente, Sharon. "Evelyn Gentry Hooker (1907–1996)." In *Before Stonewall: Activists for Gay and Lesbian Rights in Historical Context*, edited by Vern L. Bullough, 334–50. New York: Harrington Park Press, 2002.

Vincent, Merville. *God, Sex and You*. Philadelphia: J. B. Lippincott, 1971.

Waller, J. "'A Man in a Cassock Is Wearing a Skirt': Margaretta Bowers and the Psychoanalytic Treatment of Gay Clergy." *GLQ* 4.1 (1998): 1–16.

Warner, R. Steven. "The Metropolitan Community Churches and the Gay Agenda: The Power of Pentecostalism and Essentialism." *Religion and the Social Order* 5 (1995): 81–108.

Watt, David Harrington. *A Transforming Faith: Explorations of Twentieth-Century American Evangelicalism.* New Brunswick, N.J.: Rutgers University Press, 1991.

Weltge, Ralph, ed. *The Same Sex: An Appraisal of Homosexuality.* Philadelphia: Pilgrim Press, 1969.

White, Heather Rachelle. "'Love Is the Only Norm': The 'New Morality' and the Sexual Revolution." In *Cambridge History of Religion in America,* vol. 3, *1945 to the Present,* edited by Stephen J. Stein, 224–42. New York: Cambridge University Press, 2012.

———. "Virgin Pride: Faith and Sexual Identity in the Faith-Based Abstinence Movement." In *The Ashgate Research Companion to Contemporary Religion and Sexuality,* edited by Stephen Hunt and Andrew Kam-Tuck Yip, 241–53. Burlington, Vt.: Ashgate, 2013.

Wilcox, Melissa M. "Of Markets and Missions: The Early History of the Universal Fellowship of Metropolitan Community Churches." *Religion and American Culture* 11.1 (Winter 2001): 83–108.

Wilkerson, David R. *Hope for Homosexuals.* New York: Teen Challenge, 1964.

Williams, Daniel K. *God's Own Party: The Making of the Christian Right.* New York: Oxford University Press, 2010.

———. "Sex and the Evangelicals: Gender Issues, the Sexual Revolution, and Abortion in the 1960s." In *American Evangelicals and the 1960s: Revisiting the "Backlash,"* edited by Axel Schäfer, 97–119. Madison: University of Wisconsin Press, 2013.

Wood, Robert Watson. *Christ and the Homosexual: Some Observations.* New York: Vantage Press, 1960.

Worthen, Molly. *Apostles of Reason: The Crisis of Authority in American Evangelicalism.* New York: Oxford University Press, 2014.

Wynn, John Charles. *Sex, Family, and Society in Theological Focus.* New York: Association Press, 1966.

Wyrtzen, Jack. *Sex and the Bible.* Grand Rapids, Mich.: Zondervan House, 1958.

Zerubavel, Yael. *Collective Memory and the Making of Israeli National Tradition.* Chicago: University of Chicago Press, 1997.

Index

Abingdon Press, 35

Abortion, 107, 108, 109, 117, 176, 179

Abstinence campaigns, 184

Advocate, 170, 209 (n. 80)

African American civil rights movement: involvement of clergy in, 75, 76, 98, 155; and Protestant urban outreach programs, 83, 89; and homophile movement, 90; and religion, 177. *See also* Black Power

African Americans: involvement in gay organizations, 46, 67, 73, 89, 105, 154, 155–56, 166, 199 (n. 42). *See also* Race

"Age of Anxiety," 27

Alcoholic Beverage Control Board, 72–73, 84

Alexandrian rule, 11

Alinsky, Saul, 83, 87

American Baptist Gay Caucus, 211 (n. 108)

American Civil Liberties Union, 87, 171

American Holy Orthodox Catholic Apostolic Eastern Church, 67–68

American Law Institute, 78–79

American Lutheran Church, 162

American Weekly, 36

Anderson, Vann, 93, 104

Anglican Church, 39, 46, 51, 62, 70, 205 (n. 78)

Annual Reminder demonstration, 91, 99, 143, 144

Antigay tradition: religion as taproot source for, 5–6; and antigay campaign of 1977, 170, 176; of Christian Right, 180

Antihomosexual tradition: history of, 3–4, 6, 12, 13, 174, 178; biblical tradition of, 5–6, 18, 40, 68, 180, 182, 184–85; and theological-therapeutic hybrid, 19, 136, 137; and Sodom, 35, 77; in law, 37; homophile press challenging biblical interpretations, 60; role of religion in, 62, 63, 80, 163

Antivice campaigns, 77

Antiwar demonstrators, 113

Anxiety, effect on sexual development, 30, 31, 42

Associated Press, 139

Atlanta Theological Association, 211 (n. 108)

Baal, 20

Babylon, 19

Bailey, Derrick Sherwin: advocacy of sodomy law reform, 37, 38, 62, 70, 173, 174, 205 (n. 78); biblical commentary of, 37–39, 40, 62, 63, 69–70, 102, 173, 174, 175, 179; on gender difference, 103; on homosexuality, 122, 172, 173, 174, 181, 185

Balmer, Randall, 2

Barr, James, 59

Barrett, Ellen, 165

Bell, L. Nelson, 123–24

Benton, Nicholas, 161

Bergler, Edmund, 121

Bérubé, Allan, 190 (n. 34)

Bible: translations of, 1, 2, 3, 4, 17, 20, 35, 38, 60, 175, 182, 188 (n. 10), 192 (n. 74); Revised Standard Version, 1, 2, 4, 17, 34–41, 60, 175,

181–82, 192 (n. 74); King James Version, 1, 2, 4, 20, 34, 35, 181, 182, 188 (n. 10), 192 (n. 74); homosexual as term in, 1–2, 3, 13, 14, 17, 35, 36, 38–39, 40, 42, 122, 187–88 (n. 1), 188 (n. 2); New International Version, 4, 181–82; antihomosexual Bible traditions, 5–6, 18, 40, 68, 180, 182, 184–85; on sexuality, 36, 112

Bible commentaries: on homosexuality, 2, 4, 19, 20, 38–39, 40, 171, 188 (n. 7), 188 (n. 10); on sodomy, 2, 13, 19, 35, 37, 38–39, 102, 133, 173, 178–79, 181, 188 (n. 7); and conservative Protestant evangelicals, 18, 127, 128–29, 134, 180, 181, 182–83, 184; homophile press challenging antihomosexual interpretations, 60; and clergy-homophile organization cooperation, 107; interpretive changes in, 181

Birchard, Roy, 148, 166
Bird, Fred, 71–72
Birth control, 40, 104, 109, 120, 129. See also Non-procreative sex
Black, William, 198 (n. 42)
Blackburn, Clark, 115
Blackmun, Harry, 172
Black Power, 95, 113
Blaich, Allen, 163
Blair, Ralph, 180–81
Boisen, Anton, 22–23
Bonhoeffer, Dietrich, 163
Bowers, Margaretta, 25
Bowers v. Hardwick (1986), 171, 172, 176
Boyd, Nan Alamilla, 74–75, 76
Breton, Paul, 147
A Brief of Injustices (Glide Urban Center), 88
Brill, A. A., 190 (n. 25)
Broshears, Ray, 159
Brunger, Janet, 108, 133
Bryant, Anita, 170, 176
Bunch, Charlotte, 147

Burger, Warren, 171–72
Burgess, Roger, 199 (n. 42)

Calderone, Mary, 115
California Hall, San Francisco, New Year's Day Mardi Gras Ball, 71–74, 75, 76–77, 86–87, 89, 159
Call, Hal, 72, 84
Canadian Council of Churches, 116–17
Carmichael, Stokely, 95
Cassels, Louis, 112
Catholic Church: confessional of, 15; on procreation as primary end of marriage, 104; and Dignity, 140, 141, 158, 211 (n. 108). See also Independent Catholics
Catholic University of America, 147
Centenary-Wilbur United Methodist Church, 94
Central Park, New York, 145–46
Chicago, Illinois, 105
Chicago Theological Seminary, 211 (n. 108)
Chicago Urban Training Center, 83, 85
Christ and the Homosexual (Wood), 46, 63–67, 68, 96, 160, 195–96 (n. 68)
Christian Century, 77, 86, 99, 147, 160
Christian Crusade Weekly, 113
Christianity and Christian teachings: on homosexuality, 2–3, 20–21, 23, 34, 39, 40–42, 45, 59–60, 63, 69, 171, 178; theological discipline and rigor, 33; on sexuality, 42; homophile press on, 58–60, 61, 69; clergy on hypocritical practices toward homosexuals, 60–61, 69; and Wood's Christ and the Homosexual, 66–67; and legal reform, 79. See also Catholic Church; Protestants and Protestantism
Christianity and Crisis, 79, 99
Christianity Today, 131, 132, 147, 152, 174, 205 (n. 78)
Christian Life, 131–32
Christian Right, 7, 109, 176–77, 180, 183–84

Christian Science Church, 142

Christian Voice, 176

Christopher Street Liberation Day, 144, 158–59, 168, 211–12 (n. 115)

Christopher Street West, 149–50, 159

Church of the Beloved Disciple, 149

Circle of Friends, 93–94

Citizen Alert, 89

Clement, Robert, 149

Clergy: partnership with Henry Foundation, 46, 50, 51–52, 53, 55, 67, 94, 97; ordination of lesbians, 49, 165, 178; support of self-acceptance of homosexuals, 52; and homophile organizations, 67, 71–74, 75, 76, 81, 84–86, 89, 91, 93–94, 97–98, 174, 198 (n. 41), 198–99 (n. 42); and New Year's Day Mardi Gras Ball in San Francisco, 71–74, 75, 76–77; and homophile movement, 74, 75, 76, 81, 86, 88–89, 91, 94–95, 96, 99, 104–7, 155, 174; in black civil rights movement, 75, 76, 98, 155; support for British sodomy law repeal, 75, 173; reformed view of homosexuality, 87–88; and gay liberation movement, 148–49, 150, 152–56, 158; ordination of openly gay men, 160, 161–62, 178; and closeted homosexuals, 160–61, 162, 164, 210 (n. 90). See also Pastoral counseling

Cold War, 17, 27, 77–78

Cole, William Graham, 36–37, 39

Columbia University, 53

Columbus, Ohio, 98–99

Colwell, Clarence, 92, 94–95

Comfort, Alex, 183

Commission on Religion and Race, 98

Committee for Homosexual Law Reform, 154–55

Compton Cafeteria, San Francisco, 159

Compton Street riots, 159–60

Conference on Religion and Homosexuality, 160–61, 162

Congregational Church, 24

Conservative Protestant evangelicals: consolidating network of, 5; and Christian sex manuals, 10; conflicts with liberal Protestants, 13, 123–27, 133; and biblical authority, 18, 127, 128–29, 134, 180, 181, 182–83, 184; on Kinsey's studies, 26; and therapeutic methods, 41, 126–27, 175, 184; and moral regulation, 81; and sexuality, 109–10, 111, 126, 127–30, 135, 183–84; and sex education, 109–10, 123–35; and morality, 123, 124, 127, 129, 135; and Christian conversion, 127, 130–32, 136; on homosexuality, 129–35, 136, 175–76, 177, 178, 180, 181, 184, 205 (n. 78); and Christian confession, 132, 136; and traditionalism, 135–36; on gay churches, 152; political influence of, 177; and biblical literalism, 182–83; subcultural identity of, 184

Consultation on the Church and the Homosexual, 85–86, 90, 97

Consultation on Theology and the Homosexual, 95

Conversion Our Goal (transsexual support group), 89. See also Transgender communities

Cook, Charles, 49

Corbin, Joan, 57

Corinthians: Revised Standard Version's mention of homosexuals, 1–2, 35, 60, 182, 192 (n. 74); biblical commentary on, 2, 3, 38, 64, 131, 134, 175

Cory, Donald Webster. See Sagarin, Edward

Council for Christian Social Action (CCSA), 96–97, 99

Council on Church and Society, 108, 111

Council on Religion and the Homosexual (CRH): and clergy-homophile organization cooperation, 72, 74, 75, 76, 87–88, 89, 91–94, 96, 106, 147, 155, 165–66, 167; New Year's

Day Mardi Gras Ball, 72–74, 75, 76, 86–87; and Glide Urban Center, 88–89, 164; and homosexual rights, 107; and sodomy law reform, 174; and challenges to homosexual disease theories, 205 (n. 81)

Covenantal ethic, 119

Covenant House, Dallas, 148

Cox, Harvey, 83

Crocker, Bertrand, 24–25

Cromey, Robert, 81–83, 95–96, 99, 199 (n. 42)

Crompton, Louis, 209 (n. 65)

Crose, Robert, 112

Cult prostitution, 3, 182

Culture wars: oppositional forces of, 5, 179–80; and secularism, 7, 185; and history of religious and sexual change, 14, 109; and sexual identity, 184

Dallas, Texas, 93–94, 148

Dank, Barry, 208 (n. 59)

Daughters of Bilitis, 46, 72, 75, 84–86

Davis, Rebecca, 2–3, 9–10, 27, 43

D'Emilio, John, 17, 75, 76

Denver Post, 124

DeRogatis, Amy, 10, 110

De Vries, Laurence, 161, 162

Diagnostic and Statistical Manual of Mental Disorders, 137

Dictionary of Christian Ethics, 122

Dignity, 140, 141, 158, 211 (n. 108)

Donaldson, Herb, 87

Dorian Society, 94

Driver, Tom, 79

Durham, Lewis, 199 (n. 42)

East Coast Homophile Organizations (ECHO), 91, 144

Eddy, Mary Baker, 142

Egan, Edward, 55, 67, 97

Ellis, Albert, 65

Ellis, Havelock, 21–22, 179, 190 (n. 22)

Ennis, Bob, 155–56

Enroth, Ronald, 152

Episcopal Church: and pastoral counseling, 25; and Paul Moore, 49; and Henry Foundation, 51; and Cromey's sermon on homosexuality, 81–82; and urban outreach programs, 82–83, 94; on homosexual clergy, 165, 210 (n. 90); and gay liberation movement, 207 (n. 31)

Episcopal Mission Presbytery, 82

Erzen, Tanya, 184

Esalen Institute, 198 (n. 41)

Eskridge, William, 78

Ethical relativism, 33

Eucharist Catholic Church, 67

Evangelicals Concerned, 180–81

Ex-gay ministries, 184

Extramarital sex, "Sexuality and the Human Community" on, 119, 120–21

Ezekiel, definition of sodomy in, 19

Family planning, 107

Feminism, 109, 177

Fessenden, Tracy, 185

First Church of the One Brotherhood, 67

Fletcher, Joseph, 117–19

Florida: laws against homosexuality, 77; and antigay campaign of 1977, 170, 176

Focus on the Family, 176

Fosdick, Harry Emerson, 15–16, 17, 19, 20, 41

Foucault, Michel, 10

Free-speech activists, 113

Freud, Sigmund, 21–22, 24, 25, 190 (n. 25)

Fugaté, James, 59

Fundamentalist Protestants: on homosexuality, 2–3; and biblical authority, 18; and conservative Protestant evangelicals, 110, 126; on mainline Protestants as traitors to core principles of Christianity, 111, 125–26; and modernism, 180

Furies, 147

Gabriel, Paul, 74, 197 (n. 11)
Gallahue, Edward, 115
Gay (newspaper), 152
Gay Activist Alliance (GAA), 94, 138, 140, 144, 148, 207 (n. 41)
Gay and lesbian historiography, 139, 141
Gay churches, 140, 146, 152, 153, 156
Gay Freedom Day, 149
Gay identity movement: emergence of, 4–5, 13, 44, 46, 144; and therapeutic approach to sexuality, 10, 13, 48; and religious identity, 68, 141, 142, 153, 156, 162–64, 165, 168, 169; and religion, 140, 141; and "coming out" practices, 141, 160, 161, 162, 163–64, 167, 169, 170, 177–78, 184; and Stonewall riots commemoration, 145, 146; changing meanings of visibility, 161; and Wood, 161. *See also* Homosexual identity
"Gay is Good," 95–96, 104–5
Gay Liberation Front (GLF): creation of, 94, 138, 143–44, 149; and Stonewall riots commemorations, 145, 150; and Committee for Homosexual Law Reform, 155
Gay liberation movement: closet as metaphor used by, 50; and Henry Foundation, 55; challenge to therapeutic orthodoxy, 137; and Stonewall riots, 138, 141, 168; and homophile movement, 139, 143–45, 152, 168; and religion, 140–41, 142, 146, 149–50, 152–56, 158, 160, 161, 162–63, 169, 209 (n. 65), 209 (n. 80); and liberal Protestants, 147–49, 158, 177, 178, 180, 207 (n. 31); and clergy, 148–49, 150, 152–56, 158; radicalism in, 150; ideology of, 168
"Gay lib" ministries, 148–49
Gay Power Revival, 149, 208 (n. 44)
Gay Presbyterian Caucus, 211 (n. 108)
Gay pride, 168, 169, 170
Gay Pride Week, 145

Gay rights: and oppositional politics, 5, 14; and homophile movement, 90–96; and clergy-homophile organization cooperation, 106; and culture wars, 109; Perry's hunger fast for, 150, 152, 155; and sodomy laws, 171. *See also* Gay liberation movement
Gay Sunshine, 161
Gearhart, Sally, 166–67
Gender, and homosexual identity, 46–47
Gender deviance, laws targeting, 77, 78
Gender difference, and heterosexuality, 103–4
Gender ideology, and separate spheres, 11–12
Genesis: Sodom and Gomorrah in, 1, 19–20, 38, 77, 192 (n. 74); biblical commentary on, 3, 35, 38, 40, 104, 130, 131; homophile press challenging interpretation of, 60
Genné, William, 115, 118
George W. Henry Foundation. *See* Henry Foundation
Gerber, Israel, 31
Gerber, Lynne, 184
Gittings, Barbara, 97–98
Glide Memorial Methodist Church, 84, 105, 159
Glide Urban Center: Young Adult Project, 73, 84, 93; and Consultation on the Church and the Homosexual, 85; and Council on Religion and the Homosexual, 88–89, 164; resources on urban ministry, 93, 94; resources on homosexuality, 102, 166; and clergy's blessings of same-sex relationships, 104
Golden Gate Association of Northern California, 164
Golder, Evan, 160
Gomorrah, as symbolic site of sin, 19, 20
Grace Cathedral, San Francisco, 81–82
Graduate Theological Union, 211 (n. 108)

Graham, Billy, 124, 126, 128
Great Britain: and sodomy law reform, 37, 38, 61–62, 70, 75–76, 77, 173, 174, 205 (n. 78); Quakers in, 79
Green Lakes conference on Christian family policy, 116–17, 118, 122
Greenwich Village, New York, 142–43
Gross, Alfred A.: writing of annual reports of Henry Foundation, 46, 48, 50, 52, 55–56, 193 (n. 15); on clients served by Henry Foundation, 46, 53; collaboration with Henry, 48–49, 193 (n. 13); coaching gay men in skills of leading double life, 49, 50, 54, 55; on public decorum, 50, 52, 54, 70; public speaking for Henry Foundation, 50–51, 55, 66; writing on work with Henry Foundation, 50–52; on divorced private life, 52, 53, 55; on partial adjustment of homosexuals, 52, 54, 55; as mentor to Wells, 53–55, 56, 194 (n. 30); and Wood, 66; and homosexual law reform, 69–70; lack of political activism, 94
Guilt: as reinforcing homosexual impulse, 30, 31, 51, 54; effect on sexual development, 30, 42; and moral authority of pastoral counseling, 52, 69; and forum of homophile press, 61; and Wood's *Christ and the Homosexual*, 64, 66; and Marney's metaphor for human vulnerability, 100; and sex education reform, 119; and liberal Protestants, 129
Gutjahr, Paul, 182

Hadden, Jeffrey, 106
Hansberry, Lorraine, 46
Hargis, Billy James, 113
Harris, Bertha, 183
Harrison, Roger, 166
Hartford, Connecticut, 94
Hedstrom, Matthew, 17
Henry, George W., 30, 46, 48–49, 51, 56–57, 193 (n. 13)

Henry Foundation: as counseling initiative, 46, 48, 49, 52, 53, 54, 56, 97; annual reports of, 46, 48, 50, 52, 55–56, 66, 193 (n. 15); partnership with clergy, 46, 50, 51–52, 53, 55, 67, 94, 97; Cook on board of directors, 49; and double life, 49, 50, 54, 55; Paul Moore on board of directors, 49, 55; services in janitor's closet, 49, 55, 56, 57; multivocal representations of mission, 50; public decorum advocated by, 50, 52, 54, 58; official mission of, 50, 55; Gross as public speaker for, 50–51, 55, 66; lack of affiliation with homosexual membership societies, 55–56, 194 (n. 35); and integration of homosexuals into society, 56; and ONE, 56–57, 194 (n. 35)
Heritage of Pride, 212 (n. 115)
Heterosexuality: as modern therapeutic category, 6, 10; and sexual pleasure, 10, 12, 127; as healthy sexuality, 11, 12, 30, 31, 41, 42, 103, 121, 123, 130, 136, 174–75; and sodomy, 21; development of, 22, 25, 30; and Christian sexual education, 23; homosexuals as latent heterosexuals, 25, 30, 31; homosexuality as opposite of, 42, 174; and gender difference, 103–4; and Protestant debates on sexuality, 110
Hiltner, Seward, 26, 32–34, 115, 121
Holifield, E. Brooks, 9, 16, 18–19
Hollinger, David, 146–47
Homophile movement: counterdiscourse of, 42, 45–46, 47, 48, 51–52, 56, 69; audience for homophile magazines, 46; hidden meetings of, 56; and self-help, 56–63; and term "homophile," 57–58; political project of, 57–58, 61, 99; and Wood, 65, 160–61; visibility of, 70; clergy's involvement in, 74, 75, 76, 81, 86, 88–89, 91, 94–95, 96, 99, 104–7, 155,

174; and "cloak of the cloth," 74, 75, 76, 88, 98; late-1960s growth in, 76; development of, 90–96; national agenda of, 94–95; and gay liberation movement, 139, 143–45, 152, 168; and Stonewall narrative, 142; and New Left, 143; and Stonewall riots commemoration, 144–45

Homophile organizations: and Wood, 65; and clergy, 67, 71–74, 75, 76, 81, 84–86, 89, 91, 93–94, 97–98, 174, 198 (n. 41), 198–99 (n. 42); and political issues, 84, 86, 88–89, 90, 91, 94–95

Homophile press: audience of, 46, 56; as socially invisible communication, 56, 58; development of, 57–58; on religion, 58–60, 69; Christian clergy's articles in, 60–61; spiritual reflections of, 61; on Christian rationale for sodomy law repeal, 62; on Wood's *Christ and the Homosexual*, 65; on Stonewall riots, 138; and Bailey, 174

Homophile Youth Movement in Neighborhoods (HYMN), 142

Homosexual identity: confessions of "hidden homosexuals," 16, 29, 31, 43, 100–101; articulation of, 43–45, 46; and religion, 45, 46, 47, 68; and acceptable behavior, 47, 48, 50; and closets as spaces for hiding identity, 49; and double life, 49, 50, 54, 55; and wearing the mask, 50, 68. *See also* Gay identity movement

The Homosexual in America (Cory), 43–45, 48, 52, 59, 66

Homosexuality: biblical references to, 1–2, 6, 35, 36, 38–39, 40, 42, 95, 102, 122, 187–88 (n. 1), 188 (n. 2); Bible commentaries on, 2, 13, 19, 35, 37, 38–39, 102, 133, 173, 178–79, 181, 188 (n. 7); "Judeo-Christian" teachings on, 2, 20–21, 45, 59, 63, 171; Christian teachings on, 2–3,

10, 11, 12, 20–21, 23, 34, 39, 40–42, 45, 59–60, 63, 69, 171, 178; sodomy associated with, 4, 11, 18, 19, 21, 39, 40, 78, 174, 182; disease diagnosis of, 4, 16, 17, 18, 19, 21, 35, 36–37, 39, 64, 77, 78, 80, 81, 100, 101, 102, 105, 121–22, 130, 132, 134, 136–37, 162, 174, 205 (n. 81); as modern therapeutic category, 6, 10, 11; taboos against as part of Judeo-Christian tradition, 6, 17; history of changing discussions of, 8, 10, 11, 12, 41; sodomy distinguished from, 10, 21, 38, 39, 40, 179; Fosdick on, 15, 16, 19; as medical term, 17, 18, 19, 20–21, 175; and law, 17, 37, 38, 50, 52, 53; Havelock Ellis's study of, 21; Freud on, 21–22, 24, 25; medical treatments for, 24, 25; medical theories of, 24, 25, 39, 41, 42, 53, 77, 81, 100, 101, 121, 134, 136–37, 179; military regulations barring homosexuals from service, 24, 190 (n. 34); as mental illness, 24–25, 27, 29, 34, 35, 39, 43, 81, 102, 122, 131, 132, 137; therapeutic treatment of, 24–26, 27, 28–34, 37, 41, 43, 44, 47–48, 51, 64, 68, 80, 121, 133, 134, 164, 175, 184; Kinsey on, 26; Cold War rhetoric on, 27; motivational homosexuality, 32–33, 39; etiology of, 41, 53–54, 102; as opposite of heterosexuality, 42, 174; subjective perspective on, 43–45, 97; liberal Protestants on, 47, 100–101, 103, 121, 130, 132, 133, 134, 136, 153, 162, 173–75, 178, 181; Henry's studies on, 48; theology of, 96–105, 106, 135, 179–80; and "Sexuality and the Human Community," 121, 136, 137; as condition versus condemned act, 122, 131, 132, 134, 135, 136, 179, 181; conservative Protestant evangelicals on, 129–35, 136, 175–76, 177, 178, 180, 181, 184, 205 (n. 78).

See also Homophile movement; Homophile organizations; Same-sex relationships

Homosexuality and the Western Christian Tradition (Bailey), 37, 62, 102, 122, 172–74, 179, 181, 185

Homosexual membership societies, 44, 55–56, 194 (n. 35)

Hooker, Evelyn, 102, 122

Howard, John, 78

Howe, Reuel L., 27–28

"Humanae Vitae" (1968), 104

Humanistic psychology movement, 29

Humphreys, Laud, 81, 148

Humphries, Bob, 159

Hunter, James Davidson, 179–80

Husky, Rick, 165

Hyde, George Augustus, 67–68, 196 (n. 83)

HYMNAL (journal), 142, 143, 144

Identity politics, 44, 142

Independent Catholics, 67, 140, 149

Indiana University, 25

Institute for Advanced Pastoral Studies, 17

Integrity Gay Episcopal Caucus, 211 (n. 108)

The Interpreter's Bible, 1, 2, 35–36, 38, 39

In Unity, 156

Irvine, Janice, 109

Jakobsen, Janet, 172

Jamison, Gerald, 152

Jesus Movement, 150

"Judeo-Christian" teachings, on homosexuality, 2, 20–21, 45, 59, 63, 171

Jews and Judaism, 31, 45, 140, 154, 158. See also Alinsky, Saul; Gerber, Israel; Kameny, Frank; Sagarin, Edward; Shelley, Martha

Johnson, David, 27, 77

Johnson, Phil, 93–94

Johnson, William, 160, 161–67

Jones, Clinton, 55, 94, 97

Jones, Kimball, 103

Jones, Paul, 93, 103–4, 105

Jones, Timothy, 46

Jordan, Mark, 65, 146, 178

Journal of Pastoral Care, 16

Kalos Society, 94

Kameny, Frank, 90–91, 95–96, 143

Kansas City, Missouri, 93, 94, 104, 105

Katagiri, Mineo, 94

Keane, Webb, 7–8

Kennedy, John F., 113

Kennedy, Robert, 113

Kent State University, 113

Kepner, Jim, 57, 59, 62–63, 67–68, 92, 152, 154

King, Martin Luther, Jr., 76, 113, 155, 156

Kinsey, Alfred, 3, 25–26, 45, 102

Kinsolving, Lester, 159

Kissack, Terence, 139

Kite, Morris, 155

Klassen, Pamela, 8

Koinonia House, Portland, 94

Krafft-Ebing, Richard von, 21

Kuhn, Donald, 199 (n. 42)

Ladder, 46, 57, 86

Ladies' Home Journal, 36

Lahaye, Beverly, 183

Lahaye, Tim, 183

Lambert, William, 56–57

Lamont, Charles, 165

Lavender Unity, 149

Law: and morality, 7, 77–81; and homosexuality, 17, 37, 38, 50, 52, 53; sodomy as legal term, 19, 37, 190 (n. 23); sodomy law reform in Great Britain, 37, 38, 61–62, 70, 75–76, 77, 173, 174, 205 (n. 78); Henry Foundation's legal aid, 50, 53; Christian influence in, 59, 76; homosexual law reform, 69–70, 75, 76–79, 121; sodomy laws, 75, 78–79, 171–72, 173, 176; sexual psychopath laws, 78; religion separated from, 79–80, 172, 173; and clergy's involvement in homophile movement, 88, 99, 107; and Committee for Homosexual Law Reform, 154–55

League for Civil Education, 84, 85

Left, 5, 146, 163

Legg, Dorr, 56–57

Leggett, Gene, 148, 164, 165

Leitsch, Dick, 138

Lesbians: and lesbian identity, 46, 48; ordination of, 49, 165, 178; lesbian Christians hiding sexual identity in congregations, 68; historiography of, 139; organizations of, 147. *See also* Gay identity movement; Gay liberation movement; Gay rights

Leviticus, biblical commentary on, 3, 35, 39, 131

Lewis, Chuck, 72

Liberal Protestants: and therapeutic sciences, 4, 5, 8, 9, 13, 15, 16–18, 23, 36, 42, 47, 164, 174; influence of, 5, 8, 13; on spirituality, 7; modernism of, 7–8, 125, 135, 180; invisibility of, 8; emancipatory logic of, 13; conflicts with conservative Protestants, 13, 123–27, 133; and Fosdick, 15; and Freudian theories, 22; and developmental approach to sexuality, 23; and Kinsey's studies, 26; and grace over law, 37; on homosexuality, 47, 100–101, 103, 121, 130, 132, 133, 134, 136, 153, 162, 173–75, 178, 181; and legal reform, 77, 78–81; and politics of inclusion, 97, 137, 178, 179; and clergy allied with homophile movement, 99, 105–6; and sexuality, 109–10, 112–13, 114, 123, 125, 135, 163, 174, 176; and gay liberation movement, 147–49, 158, 177, 178, 180, 207 (n. 31); on sodomy law, 173, 176

Life magazine, 82

Living Church, 99

Lofton, Craig, 46

Los Angeles, California: and homophile movement, 92, 200 (n. 66); and Metropolitan Community Church, 149, 153–54, 157; and Christopher Street West, 149–50

Los Angeles Advocate, 154–55

Lucas, Don, 85

Luster, Orville, 198–99 (n. 42)

Lutherans Concerned for Gay People, 211 (n. 108)

Lyon, Phyllis, 75

Maddocks, Lewis, 99–100

Malcolm X, 113

March on Washington (1963), 90

Marinessen, Jan, 199 (n. 42)

Marmor, Judd, 102

Marney, Carlyle, 100–101

Marotta, Toby, 142

Marriage: and marital sexual intimacy, 27–28; defense of homosexual marriage, 103–4; as context for sexual pleasure, 110; Protestant support for, 111; and "Sexuality and the Human Community," 120–21; and conservative Protestant evangelicals, 127, 129

Martin, Dale, 40

Martin, Del, 75, 86

Marxism, 146

Masturbation, Christian teachings on, 3, 40, 42, 64, 175. *See also* Nonprocreative sex

Mattachine Review, 57, 61

Mattachine Society of Chicago, 105

Mattachine Society of Los Angeles, 57

Mattachine Society of New York, 65–66, 67, 91, 138, 142

Mattachine Society of San Francisco, 72, 84, 85

Mattachine Society of Washington, D.C., 90–91

McCarthy, Joseph, 27

McIlvenna, Ted, 73, 83–84, 87, 199 (n. 42)

McLean, Doug, 93–94
Media narratives: on sexual decline, 111–15; on gay churches, 152
Mental health specialists, 33
Methodist Church: publications of, 1, 2, 35–36, 38, 39; and homophile organizations, 84, 92, 93, 94; and clergy's blessings of same-sex relationships, 104–5; and suspension of homosexual clergy, 164–65
Methodist Gay Caucus, 165, 211 (n. 108)
Metropolitan Community Church (MCC): founding of, 92, 140, 149, 153, 166, 209 (n. 65); congregations of, 147, 156–57; and clergy, 149; and Perry, 149, 153–54; and Christopher Street West, 150, 169; conservative Protestant evangelicals on, 152; and ecumenicist activities, 154, 156, 208 (n. 59); and political involvement, 155, 156, 209 (n. 70); publications of, 155–56; harassment of, 157; and Stonewall riots commemorations, 157, 169; and Harrison, 166; and reform of mainline Protestant churches, 167
Military, 24, 46, 53
Military chaplains, 24–25, 190 (n. 34)
Minorities: homosexuals as unrecognized minority, 45
Minton, Henry, 48
Mollenkott, Virginia Ramey, 181
Moody Bible Institute, 153
Moody Monthly, 128
Moore, John, 87–88, 199 (n. 42)
Moore, Paul, 49, 55, 165
Morality: relationship to scientific inquiry, 7; and law, 7, 77–81, 171–72; McCarthy on moral toleration, 27; and pastoral counseling's therapeutic approach to homosexuality, 29, 42, 52, 66; and private sexual behavior, 37, 76, 173; Bailey on moral culpability of agent, 39; homophiles' counterdiscourse to, 42, 48, 69;

and homosexual identity, 47; and homosexuals' self-presentation, 54; and self-acceptance of homosexuals, 61, 69; and Wood's Christ and the Homosexual, 65, 66; and black civil rights movement, 76; and clergy's involvement in homophile movement, 76, 87–89, 96, 99, 102–3, 106; and homosexuals included in churches, 100–101; Protestant studies on, 108–9, 110, 111, 122; United Presbyterian Church on, 108–9, 110, 111–15, 116, 117, 119–22, 123, 124, 125, 133–34, 162; new morality, 109, 117–19, 123; media narratives on, 112–13; and political issues, 113–14; and sex education reform, 117, 123; and conservative Protestant evangelicals, 123, 124, 127, 129, 135; and science, 125; and moral values of Christian Right, 176–77
Moral Majority, 176
Moral regulation: and sexuality, 9, 11, 18, 22, 26, 33–34, 42, 80, 172, 185; and gender ideology of separate spheres, 11–12; medical inquiry distinguished from, 21
Moral Welfare Council, Church of England, 61–62
motive (Methodist youth publication), 146–47
Mowry, Charles, 199 (n. 42)
Muravchik, Stephanie, 9
Myers, C. Kilmer, 199 (n. 42)

Narcissism, 9
Narramore, Clyde, 130–31
National Association of Evangelicals, 126
National Council of Churches (NCC), 85, 86, 97, 98, 115, 116–17, 166, 201 (n. 89)
National Gay Task Force, 167
National Informer, 113
New Brunswick Theological Seminary, 211 (n. 108)

New Left, and homophile
    movement, 143
Newsweek, 165
New Testament: Revised Standard Version
    of, 34; biblical interpretation of, 36
New World Outlook, 137
New York Court of General Session, 50
New York Times, 138–39, 152
Nichols, Jack, 90
Niebuhr, Reinhold, 36
Nixon, Richard, 113
Noll, Mark, 185
Non-procreative sex, 42, 104, 127,
    128–29
North American Conference of Homo-
    phile Organizations (NACHO),
    95–96, 155
Northridge, William, 28–29, 31
Nyberg, Dennis, 199 (n. 42)

Old Testament: sodomites defined in,
    20, 35, 38; Revised Standard Version
    of, 35; biblical commentary on, 36;
    sexual regulations of, 60
ONE: and Henry Foundation, 56–57,
    194 (n. 35); staff of, 57; public deco-
    rum advocated by, 58; sales of, 58;
    on religion, 59–60, 61, 62; advertise-
    ment for churches in, 67, 196 (n. 83)
ONE, Incorporated, 67, 99
Oscar Wilde Bookstore, 142

Pacific School of Religion (PSR),
    161, 162
Pagan cultic practices, 20, 35, 36–37,
    38, 40, 182, 188 (n. 10)
Parade Magazine, 108–9, 111, 116, 133
Paresthesia, 21
Pastoral counseling: and post–World
    War II boom in psychiatry, 5, 16–17;
    and advice texts, 5, 28–29; history of,
    9, 41; and nonjudgment of homosex-
    uality, 13, 24, 28, 29, 33, 51, 66, 123,
    175; and Fosdick, 15–16; as synthesis
    of religion and therapeutic sciences,

18, 36–37, 42; and developmental
    approach to sexuality, 22–23, 30, 31,
    32, 34, 40–41; therapeutic methods
    of, 24–26, 27, 28–34, 41, 42,
    47–48, 51, 64, 66, 69, 121, 130, 132;
    post–World War II discussions of
    homosexuality, 25–26; and Kinsey's
    studies, 26; and narratives about
    homosexuality, 43, 47; and homo-
    philes' counterdiscourse, 47–48;
    and Henry Foundation, 50, 51–52,
    53, 97; moral authority of, 52; and
    Wood's *Christ and the Homosexual*, 69,
    195–96 (n. 68)
Pastoral Psychology: founding of, 16; on
    therapeutic acceptance, 29, 30–31;
    on women with homosexual tenden-
    cies, 31–33; on motivational homo-
    sexuality, 32–33; retrospective issue
    on pastoral counseling, 41; adver-
    tisement for Cory's *The Homosexual
    in America* in, 43–44, 48; on Henry
    Foundation, 48, 51–52; emphasis
    on heterosexual healing, 51–52;
    advertisement for Wood's *Christ and
    the Homosexual*, 63–64; Paul Jones
    on homosexual marriage, 103–4; on
    Wynn, 115; on morality, 117
Pastoral Services Commission's Con-
    cern for Sexual Variation, 97
Paul (apostle), 1, 2, 36, 40, 60
Peale, Norman Vincent, 43
Pederasty, 3
Pellegrini, Ann, 172
People of color, and homosexual
    identity, 46–47
Perry, Troy, 140, 149–50, 152–56, 157,
    158, 209 (n. 62)
Personal Rights in Defense and Educa-
    tion (PRIDE), and political activism,
    92, 93
Peter (apostle), 103
Philadelphia Council of Churches, 91
Phoenix Society for Individual Rights,
    93, 103

Pike, James, 79

Pluralism, 12–13, 33, 118

Police: and New Year's Day Mardi Gras Ball in San Francisco, 71–74, 77, 86–87, 159; discriminatory police practices, 74, 84, 89, 92, 98, 153, 201 (n. 89); and black civil rights movement, 89; and Stonewall riots, 138, 159

Political issues: and sexuality, 7, 109; and homophile movement, 57–58, 61, 99; and Protestant urban outreach programs, 83, 88–89; and homophile organizations, 84, 86, 88–89, 90, 91, 94–95; and sex education, 109–10, 114, 119; and morality, 113–14; and Perry, 155, 156

Politics of authenticity, 163–64, 168

Portland, Oregon, 94

Premarital intercourse, 3, 107, 119–20

Presbyterian Church: and urban outreach programs, 82; and social justice, 97; on homosexual clergy, 100, 165, 211 (n. 105). See also Presbyterian Church of the United States, origins of; United Presbyterian Church

Presbyterian Church of the United States, origins of, 123

Presbyterian Journal, 123–24

Presbyterian Layman, 124

Press, Walter, 199 (n. 42)

Preston, John, 165, 166

Privacy rights, 172

Program in Religion and Psychiatry, 17

Protestants and Protestantism: and Bible versions, 1; literature on homosexuality, 2–3; and modernism, 5, 7–9; Protestant metric measuring strength of religiosity, 7; mainline churches, 8, 12, 13, 16, 41, 83, 98, 106–7, 108, 109, 112, 114, 124, 125–26, 135, 136, 137, 141, 146, 149, 158, 164–68, 177, 178; and secularism, 12, 110, 111, 136, 149, 174, 179–80, 185; and pastoral counseling, 15, 16–17; and practices of homosocial kinship, 11–12, 46; and urban outreach programs, 82–85, 87, 88–89, 93–94, 101, 105, 106; and black civil rights movement, 98; on morality, 108, 172–73; and sectarian divisions, 110; decline in, 114, 177; gay caucuses of, 141, 158, 165, 167–68, 211 (n. 108); ideology of, 185–86. See also Conservative Protestant evangelicals; Fundamentalist Protestants; Liberal Protestants

Psychiatry: as therapeutic science, 4; post–World War II boom in, 5; and sexuality, 10, 11, 21, 25, 174; and Fosdick, 15, 41; on homosexuality, 20–21, 23, 24, 25, 29, 32, 35, 39, 41, 43, 78, 101–2, 136; during World War II, 24; Henry Foundation's referrals to psychiatrists, 50, 52; and conservative Protestant evangelicals, 126–27

Psychoanalysis, 22, 25, 26, 36, 37, 121

Psychoanalytic Institute of Columbia University, 25

Psychology: as therapeutic science, 4, 9; and Fosdick, 15, 17, 41; during World War II, 23–24; and conservative Protestant evangelicals, 126–27, 130–31; on sexuality, 174

Quakers, 79, 115, 141

Queer communities, 82

Queer subculture, 46, 84, 85, 88, 93

Queer youth, 89

Race: as whiteness, 12–13, 46–47, 113, 124, 126, 177; and homosexual identity, 46–47; and urban ministries, 82–83, 89; and homophile activists, 90, 95–96; and politics of inclusion, 97; and Metropolitan Community Church, 153, 154, 155, 208 (n. 59). See also African American civil rights movement; Black Power

Rado, Sandor, 25
Rash, John, 148
Readjustment Committee of the Quaker
  Emergency Service, 193 (n. 13)
Reaugh, Ernest, 148, 211 (n. 110)
Reed, William Standish, 131–32
Religion: and gay liberation movement
  demonstrations, 13–14, 139–40;
  and homosexual identity, 45, 46,
  47, 68; homophile press on, 58–60,
  69; law separated from, 79–80,
  172, 173; and clergy's involvement
  in homophile movement, 88, 93;
  media narratives of, 112–13; and gay
  liberation movement, 140–41, 142,
  146, 149–50, 152–56, 158, 160, 161,
  162–63, 169, 209 (n. 65), 209 (n. 80);
  and sexuality, 185–86
Religion and Health, 99
Religiosity, 7, 8
Religious backlash narratives, 176, 177
Religious institutions, 7, 46
Religious past, 6, 7
Religious progressives, 7–8. *See also*
  Liberal Protestants
Religious regulation, Freud on, 22
Religious Society of Friends,
  199 (n. 42)
Republican Party, 177
Respectability politics, 89, 91, 143–44
Reveille for Radicals (Alinsky), 83, 87
Richardson, Harper, 94
Right, 5. *See also* Christian Right
Roberts, David, 30
Robinson, John A. T., 117–19
Rodwell, Craig, 142–43, 144
Rogers, Carl, 29–30
Roman Empire, 27, 77
Romans, biblical commentary on, 3, 35,
  38, 40, 77, 129, 131, 175
Rose, Louise, 166
Rose, Nikolas, 9
Rossinow, Doug, 163
Rowland, Chuck, 67
Rubin, Gayle, 11

Sagarin, Edward, 43–46, 48, 52–53, 55,
  56, 59, 66
Saint Paul Theological Seminary, 93
Same-sex relationships: as interior
  condition, 1; Christian teachings on,
  2, 3, 4, 6, 10, 11–12, 19, 20, 42, 67;
  and same-sex friendships, 11–12, 23;
  and pastoral counseling, 19; sodomy
  associated with, 19–20, 174; as
  abnormal sexual behavior, 21, 24, 25,
  30, 32, 41, 42; motivating cause of,
  39; and self-acceptance, 44, 45, 46,
  52; monogamy in, 62, 103, 104; in
  Bible, 63; legal targeting of, 78; and
  homosexual marriage, 103–4; ethical
  good of, 104; and clergy's rituals
  of blessings, 104–5; conservative
  Protestant evangelicals on, 130–32.
  See also Homophile movement;
  Homosexuality
San Carlos Community Church, 160
San Francisco, California: California
  Hall New Year's Day Mardi Gras Ball,
  71–74, 75, 76–77; as mecca for gay
  culture, 75, 82, 159; North Beach,
  82; and Protestant urban outreach
  programs, 82–84; Tenderloin, 82,
  84, 87; and homophile movement,
  94–95; and clergy's blessings
  of same-sex relationships, 104;
  Christopher Street Liberation Day,
  158–59; picketing of State Steamship
  lines, 209 (n. 62)
San Francisco Chronicle, 73, 86
San Francisco Examiner, 159
Santa Ana Church of God in
  Prophecy, 153
Sarria, José, 84
Save Our Children campaign, 176
Scanzoni, Letha, 181
Science: perfectionist possibilities of,
  37; and morality, 125; and liberal
  Protestant sexuality teachings, 163.
  See also Therapeutic sciences
Sears, James, 105

Seattle, Washington, 94

Secor, Neale, 91, 101, 102

Secularism: and religion as root of sexual regulation, 7; on religion as backward and conservative, 8; and Protestantism, 12, 110, 111, 136, 149, 174, 179–80, 185; and British sodomy law repeal, 75–76; and clergy's involvement in homophile movement, 76; and separation of crime and sin, 88; and sexuality, 109–10, 185; and gay liberation movement, 140, 146

Self-acceptance of homosexuals, 44–45, 52, 53, 54, 59, 61, 66, 69

Self-actualization, 28, 31, 33, 44, 45, 68

Self-help, 9, 15, 18, 56–63

Self-knowledge, 44

Self-realization, 27

Self-transformation, 9

Sex deviance, 26–27, 77, 78, 80, 91, 98, 175

Sex education: and developmental approach to sexuality, 23; and political issues, 109–10, 114, 119; and conservative Protestant evangelicals, 109–10, 136; reform of sex education curricula, 115, 117, 118, 119, 123, 136, 162, 178

Sexual behavior: scientific study of, 4, 21, 34; regulation of, 6, 7, 11, 13, 19; as personal choice, 7, 9; perceptions of, 10; Kinsey on, 25–26, 45, 102; private sexual behavior, 37, 52, 53, 55, 62, 77. *See also* Same-sex relationships

Sexual emancipation, 185

Sexual ethics, 107

Sexual ideology, 35

Sexuality: therapeutic sciences on, 5, 8, 10, 17, 34, 40, 175; and political issues, 7, 109; medicalization of, 8, 10, 13; and moral regulation, 9, 11, 18, 22, 26, 33–34, 42, 80, 172, 185; and act/identity distinction, 10; ideals of, 10, 27–28, 32; healthy sexuality, 11, 12, 27, 28, 36, 42, 68, 79, 80, 110, 117, 121, 123, 130, 136, 162, 174–75; paradigms for, 13; debates on, 14, 108–9, 119; developmental approach to, 22, 23, 25, 30, 31, 32, 34, 40–41, 102, 130; Freud on, 22, 190 (n. 25); natural variation in, 26, 102; and marriage, 27–28; biblical interpretation of, 36, 112; Christian teachings on, 42; non-procreative sex, 42, 104, 127, 128–29; and mainline Protestant churches, 107, 108–9, 111; and secularism, 109–10, 185; media narratives on sexual decline, 111–15; and religion, 185–86. *See also* Heterosexuality; Homosexuality

"Sexuality and the Human Community" (United Presbyterian Church), 108–17, 119–25, 133–34, 135, 136, 137

Sexuality Information and Education Council of the United States, 115, 117

Sexual liberals, 78–80, 81

Sexual orientation, 179, 182, 184

Sexual permissiveness, 10, 11, 77, 112–13, 125

Sexual perversity, 77, 129–30

Sexual pleasure: responsibilities of, 9; and heterosexuality, 10, 12, 127; productive and unproductive pleasures, 11; marriage as context for, 110; and conservative Protestant evangelicals, 127–28

Sexual revolution, 109, 110, 113, 114, 127, 135, 176

Shelley, Martha, 146

Silver, Bill, 163

Silverstein, Charles, 183

Sindt, David, 165, 211 (n. 105), 211 (n. 110)

Sisley, Emily L., 183

Situation ethics, 117–19, 123, 125

Slater, Don, 57

Slavery, 185

Smith, Alex, 92

Smith, Evander, 87
Smith, George Adam, 20
Social Action, 96–97, 98, 99, 100, 101
Social class, and homosexual identity, 46–47
Social Progress, 97, 98, 99, 100, 101
Society for Individual Rights, 72, 84, 159
Society of Friends, 211 (n. 108)
Sodom: as symbolic site of sin, 19–20, 60; reconfiguration into antihomosexuality tradition, 35, 77; Bible commentary on, 38–39, 62; sins of Sodom as homosexuality, 39, 40
Sodomy: Bible commentary on, 2, 4, 19, 20, 38–39, 40, 171, 188 (n. 7), 188 (n. 10); homosexuality associated with, 4, 11, 18, 19, 21, 39, 40, 78, 174, 182; Christian discourses on, 6, 11; homosexuality distinguished from, 10, 21, 38, 39, 40, 179; and non-procreative sex, 11; definitions of, 19–20, 35, 38, 40, 190 (n. 23); as theological term, 19, 21, 38; as legal term, 19, 37, 190 (n. 23); sodomy law reform in Great Britain, 37, 38, 61–62, 70, 75–76, 77, 173, 174, 205 (n. 78); California sodomy law, 77
Southard, Helen, 115
Southern Baptist Church, 123, 124
Southern California Council on Religion and the Homophile (SCCRH), 92, 200 (n. 66)
Spike, Paul, 201 (n. 89)
Spike, Robert, 98–99, 201 (n. 89)
Stein, Marc, 91
Stigma, 45
Stiles, B. J., 147, 199 (n. 42)
Stonewall riots: and gay identity movement, 13; influence of Christianity in ritual commemoration of, 13–14, 139–40, 141, 145–46, 149–50, 157, 169–70, 207 (n. 25); grassroots activism sparked by, 74, 138; freedoms sought in, 75;

national movement sparked by, 76; commemorations of, 138–40, 141, 144–46, 149, 155, 157, 158, 169; Leitsch on, 138; narrative of, 141–50, 157, 158, 159, 166, 167, 168, 169–70, 206 (n. 8)
Strangers in Our Midst (Gross), 70
Strategy of militant respectability, 91
Stryker, Susan, 89
Sweet, Leonard, 135
Symonds, John Addington, 190 (n. 22)
Szasz, Thomas, 102

Talmij, Billie, 85
Tavern Guild, 72, 84
Teal, Donn, 207 (n. 41)
Theological modernism, 18, 34, 42, 125
Theology, of homosexuality, 96–105, 106, 135, 179–80
Therapeutic sciences: and liberal Protestants, 4, 5, 8, 9, 13, 15, 16–18, 23, 36, 42, 47, 164, 174; on sodomy as homosexuality, 4, 11; on sexuality, 5, 8, 10, 17, 18; and theological-therapeutic hybrid, 18–19; regulatory discipline of, 19; and treatment of homosexuality, 24–26, 27, 28–34, 37, 41, 43, 44, 47–48, 51, 64, 68, 80, 121, 133, 134, 164, 175, 184; and unconditional positive regard, 30, 42; and conservative Protestant evangelicals, 41, 126–27, 175, 184; homophiles' counterdiscourse to, 42; and narratives about homosexuality, 43
Thielicke, Helmut, 103, 122
Thornton, Susan, 166
Tillich, Paul, 36, 118, 163
Time magazine, 39, 139, 170
Timothy, biblical commentary on, 38
Transgender communities: in San Francisco, 82; and activism, 89, 159. See also Conversion Our Goal
Treese, Robert, 102–3

Unconditional positive regard, 30, 42, 67

Union Theological Seminary, 30, 36, 79, 148, 162, 211 (n. 108)

Union Theological Seminary Quarterly Review, 148

Unitarian Universalist Church, 141, 211 (n. 108)

United Church of Christ, 46, 64, 92, 94–97, 98, 160, 162, 164, 166, 211 (n. 108)

United Fellowship of Metropolitan Community Churches (UFMCC), 140, 156–58

United Presbyterian Church: letters of complaint to, 108, 124–25, 133; on sexual morality, 108–9, 110, 111–15, 116, 117, 119–22, 123, 124, 125, 133–34, 162

United Press International, 112

University Settlement House, 49

Upstairs Lounge, New Orleans, 157–58

Urban homosexual ghettos: and clergy's involvement in homophile organizations, 76, 89, 93; *Life* article on, 82; Tenderloin as, 84; and Perry, 153

U.S. Supreme Court: and gay rights, 90; on sodomy laws, 171

Vanguard, 89

Vector, 159

Village Voice, 138

Wahrenbrock, Ken, 92

Wake, Lloyd, 104

Warner, R. Steven, 209 (n. 70)

Washington for Jesus, 17

Wells, Robert, 53–55, 56, 194 (n. 26)

Westermark, Edward, 45

White, Dale, 199 (n. 42)

White, Edmund, 183

Wilkerson, David, 131

Williams, Cecil, 73, 89, 105

Williams, Daniel, 177

Williams College, 36

Winner, Lauren, 2

Wise, Carrol, 30–31

Wolf, Irma "Corky," 57

Wolfenden, John, 62

Wolfenden Committee, 173

Wolfenden Report, 37, 62, 70, 75, 79

Women: homosexual tendencies of, 31–33, 34; and homosexual identity, 46–47; Episcopal Church's ordination of lesbian to priesthood, 49; ordination of, 178. *See also* Lesbians

Wood, Robert W., 46, 63–67, 68, 69, 70, 96–97, 160–61, 195–96 (n. 68)

World War II, 23–24, 48, 190 (n. 34)

Wright, Keith, 97, 199 (n. 42)

Wynn, John Charles, 114, 115–17

Yale Divinity School, 211 (n. 108)

Young Adult Project, Glide Urban Center, 73, 84, 93

Young Men's Christian Association, 12, 23

Young Women's Christian Association, 12

"Zaps," 147, 148, 163, 167

Made in the USA
Middletown, DE
22 May 2017